# MYSTERY PEOPLE OF THE COVE

## A HISTORY OF THE
## LAKE SUPERIOR OUINIPEGOU

*Who were the Sea People that have eluded historians for 145 years and archaeologists for almost 30?*

## RONALD STIEBE

*Mystery People of the Cove: A History of the Lake Superior Ouinipegou*
by Ronald Stiebe
L'Anse, Michigan, U.S.A.

Copyright 1999

Stiebe, Ronald
Mystery People of the Cove: A History of the Lake Superior Ouinipegou
Library of Congress Catalog Card Number: 99-97081
ISBN 0-9676892-0-1

Illustrations and dust cover design by James M. Davidson

Printed in the U.S.A. by Lake Superior Press
Marquette, Michigan 49855

## CONTENTS

# ACKNOWLEDGMENTS

For me to express my gratitude to everyone responsible, who contributed to this research effort, would entail a lengthy compilation. It is not my intention to omit anyone, but I will attempt to identify those who were most instrumental.

The single most influential person who inspired this effort was author and historian Fred Rydholm. He provided the impetus that initiated the project, which coursed a journey that was as challenging as it was rewarding. He was there to also advise on any questions that needed to be answered regarding this new writing and publishing experience. Fred also provided assurance at a time when burnout stalled my efforts and I needed his expertise. A special thanks is in order for his willingness to inspire those of us who still have inquiring minds as we continue to search for truth in history.

Anitia Sikorsky very patiently reviewed this entire manuscript in order that it may present itself with recognizably accepted grammar, spelling, and content comprehension. Her advice and suggestions, under the competence of many years of experience, enabled me to feel confident with the completed version.

My appreciation is extended to Mr. Lawrence Dorothy and Mr. Winston Moore for allowing me to interview them on the archaeological subject matter 25 years after the event.

This effort would not have been complete without the assistance of Dr. Costellia, who took time to explain the technical terms regarding the physical anthropological report. His personal interest in anthropology was also helpful.

Also I thank Dr. Mowerman from the University of Michigan, Dearborn, for his special effort to provide me with the valuable information compiled on his data base relating to Ethnobotany of Native America, a data base that is the most comprehensive in the country.

Thanks to Dr. James Duke, U.S.D.A., Maryland Research Center, for information relating to the history and use of botanical substances.

If it were not for the many libraries, none of this material would ever have been made available for this publication. I will be ever indebted to these valuable sources of knowledge that must continue to perpetuate if research is to have any significance in understanding our history. Additionally, if it were not for the librarians and curator's efforts to access information, this project would not have been possible.

I also acknowledge Eric Nordberg, Theresa Spruce, Kay Masters, of the archives and staff at the Robert Van Pelt Library at Michigan Technological University. They were all very accommodating and always patient with my peculiar requests. The intense efforts that consumed countless hours digesting the many volumes of the French missionary journals earned myself a reputation that, at times, appeared to border on varying degrees of absurdity.

Also I am deeply appreciative for the time and energies of French language instructor, Sylvie Dangeville, also of M.T.U. Without her helpful resources, interpretation of the many French references would not have been possible.

I am deeply indebted to Brian Dunnigan, map archivist of the William L. Clements Library, University of Michigan, whose exceptional expertise laid hands on probably the most important information necessary to make this research effort complete.

My appreciation extends to Linda Panian and staff of the J.M. Longyear Research Library and Museum of the Marquette County Historical Society, an excellent facility with many resources and a helpful staff to make it accommodating.

It is only proper to acknowledge the following libraries where much of the research material was accessed. My sincere thanks is extended to all the staff who were so helpful in providing the information requested.

Libraries:
    Robert Van Pelt Library—Michigan Technological
      University, Houghton
    J. M. Longyear Research Library—Marquette County Historical Society
    L'Anse Area Schools Public Library (Library Loan System)
    William L. Clements Library of American History—University of
      Michigan, Ann Arbor
    Brown County Public Library—Green Bay, Wisconsin
    Carter Brown Library—Rhode Island
    Ontario Archives—Ottawa
    National Library of Canada—Ottawa
    Bibliotheque Gatien-LaPointe, Trois-Rivieres, Quebec—Canada
    Wisconsin State Historical Society, Archives—Madison

Lastly, but most importantly, I must thank my wife, Marie, who was very patient with me for the many hours I spent hunkered over the word processor. Only through her encouragement was I eventually exposed to this modern computer mechanism, whereas, without it, this project would never have been completed successfully.

*"Tradition fades, but the written record remains ever fresh."*

—William L. Clements Library, U.M.

# PREFACE

In the mid and late 1800's Wisconsin historians endeavored to research the history of the Catholic Church in North America, beginning with John Gilmary Shea's interest in the journals of the Jesuit missionaries, which eventually led to a staff of historians translating these extensive letters and memoirs from the original French into English.

During the course of these inquiries, Wisconsin historians sought to embrace Jean Nicolet as the first European to have discovered the State of Wisconsin. The enigmatic journey of Nicolet has been interpreted by these early historians, who adamantly insist that he arrived at the shores of Green Bay on a mission to secure peace among the resident Indian tribe of the Winnebago. It is impossible to tell the story of these native Americans without telling the story of Nicolet; however, it is this elusive group of native people that the story is about. They were called Ouinipegou (pronounced Wee-knee-pea-goo) by the Algonkin people, from which the name Winnebago is derived. The French called them Puans, but their proper name was the Sea People. The Sea People would actuate Samuel de Champlain's quest for the route to the South Sea that was thought to lead to China and Japan. Control of the northwest passage would confer great wealth on France as well as profit and honor for its discoverer.

This extensive work reexamines the journey of Jean Nicolet in order to establish the rightful place of this historic event, and to identify demographically the group of native Americans that inhabited the shores of Lake Superior. It also examines how important this group of people were to the French in their quest for the discovery of the "passage."

In addition to the historic evidence, the archaeological evidence will be examined. It is important that they correlate. This will result in establishing proof which will be necessary to convince an otherwise dogmatic audience adhering to the belief in the Nicolet myth that has persisted for so many years.

It is most essential for any serious historical researcher to retain the highest degree of objectivity possible in the course of establishing factual information. Every effort will be made to ensure that this standard is adhered to despite the efforts of earlier historians.

# INTRODUCTION

This book is as much a story of research as it is of history. The meticulous process of research requires unlimited amounts of patience and energy, which are more often the most deterring aspect of historical investigations. The process of research is academically difficult work, requiring good old fashion methods for accomplishing results. There are no computer short-cuts in this business. Without dedication and persistence, the task becomes almost unbearable, unless inquisitiveness can be satisfied with minute successes, culminating in the ultimate climax of a major discovery.

Inquisitiveness inspired the research necessary to consider writing this documented compilation of history pertaining to the Lake Superior Ouinipegou, or Winnebago Indians. Intrigue and curiosity provided the motivation and desire to understand these people, who were descendants of the forebears of the most ancient human culture known to this immediate area.

Who were these people? How did they survive? What happened to them?

Researchers are people who constantly ask questions. Finding the answer is not usually a simple process. In most cases learning the answer, more often than not, raises more questions than it solves. A process of elimination evolves, which impacts our thinking, as research is a system of constantly formulating ideas that become subject to change based upon the discovery of facts. As the process becomes more complex questions and answers must be relative, sources confirmed, information creditable and supported by factual evidence. (The building of evidentiary bridges that eventually culminates in providing conclusions which will satisfy our investigatory objectives.)

The key piece of evidence that initiated this investigation into the *Mystery People . . .* was a very early French map that historically had existed without a great deal of explanation, or at best, attempts to explain it were vague or inaccurate. My familiarity with the local area provided the knowledge necessary to orient the map to its surroundings. The key location was Sand Point, located in Keweenaw Bay or the *Cove* of Lake Superior, Michigan. For some, this map contained buried treasure. It meant desecrating a historical and archaeological site for the sake of its grave goods. For me, its treasure was vested in the historical knowledge that as yet lay undiscovered! According to the map, at this location, there existed a settlement of historic native people referred to as the Nation of Fire.

The area today is home to the native American Ojibwa people, whose ancestral heritage is not related to these ancient peoples of Sand Point. That being the case, then who were these mysterious people, for whom no one seemed to have any historic explanation?

As the process of the investigation unfolded, additional information surfaced involving the discovery and the archaeological excavation, conducted in 1970, of an ancient burial site at Sand Point. Confirmation of existing native peoples inhabiting this very location was made, although the findings were said to be prehistorical. Was there any connection between the archaeological evidence and the historic evidence on our map? The search was on!

What followed was an intensified project that required vast amounts of time, energy and persistence. Where does one even start to look for this kind of information? What resources exist? Perhaps the archives and early French history records may provide some answers. Neither the archives nor French history sounded like a very exciting place, or subject, in which to become involved.

It would take several trips to the archives before the drama would begin to unfold, as the early French records would reveal the information sought. Eventually the focus of this investigation would center on the French Interpreter—Jean Nicolet, whose journey to the western "fresh-water seas" had been somewhat of a historic enigma ever since its inception by Wisconsin historians.

If the investigation would prove to have substance, the results would change not only local history of the area, but of Michigan and the adjacent state of Wisconsin! Not to mention the impact it might have on the local native American community and especially that of Green Bay! How would this information impact past historical knowledge of Indian demographics of the Great Lakes? What significance may it have on the archaeological community as it relates to the original excavation? These questions could only be answered by correlating the historical and archaeological evidence. Was there even sufficient historical evidence available to conduct a critical research effort?

The following is an account of this effort and the exposure of the *Mystery People of the Cove*, whose historical presence on Lake Superior slipped between the cracks of historical interpretation by previous historians. Since the Ouinipegou faced near-extinction at the threshold of the historic period, the historians are not totally to blame in their accounts. How did this happen? How did their existence manage to elude us all these years? When these questions are answered there is still more mystery and intrigue which surfaces that make the story even more interesting. There are possible connections that relate to the area's unsolved mysteries; the use of copper, cairns and stone altars, ceremonial evidence of possible human sacrifices, medicinal plant uses that involve ritual ceremonies, unique burial practices and more.

This book does not pretend to answer all the questions, since this field is so extensive. These are specialized subjects for those more knowledgeable and professed in the field to embark upon. The purpose here is to identify the evidence, make it relative and offer it for their consideration.

As previously mentioned, research more often raises more questions than it can answer.

The Author.

# 1

## THE DISCOVERY

A cloud of swarming mosquitoes and black flies followed Roland Huhtala Sr. as he climbed aboard his bulldozer. He was unaware of the significant discovery he was about to make that would change history that warm June summer's day in 1967. It would mark the beginning of a series of events that none of its participants would realize as they would take part in dispelling a long enduring myth that had perpetuated for 145 years.

The job site was at Sand Point, near Baraga, in Michigan's Upper Peninsula. The property belonged to Dr. Louis Guy who had hired Mr. Huhtala to push a new road into a swampy area that he was about to develop. The new road would provide better access to a lighthouse owned by Dr. Guy on a point of land that protruded out into Lake Superior. The lighthouse had been a navigation reference for boaters traveling the waters of Keweenaw Bay, also known as L'Anse Bay.

As Roland proceeded to bulldoze his way through a stand of Norway pine near the sandy shore he came to some piles of sand that are typical of most dunes along the Great Lakes shorelines. At that point he decided to use the sand to fill in low lying areas for the prospective road. As he started to gnaw away at the corner of one of the dunes, Dr. Guy, who was standing by overseeing the project, noticed something unusual protruding from the freshly dug sand. It did not take someone in his profession long to determine what lay before him. What he identified were bones. Human bones! He immediately stopped Roland's progress on the project to inspect them closer. There were lots of bones, bundles of bones, scattered everywhere! And chunks of old burnt wood were exposed also. Dr. Guy immediately became inquisitive. There were bones from many individuals. And what about the fist-sized pieces of charcoal wood? They had obviously been there for a very long period of time, buried beneath the huge mound of sand. His first notion was that it could possibly be an ancient burial site and, rather than proceed, he decided that someone more versed in Indian history should examine the area. Rather than destroy the site further, Dr. Guy discontinued excavation at this location and decided to contact a long time friend of his, Mr. Alf Jentoft.

Alf was a life long resident to the area who was very knowledgeable about the local history of the area. He was also the secretary of the local chapter of the Michigan Archaeology Society. Dr. Guy called on him to examine and render an opinion on the discovery of the bones at Sand Point.

Keweenaw Bay is home to a native American community situated at a location just north of the village of Baraga, called Assinins. It is home to the L'Anse band of Ojibwa or Chippewa tribe. The Keweenaw Bay Indian Community was organized under the Treaty of 1854, and their ancestral occupation of the area dates back to the turn of the 18th century.

Dr. Guy approached the native American community at Keweenaw Bay with his concern over the possible burial grounds that he may have discovered. He contacted the tribal chairman, who indicated that neither he, nor anyone else in the tribal community had any knowledge of this area ever having been utilized as a tribal burial ground. At that point Dr. Guy was assured by them that as far as the local native community was concerned there was no desecration of any of their native ancestral burial grounds; therefore, being relieved of any obligation by the tribal community, he was encouraged to proceed with his road project. It was Dr. Guy's contact with Alf Jentoft that kept the road project on hold until closer examination of the piles of sand could be made. It was upon Alf's insistence that this site might be of significance to the archaeological community, and he immediately began to muster the local organization into making some preliminary incursions at the site to confirm this. Alf was the area's most ardent ethnohistorian. He was very familiar with the area's historical features and spent a great deal of his time and energies in exploring and applying theories to some of the areas local mysteries and how they related to early human habitation.

After Alf and a few of the local members of the M.A.S. had occasion to examine the site, the following letter was published by the president of the organization and sent to its members. (The date of the memo was 8-30-67.)

> so far uncovered remains of seven bodies, numerous pieces of pottery, a gorget, a perfect arrowhead, and one copper bead . . . mound is 125 feet long, 19 feet wide, and 6 feet 6 inches high. Owner having given us permission to dig it up before he levels it off for fill purposes as part of his land project. Because of this it is necessary, and almost imperative, that we should spend as much time as we can on this site, which is our first archaeological field endeavor with interesting and fruitful results expected.

There was a definite anxiety felt among members that required their immediate response if they were to recover anything from this prospective site. Indeed, it appeared as though this was some sort of burial area, but whose? The M.A.S. chapter continued to work at the site the remainder of the fall of that year and continued to do the same the following year. The chapter was convinced that this just may be a significant find and decided that the profes-

**Incursion of burial mound by heavy equipment. Members of the local chapter of the Michigan Archaeological Society confirming site as possible burial grounds.**

sional field should be alerted so that the location could be excavated properly. So far they had removed the skeletal remains of 38 individuals. Meanwhile, Dr. Guy willingly cooperated with the local chapter and kept the road project on hold.

Dr. Guy's land project was a rather extensive one. The property he acquired on Sand Point was mostly swamp, full of tag alder and lowland balsa and spruce. The lighthouse he purchased sat on a small piece of land, which for the most part, was an island. His project entailed the transformation of large amounts of fill, either dredged from the lake, or scraped from the upland forest, to be placed in the swampy lowlands. He had begun this project a number of years before. What is most startling, and was eventually revealed later, was that Dr. Guy had previously witnessed the total destruction of a burial mound even larger than the one presently being excavated. He stated that it was located inside of the existing gate and had already been pushed into the low lying swamp that it bordered. It was the largest of all the mounds!

During the summer of 1968 the M.A.S. was in contact with archaeologists from Michigan State University and the University of Michigan. It was difficult just trying to generate interest in the site since any reports of burial mounds this far north were viewed with a great deal of skepticism.

There was a great deal of excitement on the part of the local society with the arrival of professional archaeologists from the University of Michigan.

**One of 20 burial mounds located on Sand Point. Photo taken April 15, 1996 with still a foot of snow on the ground.**

However, the archaeologists already had pre-conceptions that the site would reveal nothing of any significance as far as the burial mounds were concerned. Their skepticism was founded on the premise that burial mounds had never been found this far north of the traditional mound cultures. To add to this was the coincidental occurrence of a Lake Superior seiche also occurring on the day of the inspection. This phenomenon causes the water level of the lake to rise extremely, flooding roads, basements and placing boats on top of people's docks. When the professional archaeologists arrived, the seiche was at its height and what they saw did not impress them. Their findings were that these so-called Indian mounds were only part of an old existing shoreline and the dunes had formed due to years of wind and wave action. They were identified as natural structures and dismissed as having been constructed by man. The archaeologists returned to their respective institutions to finalize their findings and conclude any further interest in the location of Sand Point.

With their spirits dashed, Alf and the Upper Peninsula Chapter members, who had been excavating and keeping records of their activities, discontinued work at the location and no plans were considered for any future efforts, at least for the time being. Members of the organization had other jobs to attend to and could only devote small amounts of their time, if any. Dr. Guy was anxious to get on with his construction project and had been overly patient up to this point. This may have been the foreclosure of the Sand Point site to any historical significance, except for the chance appearance of two people. Without them, the events following the discovery may have gone unnoticed and buried, literally!

Mr. and Mrs. Lawrence Dorothy, who were members of the Kalamazoo Valley Chapter of the M.A.S., were vacationing in the western part of the Upper Peninsula of Michigan, stopped by Northern Michigan University in Marquette. They were seeking any new or suspected locations of archaeological interest that might occupy them during their vacation time. They were directed to Baraga and stopped by the local tourist information center and museum for more information. On display were the artifacts the local chapter had exhumed from the site. They were very interested in the artifacts and looked up Alf Jentoft to inquire about their origin. Their interest sparked Alf's enthusiasm once again when they expressed the possibility of getting Western Michigan University in Kalamazoo interested in the site. The Dorothys returned to Kalamazoo with photos and specimens of the artifacts provided them. Alf eagerly awaited their response. He knew for this discovery to have any recognized historical significance it was important to involve professional archaeologists.

After having returned to Kalamazoo the Dorothys arranged a meeting with Winston Moore and other archaeologists with the Department of Anthropology at Western Michigan University.

The burial mounds were thought to be natural features that were produced by many years of wave action along the ancient shoreline. Consequently, they lay for many years without arousing suspicions as to their composition.

Based on information supplied by the Dorothys, Mr. Moore and Dr. Robert Sundick, both from the Anthropology Department, decided to journey to this most northern location to inspect the site themselves. The two met with Alf and proceeded to the site. Their initial investigation quickly revealed that the mounds in question were indeed man made. More importantly, it was determined that unless large scale work was carried out very soon by the archaeologists much of the site would be demolished. Not only was Dr. Guy anxious to proceed with his development project, but relic hunters had already begun to dig secretly at the site.

Mr. Moore, who was put in charge of the field operation, returned to the university understanding the imminent need for a quick response to organizing and getting on location, especially if the site was to be of any importance to the archaeological community. After all, Indian mounds were unheard of in this part of the country, at least as far as the most recent evidence had indicated. The site could provide some connections to the already known mound building cultures of the Mississippi, Ohio, Missouri and Wisconsin River systems—a culture whose evidence by these mounds had left archaeologists puzzled as to who these people were or where they came from, how they rose to such prominence and what may have contributed to their disappearance. Would we know anymore from the excavation at Sand Point? Would we know who they were or where they came from?

# 2

# THE DIG

With the pending conditions, Mr. Moore immediately started making plans to organize the archaeological excavation project. It would mean gathering a team together, rounding up the necessary equipment and making arrangements for local accommodations for everyone. And of course the financial expenditures of this unexpected project would have to be sanctioned by the local university heads. Mr. Moore kept close contact with Alf Jentoft, who assisted with as much as he could from his vantage point. Their arrival to the area generated a great deal of excitement for M.A.S. members as well as other members of the historical society of Baraga County. It also aroused the interest of many local residents who were welcomed to observe their activities.

The first year of the excavation the field crew would use space in the Mission facility in Assinins for their residence and final collection location. The following year, the Old Red Schoolhouse in L'Anse was used, and students would sleep on cots in the classrooms. These facilities would serve to store the collected artifacts from each day's activities. On rainy days they would spend time attempting to sort pottery remains and cleaning the skeletal remains for further examination by anthropologists.

The task of conducting this project fell upon the shoulders of Mr. Winston Moore and his thirteen field school students. In the summer of 1970, Mr. Moore arrived with his young team to begin the formal task of a professional excavation. They would spend eight weeks of the summers of 1970 and 1971 excavating the site at Sand Point. The crew members were divided into teams or groups and assigned to respective areas for their part in the survey. The areas were surveyed off into grids and the teams would commence to dig meticulously and sift each shovelful of soil for artifacts. When someone would discover a find, a cry would go out, and everyone would stop to gather around the lucky individual to observe the treasure. It might only be a copper bead, an awl, needle or arrow point, but each discovery was special and boosted morale for a task that involved, more often than not, finding nothing.

When the desired level of each excavation was reached, it was refilled with the inspected or sterile soil. First, a copper penny of the year was placed at the

The 1971 excavation crew—Winston D. Moore, upper right, his young son Andy, front row, and the Archaeology Field School students. The crew also includes Les Forcia of L'Anse and Nancy Morin of Baraga (photo, courtesy Baraga County Historical Society)

bottom level as a historical indicator for any archaeological exploration that may happen on the same location in the distant future. Digging was especially difficult in the burial mounds. The sloped surface of the mound made it difficult to plot the exact location of many of the finds. The area was overgrown with many sizeable trees that required cutting some of them down and chopping entangled masses of roots to access the buried mound remains.

Working conditions at the site were not without certain constraints. Despite the cold, snowy conditions of winter in this country, summers can be very hot. The site, tucked away in a little bay is sandy, and the tall Norway pines can make for some stagnant and muggy conditions. Worst of all, nothing surpasses the number and variety of insects that inhabit this part of the country. The site, being next to Lake Superior, and adjacent to swampy wetlands, would harbor the proper conditions for hosting swarms of these annoying and voracious marauders. But these were not the greatest fears shared by the lower Michigan student archaeologists. What they feared most, while they were intently working, was the thought of lurking bears! For most of the students, it was their first experience in the northern forest of the Upper Peninsula, and this fear was very real to them. The persistent insects, sticky hot weather, and

Initial setup by field crew and incursions into large linear burial mound. (photo, courtesy Baraga Country Historical Society)

Field crew expands excavation on large burial mound as they collect copper, stone and ceramic artifacts. They would eventually exhume the human skeletal remains of 117 individuals. Samples of a funerary pyre would also be collected and later examined at the university laboratory. (photo, courtesy Baraga County Historical Society)

the constant fear of bears tended to alleviate any anxiety that may have existed about grave digging in an ancient burial ground where the spirits of the dead may still loom!

For Les Forcia and Nancy Morin, however, the fear of the spirits of the dead may have been a greater threat than were the insects and the bears. Both were local native American youngsters, who were employed as a cooperative gesture between the university and the local Ojibwa community. They were the only two native Americans working on the project with the lower Michigan students. Anthropologists would not allow Les and Nancy to work on any of the burial mound excavations, instead they were assigned to adjacent areas of habitation. The reason for this was to protect any native cultural beliefs they may have had, which perceive that the spirits of the dead still frequent the burial areas that are so sacredly respected. The archaeologists were sensitive to this fact and did not want to create any animosity among the local community, especially in light of the fact that during these years the American Indian Movement was generating concern over the desecration of Indian burial sites by the scientific community. As work progressed into the project, an agreement was eventually made between archaeologists and the local native community to have the skeletal remains returned when their research was completed.

What would eventually be learned was that the ancient people the students were researching were not ancestral to the local Ojibwa community. In fact their occupation would pre-date that of the history of the Ojibwa and it would eventually be learned that these people were their ancestral enemies, members of the Sioux. For those native American Ojibwa, who observe their ancestral beliefs, this was no place for the living, for the powerful spirits were still present to vindicate their ancestral past. It was definitely an area that would traditionally be considered off limits to the descendants of those Algonkin members who were their ancestral enemies. (1.)

Finally, after two seasons of excavating at the site, the two field crews were involved in the manual digging of 128 square meters of soil from the living quarters of the site. Additionally, they would also physically dig 187 cubic

meters of soil from the burial mounds. They would recover 40,000 individual pieces of pottery, 232 copper items classified as tools and ornaments, numerous soil samples and the collection of 117 human skeletal remains. All thirteen students coordinating their activities as they worked under the watchful guidance of their mentor, Mr. Moore. Photographs were taken. Sketches and diagrams of the nineteen burial mounds that were identified were taken and finalized. Upon completion of the dig in 1971 this vast array of artifacts would have to be organized and examined by the specialists in their respective fields at the university. The process would extend for a period of eight years until its completion in 1980. The final analysis completed was submitted to its reading subscribers in two issues of the *Michigan Archaeologist* magazine, Vol. 26 , 1980, and Vol. 27, in 1981.

**Winston Moore inspects a small fraction of many yards of fill for artifacts with the use of water. This was strenuous work for these young students. (photo, courtesy Baraga County Historical Society)**

(1.) *North to Lake Superior,* Penny, (Carter & Rankin), 1987:37.
　　At "Le Ance" in 1840, while Penny was among the "Chippeways" he observed typical Chippewa burials (houses), some "highly decorated" with food, bells, furs, eagle quills, *scalps*, and many other trophies. He writes, "The scalps were taken last season from their ancient enemies the Sioux." He also continued to say that a "war party" had been sent out that summer "against the Sioux," and had not been heard from yet.

# 3

# THE ARCHAEOLOGICAL REPORT

After the field crews spent six weeks each summer of 1970 and 1971 digging the site at Sand Point, Mr. Winston Moore returned to Western Michigan University with a large cache of prehistoric artifacts. Now the astronomical task of deciphering the evidence of the dig would begin.

The succeeding year of this project Mr. Moore was faced with a critical decision that would impact the remaining years of his career. He had been tentatively filling in for the resident professor who was on maternity leave. Her return placed Mr. Moore's position in jeopardy. The university proposed a set of criteria that Mr. Moore felt was unreasonable. It would mean advancing his studies in addition to overseeing the continuation of the Sand Point project. Since the field of study the university was proposing was not consistent with his major interest, he decided to leave the university. For reasons of his own, he left professional academia as well. News of his decision was a disappointment to those who knew him and had worked with him in the field.

Several years went by with no one at the university taking any interest in spearheading the completion of the study. This was to have been Mr. Moore's project, his claim-to-fame, so to speak, and no one was inspired enough to commit time for futile purposes. The material from Sand Point may have lain there forever had it not been for Mr. Lawrence Dorothy's continued concern and interest.

Mr. and Mrs. Dorothy were the principal motivators in getting the university involved initially in the Sand Point site. Mr. Dorothy felt committed to seeing the whole project through, but none of the university heads were compelled to divert any time or energies toward accomplishing this. The project was stagnating, and interest in it was also diminishing. No matter who he talked to at the university, no one seemed to inspire the administrative leadership to move the project ahead.

Mr. Dorothy had recently retired after spending twenty years with the U.S. Navy. He had a former interest in archaeology and belonged to the local chapter of the archaeological society. He decided that he would advance his knowledge and skill in this interest; at 40, he enrolled at Western Michigan University. He earned his degree and then continued to work on his master's. The pottery study of Sand Point would be his thesis.

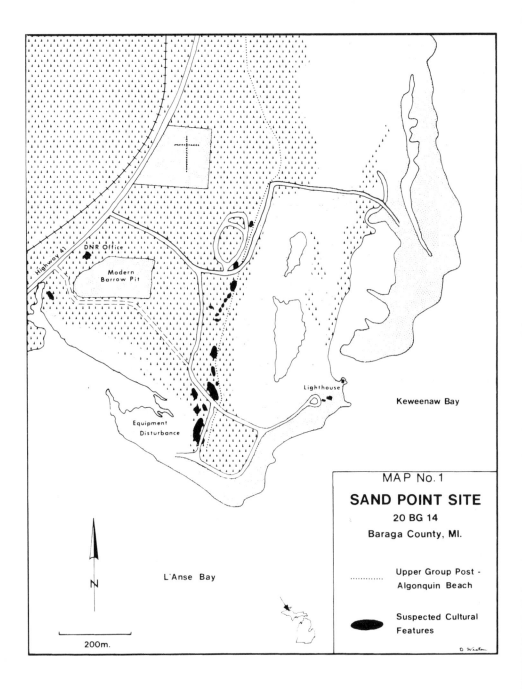

N

200m.

L'Anse Bay

Highway 41

DNR Office

Modern
Barrow Pit

Equipment
Disturbance

Lighthouse

Keweenaw Bay

MAP No. 1

**SAND POINT SITE**

20 BG 14

Baraga County, MI.

............. Upper Group Post -
Algonquin Beach

Suspected Cultural
Features

D. Weston

With his many years of experience in the military, Mr. Dorothy knew that it sometimes required breaking the chain of command to get the job done. It meant that he go over some heads and step on some toes to achieve certain objectives. Without his persistence the material from the Sand Point site might still be sitting in storage to this day without any completion of the project.

Mr. Dorothy completed the pottery study from Sand Point which was a very instrumental part of the Archaeological Report. His task entailed the examination of 40,000 individual pottery sherds. This he did every working day for two years, without any financial remuneration. To this day, Mr. Dorothy has not secured any financial gain from his learned expertise in this field. He was truly dedicated to something he enjoyed and was committed to completing what the had started. The final report may have never been a matter of record had it not been for his continued interest to move the project along.

What was of particular concern was to learn the location of a musket ball and gun flint that were recovered from the beach area of the site. They were mentioned in a historical publication printed right after the dig by Mr. Moore. If the musket ball could be located, forensic examination may collaborate information that would identify the Sand Point site as a historic location. (1.)

Mr. Dorothy did not know where or what Mr. Moore did after leaving the university and had no information for his location. He was also unaware that a musket ball was even recovered from the site. That information should have been in the archaeological report and it was not. Could this very important piece of historic evidence have gotten lost? Now, after 25 years, all of a sudden someone has taken a great interest in what probably at the time was considered to be a very insignificant item. He said he would check to see if it was anywhere with the material in storage at the university. It might be among the items listed in the lithage assemblage. Mr. Moore would also have to be found.

What was especially disturbing was to learn that some of the most important material of the site may never have made it to the university for examination. Many people were involved in the dig, and people were helping themselves to the artifacts that were being recovered. Mr. Dorothy stated that he personally witnessed a unique stone earspool that was recovered by a person who walked off the site with it. He said that it would have been the most important artifact recovered from Sand Point. (2.)

(1.) *Baraga Country Historical Pageant*, Moore, 1972:17.
   Mr. Moore also reported locating a fragment of "bottle glass" that was apparently worked or "chipped" by someone familiar with chipping stone.

(2.) Mr. Moore's report mentions a slate ear spool that was recovered (see Chapter 10:166).
   The stone net sinkers discovered were stolen during the night after they were photographed that evening.

## THE ARCHAEOLOGICAL REPORT

The following is a summary of the Archaeological Report. An attempt will be made to paraphrase a great deal of it in order to eliminate some of the details that would otherwise make the original dissertation seem palling. At the same time we must still do it justice. If the reader is so inclined to review the complete report, he may access it by researching *The Michigan Archaeologist*, Vols. 26, 1980 & 27,1981.

The editorial page preceding the report provides us with some general but interesting information about Sand Point.

The editor begins by stating:

> It is important that *The Michigan Archaeologist* present what is known about the Sand Point site because it is probable that a full site report will never be prepared. Not only is there very little published material about the Upper Peninsula, but information about this large and significant site will be useful to Great Lakes archaeologists in answering some interesting questions about the history of the region.

The report stipulates that Sand Point was apparently a location of a native copper industry, and questions that were raised were: (1) Was it used by these people for trade to maintain friendly relation with other groups? (2) Was the Sand Point site a desirable place to live because of its proximity to large amounts of float copper? (3) Was copper of greatest value as a utilitarian item?

Perhaps the Sand Point site was large because it was situated at productive fishing grounds. Raising questions such as: Did fall fishing create a situation where large numbers of people could gather and bury their dead? If this were the case, what social significance did it have?

The Archaeological Report clearly states that the data suggest a number of interesting problems concerning prehistoric life in the Western Upper Peninsula. The information gathered from the site can now be used as a guide to research further in the region and to provide information useful for solving the questions raised.

More substantial, however, is the fact that the report raises more questions than it actually answers. The summaries of each section are very brief and each author carefully generalizes his findings.

Just the same, we must apply ourselves to what can be learned from the physical evidence that was secured from the site, and allow it to be instrumental in forming certain proofs that may be reasonable and logical to our final conclusions. This would entail extending our findings beyond just the archaeological evidence and combining it where it supports the known historical evidence.

The analytical substance of the report is divided into several sections of study. They are: (1) Environment and Subsistence, Terrance J. Martin, M.S.U. &

Deborah K. Rhead, W.M.U. (2) Copper Assemblage, R. David Hoxie, W.M.U. (3) Ceramics, Lawrence G. Dorothy, W.M.U. (4) Physical Anthropology, Larry M. Wyckoff & James Addington, W.M.U. (5) Lithic Assemblage [Analyzed by James Marek for his M.A.—was never finished and to date, is yet to be completed.] And head of the Anthropology Department at W.M.U., Dr. William Cremin.

*Environment & Subsistence*

This segment deals with defining remains of plants and animals observed by archaeologists of the prehistoric subsistence of the Sand Point people. These people were identified as a hunting and gathering society.

The climate cited during the period of occupation at Sand Point was considered to have had slightly warmer temperatures than present, lending to an increase in animal species, thus having a somewhat significant impact on subsistence practices by the Sand Point people residing on the Keweenaw Peninsula.

The report explains the resource potential in both plant substance and animal life that could exist at Sand Point. They suggest that over 100 species were potentially available for exploitation in the vicinity of this site. They list several.

Wildlife in the form of game animals were also identified. Big game, such as deer were less numerous under the dense forest conditions prior to the historic period. Moose were present along with scattered populations of bison in woodland clearings, but it is doubtful they were ever plentiful in the Great Lakes region.

Among the small mammals that might have been exploited in former times were: beaver, muskrat, otter, porcupine, woodchuck, fisher, martin, badger, lynx, red fox, and gray wolf.

The report continues to state that with the absence of abundant big game, special attention was probably given to the exploitation of migratory waterfowl—being that this site is located conveniently on both legs of the Mississippi and Atlantic Flyways. Species listed include: Canada goose, mallard, black duck, pintail and waterbirds, such as the herring gull, loon, hooded and American merganser, pied-billed grebe, and osprey. Also, passenger pigeon, ruffed grouse, spruce grouse and woodcock served as sources of food.

Of all the wildlife in the area, fish offered the highest subsistence potential. These species included: northern pike, walleye, largemouth and smallmouth bass, suckers, sunfish, yellow perch, brook trout and spawning grayling. Rivers that augmented fish resources near Sand Point were the Falls, Little Carp, Otter and the Sturgeon. On Lake Superior such fish as sturgeon, whitefish, lake trout, burbot and suckers were found.

The above mentioned resources are strictly potential subsistence food sources. The following are the actual recovered specimens of over 700 soil samples constituting 314 cubic meters of soil. The samples were collected with the intention of chemical rather than botanical analysis, and the samples were small: 38 identifiable botanical specimens from the site, fragments of acorn, lambs quarter, cherry and plum, squashberry, sumac, and snowberry. The report concludes that unfortunately, little can be gleaned from the actual subsistence usage of floral material secured from Sand Point. Lack of material may be explained by (1) small numbers of species having subsistence value in the local environment (2) the large percentage of these that may have provided greens or fruits for consumption, leaving few or no inedible parts to be preserved in the archaeological record (3) high acidity of soil would inhibit preservation of organic remains, and (4) purpose of the excavation, placing an emphasis on mortuary rather than the habitation area of the site.

The remains of the wildlife collected were taken from 503 elements. Soils yielding bone fragments identified species. The findings indicate a surprisingly small quantity of animal remains considering the large amount of lithic material (hunting points) and ceramics (pottery) that were recovered during excavation of the living areas.

Those animals identified by bone fragments from nine species of mammals included: white tail deer, beaver, muskrat, unidentified canid (dog or wolf). Also elements of Canada goose, unidentified duck species, turtle, fish and freshwater mussel were present in small numbers.

The most surprising aspect of the Sand Point site is the very small number of fish remains present. Two species of fish identified were the brook and/or lake trout, and the whitefish. Both being fall spawning, they should be represented by a large number of bones, especially when considering the site's proximity to Keweenaw Bay. There is some evidence that the water level of Keweenaw Bay may have been lower during the occupation of Sand Point. At the time of the burial mound construction, the mound closest to the shore displayed evidence that some of the burials were below the water table when the structure was excavated. A slightly lower lake level would have resulted in a much greater land area available for occupation. This would signify a greater portion of the beach area being exposed to processing of fish, the area being under water and inaccessible at the time of the excavation.

This section summarizes by concluding that the only plant foods recovered were acorn and lambs quarters and those only in minute quantities. It was also suggested that plant food procurement emphasized foods that would not result in large quantities of preserved parts, (e.g., greens, sap, cambium). The animal remains indicated a moderately diffused subsistence with concentration on small and medium sized mammals and migratory waterfowl typical of the Canadian biotic province. The very small number of fish remains is contrary to what would normally be expected in this situation. The archaeologists hypothesize that due to the risen lake level, expected fish processing areas along the shoreline are presently submerged and inaccessible to archaeological exploration.

## Late Woodland Copper Assemblage

Besides the use of pottery and stone tools, the Sand Point inhabitants were engaged in the technology of a modest copper industry.

The finished copper artifacts are categorized as: ornaments and tools. A total of 232 items were recovered. The ornaments were described as a crescent (decorative piece for personal adornment), a necklace, spiral pendant, beads, and tinkling cone.

Twenty-eight copper tools were recovered from Sand Point. Most were classified as awls and barbs (fish hooks). A twist drill was identified displaying six single helical twists that make its appearance not unlike that of a modern drill bit. A harpoon tip was found along with two copper projectile points.

Under a separate heading labeled "Discussion" the report elaborates on the author's findings as to the relevance of copper to the Sand Point location.

The report explains that Sand Point is located southeast of one of the richest veins of native copper in the United States. Despite numerous confirmations of concentrated activities at copper mines, especially on Isle Royale, Sand Point now represents one of relatively few so-called "work shop localities" in Michigan.

The report states, however, that there is little if any evidence to support the contention that the copper utilized here was obtained through the laborious activity of mining and then transported back to the site for further processing. It suggests that fragments of float or drift copper, which could be located along beaches and streams, were collected by aboriginal craftsmen . This information is supported by efforts that required greater amounts of time and labor and a specialized extractive technology. Float copper from the Keweenaw Region would have been easy to obtain but would still be a limited local resource for prehistoric groups occupying the areas of Minnesota, Wisconsin, Michigan and Northern Illinois and Iowa. The report states that some of the copper used at Sand Point may have in fact been mined. Though the focus of the report suggests the emphasis on float copper, the processing entails crystalline chippage that may be represented by debitage left scattered on the site after copper ore had been extracted from the conglomerates.

The report includes the mention of two other prehistoric site locations in the Upper Great Lakes Region to the east of Sand Point. They are the Naomikong Point site at Whitefish Bay in Chippewa County and the Juntunen site located on Bois Blanc Island at the straits of Mackinaw in Lake Huron. Mention of these sites is for the purpose of establishing a chronology that is relative to the use of copper in each, concluding that the copper working industry at Sand Point precedes that of the other two sites and was fully developed by A.D. 1150. (The earliest dates being established as A.D. 1138.) The inhabi-

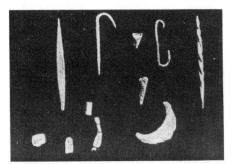

Copper artifacts from Sand Point. (Left to right, top) an awl, a fish hook or gaff hook, a conical bell, an unknown object, a twisted drill bit. (Lower) copper beads, a conical projectile point, a lunate ornament. (photo, courtesy Baraga County Historical Society)

Stone fish net weights that were instrumental in the wholesale harvest of fish for sedentary occupation. This significant find established the dependence on fish for winter survival. Unfortunately, these stone artifacts were stolen during the night. (photo, courtesy Baraga County Historical Society)

tants of Sand Point appeared to have developed and expanded their copper working technique prior to their counterparts at the straits of Mackinaw.

It was stressed that during this time a shift occurred in changing subsistence strategies. This reference primarily was directed toward a more efficient means of procuring fish. The site turned up stone net sinkers that evidenced the transition to the use of nets and weirs, over the copper hooks and barbs, as primary tools of harvesting fish.

The report suggests that considerable use was made of float copper to fabricate a variety of items. The number of copper implements indicated that their industry involved activities that included skills where perforation and/or drilling were common place practices.

It concludes by saying:

> Much has been written about the use of copper in the Upper Great Lakes region during the Late Archaic period but many questions remain to be addressed in regards to similar yet distinctive developments during the late Woodland period, a few of which have only been touched on here. Questions directed toward explaining the long hiatus between the "Old Copper Culture" and the subsequent reintroduction of copper working by later traditions, how the mineral was acquired, in what manner it was worked, and why, should make for enlightening research in the future.

## Physical Anthropology

This segment consisted of the examination of the human skeletal remains exhumed at Sand Point. It may very well prove to be the most interesting of all the sections of the report.

Initially upon examining the remains, the most basic information one attempts to learn is the cause of death (natural or homicidal), age, sex, and any deformities that may have been induced even after death.

Physical characteristics are determined to learn if the site was continually occupied by the same people, and what similarities existed among people outside of the site, community or region, also to detect any evidence that may be supplied by the ceremonial burial ritual itself, in this case not only bone bundles, but the observance of cremation.

Let us begin by examining some of the details at the site of the recovered remains. Of the nineteen burial mounds at Sand Point, skeletal remains were removed from only three. Those excavated were directly affected by the land development project that was underway and ultimately would have been destroyed.

Evidence indicates that all of the burials examined at Sand Point appeared to be secondary burials, meaning that a former aspect of the burial process involved pre-disposition of the corpses. Either they were previously buried somewhere else or placed on a raised platform for a period of time and the bones—those that were recoverable—were reburied at a later date in the mound structures. The bones were buried either singly, in ossuary burial pits, bundled (bound) long bone burials, or cremated. The most common burial accounting for 84% of the excavated individuals, were ossuary burials. They contained the mixed bones of two to fourteen individuals.

A total of 117 remains were recovered from the three mounds. The largest mound measured approximately 100′ feet long, was between six and nine feet high, and was the source of 91 of the total 117 remains. Only half of this mound was excavated and it yielded the greatest number of individuals. Within the portion of the mound that was excavated were uncovered: eight ossuary pits, eight single burials, and the cremated remains of four individuals who were found in association with a burnt wooden ramp structure built into the mound which apparently served as the funerary pyre.

The other two mounds were constructed quite differently. They were round in construction and lacked the elaboration of the large long mound. One of these, partially excavated, contained four ossuary pits. Both male and female adults and sub-adults were buried in this mound. Some were bundled burials and some appeared to be just thrown into the pit with no apparent attempt to isolate the individuals. A total of nineteen individual remains were recovered. The remaining mound was completely excavated. It contained two ossuary burial pits; removed were a total of five adult males.

Analysis of these skeletal remains was indeed a very arduous task. The mixing of bones in the ossuary pits made it especially difficult to sort out what belonged to whom. Add to this the problem of bone preservation, making determination of age and sex difficult, and in some cases impossible. In most cases the skull portions could not be associated with the correct individual remains. The report is quite explicit as to the methodology employed for the results that were collected. Of particular interest is a formulated system used to determine intra- and intersite biological relationships. It involves measured skeletal data used statistically to compile a measurement called a T-score. This computation is then compared with other populations of Eastern Woodland Peoples who compose a base population of over 1200 adult males and females from 30 other sites within the Eastern Woodland area. Without going into a great amount of detail or the techniques employed, we will instead rest with the results.

It was concluded that the individuals of Sand Point, despite the fact that they were removed from three separate locations, represented a single biological population within the site. Based on the information formulated the report states that the three mounds do not represent different populations.

A mortality profile was calculated for the 87 remains that could be assigned an age. The remaining individuals were determined to be adults. This would indicate the frequency of death in each age group. One startling observation for Sand Point was the under-representation of juveniles. Only twenty-five percent of the 117 Sand Point people were under the age of twenty with less than four percent (one individual) of these sub-adults being under the age of one. The report indicated that by comparison adult mortality was typical; however, it was the juveniles and infants that were under-represented in the Sand Point burial population. This mysterious lack of infant and juvenile individuals was explained in the report as having been due to any number of factors:

1.) Rapid decomposition due to the fact that immature bones do not preserve as well as adult bones.
2.) The small bones may have been overlooked during excavation.
3.) Different burial practices for different age groups—the most likely explanation.

Also there was a high number of adult deaths between the ages of 20-30. This, the report explains, was probably due to many female deaths related to complications of pregnancy and childbirths.

*Physical Examination of Mounds and Burial Practices*

Specific examination of the skeletal remains showed bone deformations. These consisted of holes that were inflicted on many of the long bones, (tibia, femur, humerus, etc.) to include holes in the pelvises and some of the skulls. Most of these insertions were the result of a blunt instrument that only crushed the cortex of the bones (near the ends), and were approximately one inch long by one-half inch wide.

The practice of bone deformation associated with the burial process, although widespread among Indian tribes, has no definite explanation. The report suggests that it was likely part of a ritual involving a belief that the bones contained spirits, or a soul within. By damaging the bone you were "killing" the soul, thus preventing the soul from being reincarnated, a practice that may have been imposed upon murdered enemies or other undesirable persons to prevent them from being born again.

Significant to the Sand Point burial mounds was the observance of cremation which was associated with their burial practices. Within the large linear mound was evidence of the construction of an elaborate wooden ramp structure that was utilized to cremate the skeletal remains of four children. The funeral pyre was constructed on top of an earthen berm that was raised on its northern end and sloped towards the south. The bones of the four youths were placed atop the substantial wood structure and set ablaze, after which the burnt remains were covered with a layer of fill from the adjacent area. It might be added that bone burials had been deposited in the large mound prior to the ceremonial cremation and others were also deposited in the fill atop this as well, indicating that this single mound was utilized over a period of time to bury and cover their dead in periodic intervals as the occasions arose. Thus the layers of fill would accumulate and give additional height to the mound over an extended period of time.

In conclusion, the report states that such a variety of methods of burial, i.e., single, multiple, bundled long bone burial, cremation and bone deformation, suggests different treatment for individuals according to age, status or other reasons.

In the case of bone deformation, for instance, among certain historic tribes of the Ottawa, Ojibwa and Potowatomi, cremation of the dead was reserved for individuals belonging to the family members of the Great Hare. The Ojibwa also cremated the bodies of warriors slain in battle. This, however, was not the case at Sand Point since the cremated remains were of children and the fact that the one individual that apparently died in warfare was not cremated. The fact that there was an under-representation of infants and juveniles in the mounds suggests they may have been buried elsewhere.

*Pathology*

The most prevalent diseases revealed by the examination of the skeletal remains showed that the Sand Point people seemed to suffer from some infection shown by bone inflammation. In fact, bone inflammation of the form known as *periostitis* was quite common. Approximately twenty-five per cent of the adult population showed varying degrees of this disease.

All five individuals (adult males) from the mound that was totally excavated showed some form of bone inflammation on the long bones. The most common site of infection was the tibia, followed by the fibula and the femur.

*Biological intersite comparison*

The report continues with comparing biological relationships outside of the site with other aboriginal groups in the Great Lakes Region. To do this, the T-score system was employed by comparing Sand Point populations to 30 others.

The results indicated that four populations were significantly similar to Sand Point. They were:

1.) The Winnebago Focus—which is confined to Wisconsin and generally thought to represent the Winnebago Indians.
2.) The Robinson site in Oneida County, Wisconsin, dated 1000-14000 A.D.
3.) The Old Birch Island Cemetery site, Manitoulin District of Ontario, dating 1750-1800, (historical)
4.) The Sauk Indian population, Rock County, Illinois, dated 1790-1820, (historical).

The report goes on to state that the comparative site studies of the Sand Point people and the Robinson site people, in Oneida County, Wisconsin, were closely related. Apparently similar characteristics were evident with the occurrence of bone deformations.

The conclusion of the intersite comparisons state that:

In all probability the Sand Point and Robinson people represented an Algonquian population due to their similarity to the Old Birch Island Ojibwa. This conclusion is also supported by the close similarity of the Sand Point to the historical Fletcher site population in Bay City, Michigan determined to be an Algonquian occupation.

*The Ceramic of Sand Point*

Some 40,000 pieces of pottery were collected at Sand Point. Out of this assemblage there was not a single complete vessel. The pieces were to be categorized in the field, bagged and labeled. However, due to the inexperience of the members of the field crew, much of the work involved resorting the material back at the laboratory.

The task of sorting, washing, drying, and re-examining the sherds was astronomical and tedious. The were counted, weighed and cataloged, then finally examined under magnification.

Without going into the exact details of pottery classification, we will only mention that it is quite extensive regarding the ware, types, styles, etc. The author mentions that the Sand Point ceramic type appears to bear close resemblance to certain Juntunen site ceramics; therefore, some of the same methods were used to describe the ceramics of Sand Point.

In the course of attempting to classify certain types of pottery with those at Sand Point the author makes an interesting statement worth repeating.

This rim section of a very large Late Woodland pot shows the impressions made by a twig wrapped with a string. The size of this pot is calculated at about two feet across with a capacity of more than five gallons. (photo, courtesy Baraga County Historical Society)

Although I am convinced to the validity of the topology arrived at herein, I am hesitant to add to the proliferation of similar already named types of Late Woodland pottery, in the Upper Great Lakes.

If we view artifact analysis as a means to discover and understand human behavioral patterns, an objective sometimes forgotten in the impersonal world of the laboratory, we should remember that an archaeological site and its artifactual assemblage represents a community of living, working people who manufacture the greater part of their own tools and utensils. Sand Point pottery, for example, and for the most part, was not made by Heins Creek, Juntunen or Aztalan people, and it would serve little purpose to so classify it, leaving the Sand Point people, as it were, without a pot to call their own. Furthermore, I believe that I can demonstrate real differences of Sand Point types from similar types in surrounding areas.

Accordingly, he established a ware group which he believes differs sufficiently from previously defined wares to warrant its own designation, calling it the Sand Point ware group. It was represented by 152 of the 204 pottery vessel samples collected from the site. The largest vessel of the Sand Point collection was measured at 40 centimeters in diameter.

Other classifications of pottery were identified and represented as: Black Duck ware—one vessel; Heins Creek ware—one vessel; Juntunen ware—eighteen vessels; Unclassified—fifteen vessels (believed to be a local expression of Upper Mississippian and Oneota pottery ware) and Mississippi ware—ten vessels.

The information supplied for dating the pottery is very confusing and when presented in the report raises many questions as to the credibility of the information as supplied by the samples for carbon dating. For instance, three carbon dates were obtained from three samples of wood charcoal. The first sample was taken from the large burial mound and was dated A.D. 1055. A second sample was retrieved from the same square, but one foot lower and was dated a later date of A.D. 1200. To this, add the variable allowance for a possible 55 year deviation in the dates suggested and it still leaves a time lapse of 55 years between them.

The reason for this mysterious juxtaposition of dates relative to stratification was unknown. The report does not state specifically whether both samples were secured from the same pieces of carbonized log that were part of the same funeral pyre used in the ceremonial burial. It is therefore possible that the carbonized specimens may have been from fill gathered from a habitation location and deposited into the mound during the course of inserting and covering a later burial. Mr. Moore cited evidence of this in the course of excavating one of the mounds. It would seem reasonable for this to occur since digging soil from the forest floor would be especially difficult when contending with entangled tree roots.

Due to their burial customs involving the periodic displacement of soil from various locations, especially including the habitation site, it would make it virtually impossible to arrive at any conclusions that would be based on the placement of a feature within a certain soil stratification. Unfortunately this would have to apply to the entire site. The following example will illustrate this problem:

A third carbonized sample was collected from wood charcoal remains from the hearth of the habitation area. It was recovered near the bottom of the artifactual bearing levels (about eighteen inches below the surface). The carbon dating derived at was A.D. 330. Mr. Dorothy stated that the ceramic from near this feature was generally nondiagnostic but seemed to be consistent with other styles found on the site. The only type found in this habitation as differing temporally was the Juntunen Drag-and-Jab, which was firmly dated by previous documentation at A.D. 1300, this being much later than the other Sand Point styles. He concludes, "The A.D. 330 - date therefore appears to be highly inconsistent with Sand Point pottery styles."

The report continues to explain the reason for the various ceramic type distributions in the burial mound. It explains that the only major types which were significantly different were the Mississippian pottery and the Juntunen

Drag-and-Jab. Of the former, only one vessel was found in the habitation area and only one Juntunen type was found in the burial mound. Mr. Dorothy concludes:

> These were both minor and presumably exotic types at Sand Point and if dates for the burial mound are correct, might indicate a relatively earlier occurrence of the Juntunen type at Sand Point, or a relatively later date for the habitation area for the Juntunen pottery as compared to the burial mound pottery at Sand Point.

The report also states:

> . . . the date of A.D. 330 does not correlate well with the pottery found in direct association with the sample. Rather, it is suspected that this date is in error with this feature and the habitation is in general, being of the same age or perhaps somewhat more recent than the activity associated with the construction of the burial mound.

This discrepancy has been explained by the fact that fill from the habitation area was removed and found deposited in the burial mounds, confounding any possible means to associate stratification of features with any chronological accuracy. (1.)

The A.D. 330 date from the habitation area was not considered as a factor in dating the site. Archaeologists concluded that the date of the site was from A.D. 1100-1400, which was apparently based on the majority of the ceramic remains found at the site corresponding to the two carbon specimens of the one burial mound. It must be realized, however, that due to the cultural burial practices that involved periodic disturbances to the site, if the carbon dates prove anything, they merely date their respective samples regardless of where they were found. Additionally, the dates of the site correspond to what is referred to as the late Mississippian period.

Therefore, it would appear that the Sand Point site may have been an important locus even prior to A.D. 1100, if for only seasonal occupation, as the A.D. 330 date may suggest. Equally important is the fact that this location may have been habitated beyond the date of A.D. 1400 and into the historic period!

Our ceramic expert, Mr. Dorothy, concludes his segment of the report with these very noble words:

> Perhaps, as others have observed, burial mounds and complexes may not be the ideal places upon which to hypothesize cultural dynamics, and especially at sites such as Sand Point *where cultural remains show no clear association or stratification*. The diversity and cross-cutting of pottery characteristics in this area of the upper Great Lakes region is as puzzling to me as it has been to others working in the area. Perhaps greater attention should be paid to the more conservative practices of burial custom and lithic technology as cultural indicators. On

(1.) This fact was reinforced by Mr. Moore, who was located and interviewed in the spring of 1997.

the other hand, *perhaps our confusion arises from our inability to decipher the information contained in our data.* Sand Point fills a geographical hiatus between Wisconsin and the Straits of Mackinac. It is beyond the scope of this report to synthesize all data now available, but it is hoped that the data presented here, combined with that of previous reports, will lend itself to such a clarification. [Italics added]

*Lithage Assemblage Report*

At the time of the publication of the Archaeological Report the lithage assemblage report was not available. It was reported to have been in the process of being analyzed and was not available in time for publication.

However, the individual who was to have analyzed the lithage assemblage also left the university and consequently it was not finished. In fact, as of this writing, it still has not been completed; therefore, that information is not available and there is no indication as to when it will be completed.

This portion of the research is very significant to the study since among its works are at least three very important artifacts: the unique stone earspool, the musket ball and the gun flint.

After a year of attempting to find Mr. Moore, he was located living in Michigan not far from the university. He stated that the musket ball and flint should still be among the artifacts in storage, along with his field notes.

When asked about the musket ball and flint, he stated that they were found on the beach area of the site within approximately ten yards of each other. The beach area was not formerly dug as a designated area, since it was considered too disturbed to be of significance; meaning that the area was exposed to a great deal of human foot travel; however, no heavy equipment had been in this area. Archaeologists were examining the area because of the extensive amount of pottery sherds that were visible on the beach as well as in the water.

Mr. Moore stated that the musket ball was the size of a marble and was in good condition. He also stated that a slate earspool was included in the inventory of recovered material.

Finally, contact was made with the university to locate the musket ball in hopes that further testing could be conducted to reinforce our suspected historical correlation of the site itself. University officials were unable to locate it, and it appears that this very significant piece of evidence has been lost to research. How this happened is unknown.

It was further disclosed that the skeletal remains had not been returned to the site as agreed upon when they were exhumed 25 years ago; however, the university just recently initiated steps to do so.

# 4

# THE COVE

It would be the cove of Keweenaw Bay that the ancient people of Sand Point would choose for their habitation and ritual burial grounds. This place would provide protection from the worst of winter conditions that only those who live here can understand and truly appreciate. More importantly, it was a location that would provide large amounts of fish that would adequately supplement their food needs if they were to survive the cold lengthy winters.

Not only did this "Grand Lac" called *Superior*, provide an abundance of fish, but the many streams and rivers that flow into it were teeming with spring and fall runs of fish as well. The most spectacular of the Lake Superior fish were the lake trout and whitefish. The streams ran with large sturgeon in the spring. In the fall the large spawning lake trout followed the shallow lake shores. Fish appeared in such large numbers that they would stagger our imaginations today. Equally abundant were "clouds" of waterfowl that appeared in the spring and fall, which invaded the marshes as well as the shallows of the open bay.

Not only were the rivers of the *Grand Lake* important for food, but they served as important highways to connect their settlement to others in the area and beyond. They used canoes to access the rivers that provided easement to the interior of many distant lands. From river to river they portaged to link trade routes that were essential to the Sand Point site. They accessed routes that led them into the Mississippi River and as far away as the ancient city of Cahokia.

The cove is located at the southernmost end of Keweenaw Bay. The term 'Keweenaw' means, 'Place of the Portage' or the 'Carrying Place'. It was this location that was used to access a short-cut across the prominent peninsula of land that juts well into Lake Superior. This peninsula will not only prove to be a very historic place, but also very ancient grounds for prehistoric man as well. The reason for this is its unique abundance of pure copper. A short-cut was accessed at what today is called the Keweenaw Waterway or the Portage Ship Canal. The canal construction of this waterway has actually severed the penin-

Aerial view of the "cove" on Keweenaw Bay with Sand Point protruding into it from the northwest and Pequaming Point from the southeast. Present day village of L'Anse is on the south side of the bay and Baraga on the north.

sula from the mainland, where today, it is an island connected by a lift bridge in present day Houghton.

We can not be sure what these early dwellers called the place on Sand Point, but the first historic explorers would call it 'Anse,' a French term meaning 'bay.' Even today the existing village of L'Anse, meaning 'The Cove,' located on Keweenaw Bay, is a testament to this early reference by these explorers.

L'Anse ranks as one of Michigan's oldest place names. It is unique in the state as it shares its ancient French name with no other geographical designation along Michigan's many miles of Great Lakes shore. On many of the early maps of the area the Upper Michigan Lake Superior shoreline was one of the first to show up as it lay along the main route into the heart of New France. L'Anse already had a familiar place in American geography 200 years before many of its neighbors. (1.)

One of the first French fur traders to enter western Lake Superior was Pierre Esprit Radisson in 1659. The first European reported to have entered the bay was the missionary, Father Rene Menard, in the same year. New information, however, will demonstrate this to be inaccurate as historical discoveries will reveal that other French explorers had preceded him and Radisson.

---

(1.) *Baraga County Historical Pageant*, Carter, 1969:8.

The present day village of L'Anse is located across the bay on the opposite shore from Sand Point. It was near this location that the French constructed a fur trading post in 1800. Activity in the French fur trade had long preceded this date as trade was commencing between the very western reaches of Lake Superior and the location at Mackinac. But for most historical interest, this generally has been the period that commemorates the historical beginning of L'Anse. The French fur trading post of the North West Company was essentially established to accommodate trading interest with residing native American Ojibwa that had gathered here. Close to follow were the missionaries who accompanied them and began their exploits to civilize these native people.

The first Europeans to L'Anse would become embroiled in controversies that would divide the existing native community. The Methodist mission that was established at Zeba was divided, which encouraged the deployment of the missionary Father Baraga from the Catholic mission at LaPointe to assist in resolving the conflict. Baraga assembled the resisting flock at a location called Assinins, across the bay near the present day village of Baraga. Hence, we have the two communities as they stand today.

A native American Ojibwa tribe resides on Keweenaw Bay as a result of the Treaty of 1854, thereby establishing the present day reservation for the L'Anse band of the Chippewa. The legends of the Chippewa, as well as the historic evidence, supplies us with how these Algonkin migrants moved westward from their previous homelands at present day Sault Ste. Marie; they eventually settled into western Lake Superior and Keweenaw Bay.

This is a very brief overview of the history of L'Anse during this early period, which emphasizes how important the cove was to all of these early inhabitants of Lake Superior. Today, Lake Superior is just as important to its modern inhabitants as it was for the preceding prehistoric occupants. In recent times, however, the dependency on the waters of the bay has been principally for recreational use, yet some of the native Ojibwa still fish the depths of the bay for a livelihood. The number of recreational and sportfishing boats far surpasses the number of tribal fishing boats using these waters.

The presence and influence of the modern-day Keweenaw Bay Indian community is very evident today. Casino gambling and the tourism it brings to the area have provided prosperity to this once depressed population of native people. Motels and restaurants accommodate the traveler. The long cold winters and large amounts of snowfall are no longer a time of desperation, but instead have become an asset to the native community with the popular interest in snowmobiling and cross-country skiing. Extensive snowmobile trails now replace the foot trails that were once important for accessing hunting grounds. The spirit of the native American is still very evident in the annual presentation of the tribal Powwow that takes place at the Indian Camp Grounds on Sand Point.

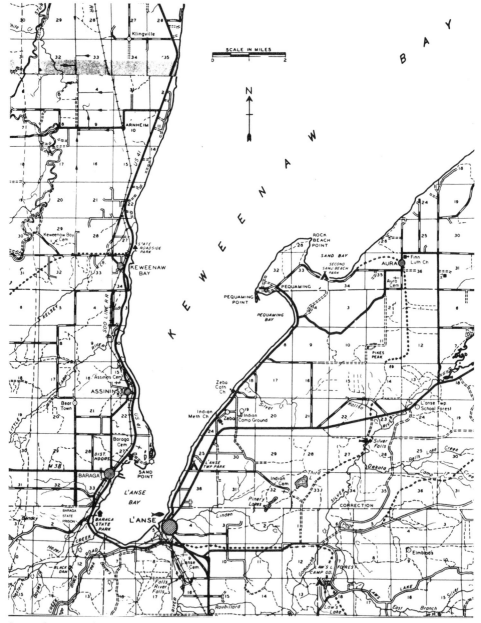

Located on a southeastern shore Sand Point was located at the heart of the copper country of the Keweenaw Peninsula that extended well into Lake Superior.

But who were the ancient dwellers of Sand Point? We have already mentioned that the Ojibwa migrated into the region during the historic period. The Archaeological Report reveals that carbon dating of the site predates that of the Ojibwa and corresponds to the classification of the late Mississippian mound building culture, an occupation which may have occurred as early as 330 A.D. On the basis of the scientific results, it definitely appears that the residing Chippewa are not the descendants of the Sand Point people. That being the case, is there any historical evidence that may allude to who these people were?

Baraga County Historical Society sponsored a historical pageant in 1969 and solicited several historians from around the area to contribute articles of historic interest for their booklet.

One of these historians was Mr. James L. Carter from Northern Michigan University of Marquette. His article was titled, L'ANSE SHOWN ON 1688 MAP and included an enlarged map of Keweenaw Bay from a map published by DuVal of Paris in 1669. What is so striking about this map is an Indian settlement that Mr. Carter identifies on the map that is none other than that of Sand Point. This "settlement of Indians" was indicated by "a cluster of dots at the present site of L'Anse-Baraga." Next to it are the words "Nation du Feu," meaning "Nation of Fire." What possible correlation could this historic map have with the known location of a native "settlement of Indians" revealed by the archaeologists digging at Sand Point? This question would provide the impetus for launching a grand historic research effort into finding the answer. (1.)

What had Mr. Carter hit on with his identity of Sand Point containing a "settlement of Indians?" Ironically, he had no way of knowing, since his research and article preceded the discovery and confirmation of the archaeological dig, which did not occur until 1970. The results were not published until 1980.

It would appear that had the archaeologists accessed the map prior to their investigation of the site, they may have easily confirmed the historical existence of this habitation. It appeared that someone else already had. When Mr. Winston Moore surveyed the site at Sand Point, he reported that every one of the mounds had been previously intruded possibly 30, 40, 50, maybe even 100 years before. The intrusions into the mounds were solely for the purpose of securing grave goods; these relic hunters abandoned their efforts, having found none. Someone must have accessed a source that led them to the site long before archaeologists in 1970. Could it have been this same map that tipped them off to the possibility of this location being that of a "settlement of Indians?"

---

(1.) *Baraga County Historical Pageant*, Carter, 1969:8.

The famous map of DuVal's was first introduced to the American public in 1931, published by the Michigan History Commission and titled *Bibliography of the Printed Maps of Michigan*, by Prof. Louis Karpinski.

Is it possible that the dates of the intrusions implied by Mr. Moore, correspond to that of the publication of this map, especially since relic hunters somehow must have been able to identify and find the location of Sand Point?

The next logical place to continue the investigation was to travel to the nearest university to locate a copy of this map. At the archives extensive efforts were made to research every available source that would provide us with everything there was to learn about this curious map. Somewhere, hidden away in some obscure historic annals, lay the answers.

# 5

# THE ARCHIVES

The last time I had seen the inside of a library was during my high school days, some 30 years ago. So prior to my arrival at Michigan Technological University in Houghton, I tried to refresh my memory as to the procedural aspects of the library.

After consulting the librarian at the information desk, I soon realized how inadequate my former impression was. The librarian politely marched me over to a computer screen, and immediate culture shock set in. I was computer illiterate and admitted it. No card catalogs here! She was not about to hold my hand, despite my lack of knowledge, and proceeded to give me a hands-on crash-course in the use of their new filing system.

The reality of not facing the modern electronic world of cyber-space was no longer avoidable. If I were to advance my research, it would require that I adapt to the system and rid myself of any former prejudice and disdain for these modern toys. Perhaps I would modify, but I would never allow it to substitute for doing things the old fashioned way. Besides, there were not any book reader diskettes for the subject material that I was researching anyway. Hyper-links and hotspots were useless to me. This experience, however, would eventually lead to purchasing a word processor and joining the propeller-headed world of computer enthusiasts.

To begin with, university libraries are not places most ordinary people would find themselves in their spare time. (Too academic, too boring and uneventful). If fact, very few of the full time attendants of the university ever find themselves on the third floor of the Archives. But that is where my search was taking me, and with any investigation, you follow the trail, wherever it leads you.

By beginning on the first floor of the map room, I found myself seeking out 17th century maps. The volume I was searching for was Karpinski's bibliography that displayed the 1669 map of DuVal's. This compilation had several other map references that were also useful. In the course of studying this map, much could be learned from closely inspecting it in its entirety. What makes this map especially significant are the dots that are shown. They specifically designated concentrations of native people or settlements. The fact that there are four dots denoting the Sand Point location would indicate a rather sizable number of people in the village complex. In fact, the map is literally covered with dots, especially along the coastal areas of the bays.

What possible connection could this historic "settlement of Indians" have with any of our known history? Could this information be hidden away in some annals, eluding us in the course of our interpreting the past history of the Great Lakes? There is no doubt that the location cited on the map, and the excavation of the Sand Point site, in 1970, are the same location.

I was convinced that the dots were not just arbitrarily placed on the map, despite the fact that there were so many of them at other locations. The ones denoting Sand Point were just too obvious and discriminate, indicating that someone had to have been there to know that a "settlement of Indians" did in fact exist here. For this location to show up on a French map meant that it must have been placed there with the knowledge of a Frenchman.

As we continue to examine this most important map we notice Karpinski's caption at the bottom of the page that states: *"This map is based directly upon the Champlain map of 1632; Lake Erie is named, and the name, Lac des Puants, is incorrectly applied to Champlains Superior."* (see Chapter 7:58) What could the author mean? That Lake Superior was incorrectly called the "Lac des Puants"? What basis would this author have for making such a claim? And what did these French words mean? Since the entire map was in French, I was at a loss to determine what all the other references meant. The reference to the word "Puants" was also used at a location on a large river system west of the peninsula. The translating of these French references would be anticipated with great excitement. Since I was at a loss to interpret the language myself, a French language expert would have to be sought out in order to compensate for my language deficiency. Fortunately, the university had a French language program and the instructor was very qualified. She had spent her entire life as a native of France and had only been in this country a couple of years; her French was perfect. It was her English that I was having a problem with; however, she was very friendly and accommodating.

With this map as the only lead, it then became apparent that locating additional information may be difficult, if in fact, it even existed. It was a long shot, but I was convinced that somewhere buried away in some ancient records there just might be some answers. The most likely place to find that information was in the archives.

From the bottom floor of the map room one had to ascend three flights of stairs to where the archives were located. The first impression of the archives is a rather forbidding one. It almost conveys the impression that you should have a security clearance prior to entering. This is all quickly dispelled by the friendly reception of the staff. They were very helpful and willing to assist in every way.

My research would entail searching for material that would have to provide me with historical data that would directly correlate with the particular information on the map. It would mean seeking out sources that would cover the early exploration of America by the French in the early 1600's. To learn of the first historical records of the Great Lakes region, there were several sources that would eventually have to be plowed through. The one I dreaded most was the one I chose first. It would be the 73 volumes of the books referred to as the *Jesuit Relations and Allied Documents*. Other sources would include the journals of such Frenchmen as Champlain, Sagard, Radisson and Perrot, just to mention a few. (1.)

I became a regular presence at the Archives since these publications could not be removed from the premises. All of the publications were over a 100 years old and the availability limited. Bear in mind that the original information contained in these volumes was recorded over 350 years ago. It was a trip back in time to be able to experience holding these antiquated treasures. Care must be taken when opening the covers. Some are so brittle that you can hear them creak if you open them up too far. Pages that are all irregular, no two cut the same size, make it necessary to turn the pages from the top since the margins are uneven, and map print so small that reading it requires the use of a large magnifying lens. Lots of notes would be taken with lots of paper and pencils.

There I was confined for eight hours at a time, in this vault of literary antiquity. (Doing it the old fashioned way.) I soon began to wonder if this was all really worth it.

Each trip to the archives would reveal an additional piece of encouraging information that would provide the incentive to keep me returning for another round of eight hours of punishment. Besides, I was already too committed to quit now, and I was learning some neat stuff that was buried away in these old books. They just needed someone to blow the dust off them and bring them back to life. After all, there was a story here and if I did not tell it, it was not going to get told.

After an extended period of time exploring the historical records of the *Relations,* some revealing pieces of evidence began to emerge. For instance, references to the Puants began to surface and give meaning to who they were in relationship to their historic place in early French history. Also, some key names began to appear that were part of these events that are part of the story.

It would be in the archives that the most critical evidence would be revealed about our discovered map of Karpinski's, a map that he identified as the Du Val map of 1669, and as succeeding that of Champlain's map of 1632.

(1.) The Internet may be accessed for research of the *Jesuit Relations*. A recent experimental website was brought on line in a joint project of <u>Le Moyne College</u>, the <u>Jesuit College of Central New York</u> and <u>Ste. Marie Among The Iroquois</u>, a facility of Onondaga County Parks. http://vc.lemoyne.edu/relations/

At the present time the project continues to undergo completion as many of the volumes are not yet on line.

The evidence that would prove fatal to Mr. Karpinski's bibliography would not be found in the M.T.U. Archives, but would necessitate a journey to the archives of Mr. Karpinski's own library of research where he produced his bibliography some 66 years before, the William L. Clements Library located at the University of Michigan in Ann Arbor.

It was after inserting the sixteenth quarter in the parking meter and crossing University Avenue, on the university campus at Ann Arbor, that I approached this rather old Greek-style building. It appeared to have been one of the original buildings and was the library of American history. It was necessary to enter the building from a rear entrance. Walking around to the rear of the building, I found myself digging into my pocket to offer a begging fox squirrel my last butterscotch candy. As usual, we were in the basement again, digging into maps, particularly maps by DuVal. The facility was especially sensitive to security and for very good reason, the map curator produced an original French map published by DuVal.

Since Karpinski's publication of the *Printed Maps . . .* , new discoveries have emerged for the researcher of DuVal's maps. The research into this map became rather complex and necessitated some intensive efforts to complete. Contrary to Karpinski's thinking, DuVal's 1669 map does not succeed Champlain's map of 1632 that is so well known. In fact, it will be shown that the DuVal map was also drafted by Champlain in 1616 and is the very first historical map of the Great Lakes region. (Details of the 1616 map and DuVal's 1669 map are covered in Chapter 7.)

Before we can truly understand the significance of these maps and how they originated, it is just as necessary to know who may have contributed to their inception. By identifying these individuals we can know what part they played in the events of the European exploration of America. Only when we understand their roles, the conditions and methods they employed to acquire the knowledge and information that are testament to their witness can we understand how to interpret these events from their maps and journals. Only when we have examined all the records available can we expect to formulate any conclusions upon which to base our convictions. Let us advance further into our research and find out who some of these players were and how their efforts are all part of understanding the big picture of the history of New France, and particularly, the exploration of the Great Lakes.

# 6

# THE FRENCH

Since the initial piece of evidence is a map of French origin it is going to necessitate researching the occupation and exploration of the region in question by these early Europeans.

In order for us to make our research relative to the map references of the DuVal map of 1669, we must associate the map references with those French participants who were responsible for them. As we acquire more knowledge of their experiences in this region, we will be able to correlate the historical evidence, as it appears on the maps, with that of the historical record of events. This task will not be an easy one.

We have already mentioned accessing the *Jesuit Relations*. It is the most extensive and reliable source of information relating to this period and will prove to be the most complementary to the maps in question. The missionaries and their memoirs will be included in a separate section in this chapter.

### Samuel de Champlain

Considered the Father of New France, Champlain was the driving force behind most of the events that occurred during the period of our inquiry. His cartographical contribution to our knowledge of the early Great Lakes is evident by the maps that he made identifying the new lands that were so important to the explorer. His journals will inform us of his actions and thoughts as they relate to developing a new colony. He emphasizes how important the native people were to the French, without whom they would never have been able to claim the vast territory that was considered New France.

Champlain's greatest contributions to the researcher of geographical inquiry are his maps of North America, maps explaining the region of the St. Lawrence and the western Great Lakes that he first identified as the "Mer douce" or the "fresh-water seas." He solicited information from the native people as well as made personal journeys into the unexplored waters in order to chart them for the first time. His most important journey of 1615 to the Great Lakes would provide us with key information that would supplement other recorded historic evidence for the occupation of a "settlement of Indians" on Sand Point.

Champlain was caught up in the exploratory hype that was cause for the European countries of England, Spain and France to search out a route through the newly discovered land mass that was impeding access to China and Japan. The search for the northwest passage was the driving force behind the efforts of all the explorers, especially Champlain, who in 1610 was rivaled by the exploits of Henry Hudson, in present day Hudson's Bay. The threat of the English finding the route, thought to exist in this northern region, compelled Champlain rigorously to persuade French authorities to continue supporting the colonial effort. The basis for his argument would rest on his "judgment" that a route lay west of the present occupation of the new colony, through the western Great Lakes. Due to lack of wealth by France in comparison to that of England and Spain, the discovery of the northwest passage and control of the route would certainly be worth the investment.

In order to keep his idea alive it would be necessary for Champlain to travel almost annually back and forth from Quebec to France reporting on his progress. A voyage encompassed a whole month and was not without peril. On one occasion a vessel ran atop a whale causing it to take on so much water that it had to return to Quebec. Eventually, vessels would be lost at sea due to storms, a loss of both cargo, passengers and crew.

Champlain was relentless in his constant struggle to perpetuate his ideas. He would battle rival opponents seeking his office and contend with continual conflicts with investment merchants, power struggles within the Church, appeasing the King, and mutinies among his colonists. The natives of this new land would be equally demanding as they rivaled for French trade.

Champlain would be compelled to form alliances that would increase social tensions already existing among the tribes. Skirmishes would totally disrupt trade, French exploration, and native demographics; eventually they escalated into a major conflict that would necessitate the deployment of a regiment of elite French forces to resolve.

The Indian tribes were a major problem for Champlain despite the problems back in France. His initial concern was bridging the language gap that existed between these two very different cultures.

*The Interpreters*

Because of France's lack of wealth to finance the colonial effort, Champlain was compelled to utilize the local populations of native people and their beaver to finance it. His economic plan entailed soliciting natives to travel to a location where French middlemen would make contact and trade fur for French goods. These middlemen were key people in the economic system. Since the language barrier was a principal obstacle in organizing this system, Champlain needed to recruit candidates who could learn the native language. For this task Champlain chose young "grown up boys," mostly in their teens.

They would have to be a rigorous lot since they were sent into the native communities to live in order to learn the languages.

In addition to learning the language they were also instructed to learn everything they could about the people, their country, the lakes, rivers and mines. They would spend the winter with the various tribes and make the annual journey down river to the *Sault* or rapids at LaChine, where they would exchange fur for the prized knives, kettles, axes, beads, etc. These "boys" were instrumental in bridging the existing language problem.

Additionally, Champlain failed to maintain a monopoly on the fur trade. An open market created competition that he met by sending these hardy "lads" into the wilderness to befriend or create native alliances. The Interpreter was sent to every major trading nation in order to control the market. Likewise, as the industry and competition progressed, along with the threat of Iroquois rivals, the need for additional fortifications, or trading posts, were eventually required.

These adventurous "lads" were exposed to extreme conditions of survival and were apparently well selected to perform in these capacities. Just where these grown up boys originated is an interesting subject for discussion, since they seemed to adapt so well to the life style of the wilds; engaging in stealing, lying, and taking advantage of the sexual promiscuity of the young native girls. The record speaks of their delinquency in the capitulation of Quebec, due to the traitorous participation of several of these "domestic" delinquents. Punishment for their misdeeds or lack of cooperation was to send them back to France!

Of these Interpreters only a few become historically distinguished. One of these was Etienne Brulé (pronounce Et-jen, or the English is Stephen). Another is Jean Nicolet (pronounced John). These two are legendary, each in his own right. As for character, they could not be farther apart on the spectrum.

The reason these two are important to us is that they are to play key roles in providing the historical record with some very valuable information that is essential to this investigation. In fact, Nicolet will provide us with the vital evidence that will eventually prove who these mysterious people were and how they directly correlate to the location of Sand Point. The investigation will intensify as Nicolet becomes a principal witness to solving this mystery, which will be revealed as the focus of the investigation narrows.

*French Traders and Explorers*

Three traders that are key characters to our research also deserve mention.

The first two are really a trading team, Pierre Esprit Radisson and his brother-in-law, Medart Chouart, or more commonly known as des Grosiller.

Radisson has got to be the most daring and aspiring trader of New World French history. No one covered as much country, in such a short span of time, as these intrepid explorers did. They engaged in their exploits during a period when the St. Lawrence and Ottawa Rivers were under attack by the Iroquois. Traveling with natives as their guides, they accessed Green Bay and the Wisconsin interior, not stopping until they had entered the Mississippi River. They no sooner returned when they were off again into Lake Superior and west into the Sioux country. They constructed a fort at Chequamegon and two years later returned. Upon their return they ran into some problems with the French authorities. They defected to the English and eventually ended up in Hudson Bay where their trading exploits earned them credit for starting the famous Hudson Bay Company.

Radisson was very experienced in dealing with native people. He was not in New France a year when he was captured by the Iroquois. Although his two companions were killed, he was spared and adopted into the tribe and lived among them for a year. A mere sixteen, he eventually escaped and returned to the service of the French. As a result of his journeys, he records and leaves one of the most confusing accounts of any historic journal.

Grosiller came to New France as a missionary donné. As an explorer he communicated his activities to the Jesuit missionaries, who recorded them in their journals.

One important thing to mention is that despite the many separate journals that were kept by these individuals, many of these observers knew each other and of their exploits. There was no doubt that they were cognizant of each other's travels and activities. This is reflected by the missionaries explaining the progressions of discoveries of these new lands and recording them in their journals. They failed to mention names, but the information they had learned was from many of the explorers, who were the first to come in contact with the native groups that were the focus of the missionary purpose. In most cases, it was only after initial contact with the explorers that the missionary would venture into what was previously uncharted waters to open new missions.

The last trader is Nicolas Perrot, who left us a great deal of information and came on scene after Radisson. He moved into Green Bay a number of years after Radisson's previous exploits to this region. Like Radisson, Perrot built a fort and traded with many of the tribes that had fled into this region due to the onslaught of the Iroquois war. Perrot spent over 30 years of his life among the Indian people. He gained a great deal of respect from both the French and native groups. Fortunately for us, he kept extensive journals from his many experiences in the Green Bay area. His witness and testament provided the details of the inhabitants of Sand Point. A rendition that highlights the very nature of these fearsome people and explains how they were nearly annihilated, causing their departure from the shores of Lake Superior. (1.)

---

(1.) *The Indian Tribes of the Upper Mississippi Valley & Region of the Great Lakes*, Blair, 1911:I:288-301.

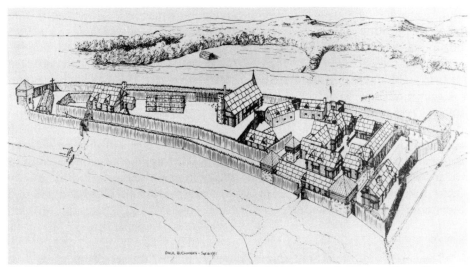

The elaborate fort of Ste. Marie was located on the Wye River, one mile from southern Georgian Bay. It consisted of two compounds, one for the French, another for the natives. Access included a water channel with three locks and a loading area. Constructed in 1639, it was burned to the ground by the French fleeing the Iroquois in 1649. From *Sainte Marie Among the Hurons* by Wilfrid Jury and Elsie McLeod Jury (Toronto: Oxford University Press, 1954). Reprinted by permission of Oxford University Press Canada.

## The Donné

This group of volunteers or "domestic" participants that donated (donné) their labor, talents and *lives* for the service of the missionaries, deserves mention. Not only as a group of religious servants, but because they were recruited to build a fort at a most significant location in the "upper country." The location, called Ste. Marie, was the center for the Huron mission that became so well known on Georgian Bay. The Hurons were the most important ally and it was necessary to maintain friendly relations with them. It was helpful that they were sedentary, but more importantly they were familiar with the western reaches of the Great Lakes where they had been trading with people that the French were particularly interested in—the Sea People, who would lead them to the Pacific Ocean. Ste. Marie was an especially important location for the French, not only as a mission location, but because it was the most advanced French habitation in the western wilderness.

By 1639 it was deemed necessary to build a fort at the location, and it was undertaken by the missionaries, who recruited young volunteers to build it. The fort endured for ten years. What was important about the location was that it served as an outpost for French explorers who were plying their way into the western waters of the Great Lakes. Brulé was assigned here in 1610 and would spend the rest of his life here. Nicolet used this location to begin his famous and controversial journey, where he likely returned and spent the winter before continuing on to Three Rivers. It was at Ste. Marie that des Grosillers began his career as a donné doing his part for the service of the missionaries.

During the period of 1639-1649, as many as 40-60 Frenchmen had occupied the fort, which was considerable when you realize that the total French population of Canada was only 250. It was also during this time the missionary volunteers would participate in the exploration of the Great Lakes. They would pick up where the explorers Brulé and Nicolet had left off. Practically nothing is recorded of their exploits into the western Great Lakes, but they were there, confirmed by information that was finding its way into the missionary journals during this period. We will examine the evidence during this discourse in order to add the missing pieces to the exploratory puzzle that have plagued our understanding of the discovery of Great Lakes. (1.)

*The Missionaries*

The earliest missionaries to New France were the Recollets, who, other than Gabriel Sagard, left us very few records. The Recollets were replaced by the Jesuit order of the Society of Jesus, and it is from these missionaries' journals that we have access to a mountain of information relative to the native American people of North America.

As previously mentioned, the missionary journals would come to be known as the *Relations* and were eventually compiled into the volumes we know today as the *Jesuit Relations and Allied Documents*. (2.)

The *Relations* would concern themselves mainly with the apostolic efforts of the Jesuits and their associates. They covered their travels and methods of organization, as well as studies of the native people, their language, instruction and spiritual ministrations.

Because the focus of the Jesuit was on the native American, they provide us with extraordinary information about the natives' customs and beliefs, their physical features, their games, tribal divisions, occupations, rivalries, wars, alliances, hunting and fishing, dwellings, food, etc.

The *Relations* also provide us with many geographical details, about rivers, lakes, streams, and the trips they engaged to access various parts of the country.

Most important was information that had historical significance to the French exploration of the New World. The journey of Jean Nicolet would be revealed through the witness and testaments of the missionaries. They would also articulate other events that would have great significance for this research effort.

The search for historical information relative to the exploration of the Great Lakes region is very perplexing when studying the missionary journals.

(1.) *Sainte Marie Among the Hurons*, Jury, 1954.
(2.) *Jesuit Relations and Allied Documents*, Thwaites, (73 Vols.; 1899)

Especially difficult is assembling these events into any chronological order, due to the bits and pieces of information which are found fragmented throughout their writings. It almost appears that many of the really important events that deal with the exploration of the Great Lakes are intentionally omitted. This is the case with Nicolet's journey and the native group with whom he had contact.

One explanation for the intentional omission is that the French were desperately searching for a passage that was thought to exist via the Great Lakes leading to the Pacific Ocean. Information alluding to, or giving explanation to the discovery of such a route, would seriously jeopardize the ability of the French to control it. Therefore, it appears that the missionaries avoided specific reference to searching for the passage in their letters, since these were published in France and made public. Should the passage be discovered and the English wish to seize it, the French would have been unable to defend it; they lacked the resources and man-power presently existing in the colony. Surely, had the French discovered a passage it would have been cause for war between these two countries, who were both attempting to locate an access thought to exist in this region of the North American continent.

Consequently, the missionaries had to be careful when reporting events in their letters. Quite possibly references alluding to any efforts for exploration of the "passage" may have been edited out when they arrived in France. As an example, the missionaries' account of Nicolet's journey does not so much as mention his efforts to search for the sea route, except they slip up and describe a Chinese robe that happened to be part of his attire. Other exploratory efforts appear to have been kept out of the missionary letters. It is not that the missionaries are not interested, because eventually their letters begin to divulge references to the search for the "South sea," but only after Champlain's death. It is not until 1658 that the cat is let out of the bag. (1.)

These circumstances make researching this information from the *Relations* especially challenging. These bits and pieces of the exploration puzzle, which are scattered throughout the missionaries' memoirs, will have to be gathered and fit into logical order so we can sort out what was really going on in the Great Lakes. The French purpose in North America was based on the tireless efforts of Champlain to locate this mythological "passage."

What will be presented from these journals is documented evidence supporting the conviction that the journey of Jean Nicolet was made into Lake Superior, where he made a peace with a group of native people the French called the Puans, or the Sea People. With the corroborating evidence of other French witnesses, it will then prove beyond any reasonable doubt that the location arrived at was none other than Sand Point in Keweenaw Bay.

The preponderance of the evidence will conclusively establish that the Sea People were indeed the *Mystery People of the Cove.*

(1.) J.R. Vol.44:247, (see Chapter 8:102).

# 7

# THE MAP

It was almost like living a chapter out of Robert Louis Stevenson's novel, *Treasure Island*. This mystical map held a secret that may not lead to gold or silver, but it would reveal treasure of a different nature, that treasure being the existence of an unknown settlement of Indians on the shores of Keweenaw Bay. This map shows a settlement at a particular geographical location, but how can it be proven that it actually existed? The information on the map would have to be confirmed by documenting the location of such a settlement. The only way of doing this would be to dig historically for it, just as the archaeologists did at Sand Point.

The map is a very early French map that is pivotal to the entire research effort. It is the famous map of DuVal's that would eventually prove to date as early as 1616. A map that would prove to be the very first of the Great Lakes region.

Locating this map originated with an article that appeared in a local historical publication by the Baraga County Historical Society. The organization was producing a pageant in 1969 and requested various authors of history to contribute articles for the pageant souvenir book. The article containing this map was authored by Marquette resident and researcher for Northern Michigan University, Mr. James Carter. It was titled *L'Anse Shown on 1668 Map*. (The date is a misprint and should read 1688.) The map featured was a map published in Paris, France and was identified as a map originating in 1669 (This map was an undated map that was first located by Louis Karpinski in 1930 and was given this date by that author. Later research would place the date at 1670). (1.)

Mr. Carter's article stated,

> The first map on which the author was able to locate the bay [Keweenaw Bay] was one drawn by DuVal of Paris of 1669. It was labeled *Tekari endiondi*, and a cluster of dots at the present site of L'Anse-Baraga indicated a settlement of Indians was located there. Near the Indian village were the words, *Nation du Feu*. The most common meaning of *feu* is 'fire,' and perhaps "Nation of the Fire," would be as close a translation as any to the meaning intended by DuVal.

(1.) *The Bibliography of the Printed Maps of Michigan*, Karpinski, 1931:Plate IV.
   *Mapping of North America*, Burden, 1996:228.

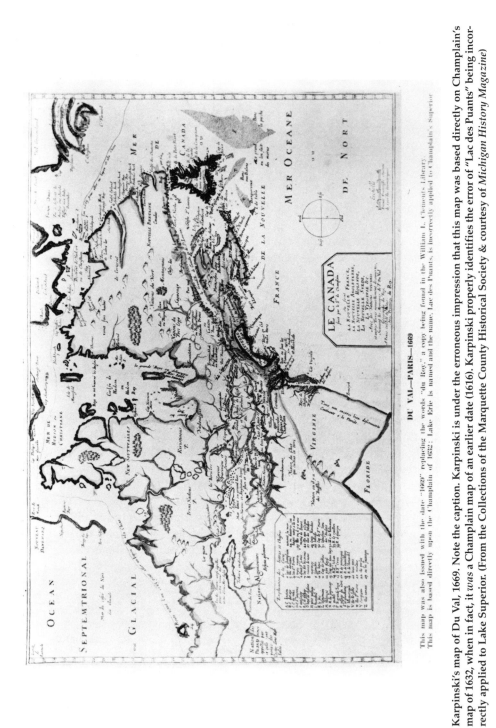

DU VAL—PARIS—1669

This map was also issued with the date "1626" replacing the words "du Roy," a copy being found in the William L. Clements Library. This map is based directly upon the Champlain of 1632; Lake Erie is named and the name, Lac des Puants, is incorrectly applied to Champlain's Superior.

Karpinski's map of Du Val, 1669. Note the caption. Karpinski is under the erroneous impression that this map was based directly on Champlain's map of 1632, when in fact, it *was* a Champlain map of an earlier date (1616). Karpinski properly identifies the error of "Lac des Puants" being incorrectly applied to Lake Superior. (From the Collections of the Marquette County Historical Society & courtesy of *Michigan History Magazine*)

Sand Point stands out as a well defined point of land on the early maps of Champlain's, where a "settlement of Indians" existed. This point is well illustrated in association with the Keweenaw Peninsula.

Emphasis is placed on the location of the "Indian village" that Mr. Carter cites from the DuVal map. He identifies this bay as that associated with the Keweenaw Peninsula in Lake Superior. This settlement is situated on a well defined point of land near what is present day Baraga. The question then arises, what does this historic "settlement of Indians" have in common with the archaeological site at Sand Point? As Mr. Carter's article was being put to press, the discovery of Sand Point was just being made. It would not be until 1970 that it would become officially known to the archaeological community.

The Baraga Historical Society commenced to celebrate their pageant with Mr. Carter's article *already* mentioning the "settlement of Indians" that was about to be confirmed and put on the archaeological maps. A *rare instance* of the historical evidence being substantiated by the archaeological evidence.

This was just the beginning of this research effort to locate historical data that would correlate the historical mention on DuVal's map with that of the archaeological evidence, confirming that there was indeed an "Indian settlement" at present day Sand Point in Baraga.

DuVal's map would prove to be the most interesting challenge, as this famous map has a lengthy history of its own. The story begins with Louis Karpinski, Professor of Mathematics, University of Michigan, Ann Arbor.

It is only proper that Professor Karpinski be given ample credit for introducing us to the DuVal series of maps. He had a secondary interest in history and due to his close acquaintance with the University dean, Mr. Clements, was sent abroad in 1930 to attempt to secure early maps of North America from the countries of Spain, Portugal and France. His greatest success would be from the country of France where he would secure 642 map copies, many of the Great Lakes region. The value of Karpinski's success was made known in the Library of Congress annual report which made special mention of the collection as marking notable progress in the attempt of American libraries to secure pertinent documentation of American history from European archives. The results of his success would be published in the well known volume, *The Bibliography of the Printed Maps of Michigan, 1931*, published by the Michigan History Commission. (1.)

It would take a trip to the Clements Library to examine Karpinski's efforts to secure the DuVal maps and to learn of the latest discoveries of these maps. It is this segment of the research effort that becomes very exciting and challenging as the evolution of the DuVal 1969 map becomes known.

Upon examination of Karpinski's publication, the maps shown are listed in chronological order. He has his DuVal map of 1669 listed following the Champlain map of 1632, with a caption below, stating that the DuVal map, "is based directly upon the Champlain map of 1632." What Karpinski was not aware of at the time was that the DuVal map was a Champlain map, and instead, the 1632 was the later rendition. This would not be known by historians for another 20 years, when an amazing discovery would reveal that the DuVal 1669 map was a very modified state of an early Champlain 1616 map. This early map had been severely transformed into the DuVal 1669 map.

It is important for us to understand the progressive changes that impacted this map since there are many references on the map that seem contradictory and confusing. For example, in the map caption Karpinski states that, "Lac des Puants is incorrectly applied to Champlain's Superior."

If this map is to have any meaning for us, we must isolate those references that are confusing, and determine how and when they originated. We must be able to peel away the layers of information that have been added to the later dated maps and determine what was original in order to see how this affected the location of the "Indian settlement" on Sand Point. As we shall find, these additions to the Great Lakes changed the geography of the original map entirely.

### Champlain map of 1616

It was in 1953 that the discovery of an original copy of the so-called DuVal 1669 map would be revealed by a Paris bookseller. Historians would rival to examine and give credence to this new found "Proof" as it was called.

(1.) *Manuscript Maps of European Archives*, Karpinski, 1930, Vol. 14.

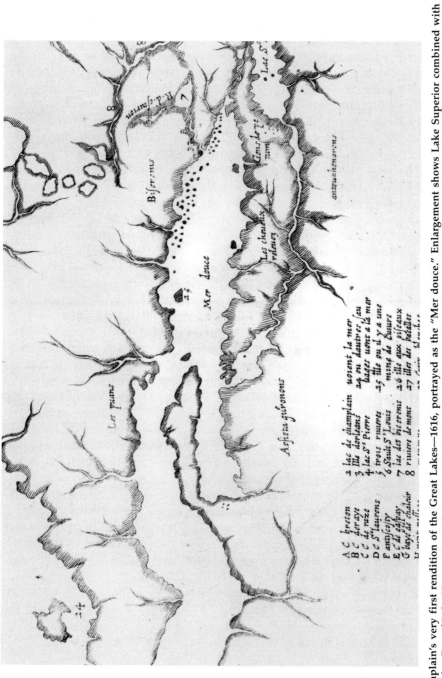

Champlain's very first rendition of the Great Lakes—1616, portrayed as the "Mer douce." Enlargement shows Lake Superior combined with Georgian Bay of Lake Huron. Note Isle Royale (25), the Keweenaw Peninsula, and the "settlement of Indians" on Sand Point. (The John Carter Brown Library, Providence, Rhode Island)

Identified as an "unfinished" map it was confirmed that the map's founder was indeed Samuel de Champlain. The events of the evolution of the famous map began to unfold. (1.)

The map was to have accompanied Champlain's journal of 1615-16 (*Les Voyages of 1619*), but for some unknown reason, it never was completed and the copper map plate was eventually sold to the map maker DuVal, in 1644. The Proof copy that was discovered in 1953 was a copy that was struck from the original copper plate prior to the additions that followed the map's completion in 1650. This map was then published by DuVal in 1653 and was the first of the published maps. The map would continue to evolve with several other states to follow (in 1664, 1670, 1677) and with several publications that were undated.

It would be learned that the undated DuVal map that Karpinski titled as 1669 would prove to be a 1670 state. For our research purposes, the most significant maps are the Proof and the first published map of 1653. These two have the most critical information, but we will also compare the additions through Karpinski's map of 1669 (1670). What is really important is to examine the relationship of the original Proof to the first published state of 1653 if the settlement of Indians on Sand Point is to have any historic meaning.

It is important to emphasize the original Proof since it is the initial state of the map and contains the information intended by its original founder. Champlain had compiled the map for a definite purpose as only the original can demonstrate. The map then began to take on new character as additional information was added to its first published version by DuVal and continues to do so with each of the succeeding states, of which there are a total of seven. (2.)

Researchers also established that the Proof copy was unfinished. This meant that neither the cartouche, nor the geographical delineations at the margins were complete. Otherwise the information that is identified on the Proof demonstrates or, ". . . marks an important intermediate state in the slowly developing knowledge of New France and its Indian nations which took place in the first half of the seventeenth century."

Thus, the original as composed by Champlain, has been, ". . . engulfed by the addition of a very large number of place-names, so large a number, indeed, that the '1616' map is lost in the map of 1653. The contribution of the earlier map to current geographical knowledge thus was effectively obscured by the DuVal revision of 1653 and remained so until the discovery of the single known print identified as the 'Proof,' of 1616." (3.)

The 1616 map is of special importance to us due to the nature of the "Indian nations" that are so numerously depicted on this original. They appear in the form of literally hundreds of dots that can be found over the entire map. Viewing an original is the only way to fully appreciate this fact.

(1.) *An unknown Champlain map of 1616*, Wroth, 1954, Vol. 11.
(2.) *The Mapping of North America*, Burden, 1996:228.
(3.) *An unknown Champlain map of 1616*, Wroth, 1954, Vol. 11:88.

Also, the following year is a critical one for Champlain, who was preoccupied formulating extensive reports for Louis XIX and the Paris Chamber of Commerce. The reports would contain considerable amounts of statistical information for future investment potential for French interest. It may have been possible that this 'unfinished map' was to accompany those reports. Champlain is well known for the accuracy of his maps and the fact that he does not depict that which is unproven. There is no effort to depict the area south of Chesapeake Bay, indicating that the map was probably intended for a specific purpose and not general circulation. It could be that he was intending to entice extra interest in certain quarters. (1.)

We only have to refer to Champlain's journals to understand how paramount the native people were to the French occupation of North America. Champlain drew most of his information from the native people when he was attempting to learn about unexplored lands and other native nations. (2.)

When Champlain returned to France following his exploits of 1615-16, he would need to document the most valuable resources to the French investors of New France, which were its people. Champlain was making every effort to ally the native people in order to enhance the much needed trade in fur that the colonial effort was depending on for its economic survival. This map would suffice to demonstrate that fact to the King, investors and the Cardinal. We must not forget the religious assets that Champlain was willing to tap in order to further enhance France's foothold in the New World. (3.)

For the first time in the geographical exploration of the New World the presence of the Great Lakes was confirmed by Champlain's personal exploration of the "Mer douce." His journals can not hide the fact that he was adamant toward locating a route through the Americas and in his "judgment," this was possible via these "fresh water seas." Great fame, fortune, and power would come to the man and his country that would discover and con-

(1.) *The Mapping of North America*, Burden, 1996:229.
(2) *The Voyages and Exploration of Samuel De Champlain*, Bourne, 1911; II:59.
    "Whereupon I perceived that it was very necessary to assist them, not only to make them love us more, but also to pave the way for my undertakings and discoveries, which, to all appearances, could not be accomplished except by their help . . . ." (1616)
(3.) *France in America*, Eccles, 1972:23,24.
    In 1617 Champlain appealed to the French Chamber of Commerce to undertake a major colonization program. Submitting a detailed estimate of the products the country could provide—fish, fur, timber, minerals, grain, and leather—valued at 6,400,000 livres a year, he requested that four hundred families and a garrison of three hundred soldiers be sent to Quebec. He voiced the fear that unless this were done the Dutch or the English would seize control of the St. Lawrence and go on to eliminate the six to seven hundred French ships from the well established cod fishery off the Grand Banks (these areas are noted on his 1616 map). The costs of this ambitious program, he estimated, would be a modest 45,000 livres a year, and once the water route across the continent to the Pacific was discovered, the customs duties on Asiatic goods using that shorter and safer route would flood the royal coffers. The Chamber of Commerce found this proposal very interesting, but thought it something the Crown should undertake.
    The Crown was unable to undertake such a proposition due to rebellious great lords that had joined the ousted queen mother. Nor would the French business community provide the backing Champlain sought. The only other agency that remained: the Church.

trol the route that would open up the Asian markets of China and Japan. Champlain had his eye on the prize and was ever resourceful at persuading the proper authorities of his ambitions. (1.)

## The "Mer douce"

As we compare the 1616 map of Champlain's and DuVal's first published version of 1653, we notice the particular place-names and ethnic groups that have been added. Consequently, it has changed completely the geography of Champlain's original map. What we are going to examine are the additions and make an effort to trace their origins in time and place.

What we must first do is to identify the western Great Lakes geography of the 1616 map. There is no doubt that Karpinski is convinced that this body of water encompasses the whole of Georgian Bay and that of Lake Superior. The fact that Lake Superior is portrayed in this map is unmistakable by the presence of the very obvious and evident "Tongue" of land or peninsula that is the present day Keweenaw Peninsula. Also present is Isle Royale, which is depicted in the legend as the "island where there is a mine of copper." Champlain has failed to include the St. Mary's River (Sault, meaning falls or rapids) that separates the two, which is easy for us to understand once we learn how he first became knowledgeable of this portion of the western "fresh water sea." (2.)

Champlain has entered Georgian Bay at the confluence of the French River and lacked any personal knowledge of the country north and west of this. Yet

(1.) *The Voyages and Exploration of Samuel De. Champlain*, Bourne 1911. Two volumes.

Champlain's journal of 1632 describes the several failed attempts by other voyagers to find the "passage."

He then explains how important locating the northwest passage is: "All this is only to show how much honor, if this passage, which was so greatly desired, had been found,would have come to him who lighted upon it; and how much advantage to the state or realm which would have possessed it. Since, then, it is our own opinion that this enterprise is of such value, it should not be despised now, and that which cannot be done in one place can be accomplished in another, in time, provided His Majesty be pleased to assist the undertaker of so praise worthy a project."

The above was stated by Champlain in 1629 and was apparently a deciding factor for his return in 1633. Having convinced the Cardinal and the King of his worthy accomplishments in his writings of the 1632 publication, he was promoted Governor to New France. When he returned, it appeared that finding the "passage, an enterprise of such value," that Champlain desired this 'honor' bestowed upon himself despite his age and health.

Equally important to Champlain was Cardinal Richelieu who was a very important and powerful individual. Champlain dedicates his 1632 Journal to the cardinal and reports:

"Cardinal, Duke de Richelieu. Head, Grand Master and Superintendant-General of the Commerce and Navigation of New France.

. . . of the situation in New France . . . the facility with which a safe and important commerce can be carried on there: the great profit to be derived from it; . . . .

. . . For in order to begin and complete these enterprises with honor and profit, one must spend long years in sea voyages and be experienced in such discoveries."

There is no doubt that Champlain, in the course of expressing his opinion regarding the "passage," was greasing his skids for a return trip to New France to win this "honor" by convincing the Cardinal and His Majesty of the importance of this discovery. His anticipation is evidence by his returning with the "grand robe of China damask." His eye was on the prize.

(2.) J.R. Vol. 54:149. Claude Dablon 1669-70.

"The Lake [Superior] has almost the form of a Bow, more than a hundred and eighty leagues long; the South side serves as its string, and the arrow seems to be a great Tongue of land [Keweenaw Peninsula] projecting more than eighty leagues into the width of the Lake, starting from this same South side at about its middle."

his map includes the western expanse of Lake Superior as is depicted on his map. But how did he acquire the geographical information that seems to identify the Keweenaw Peninsula with such accuracy? It was through the native people that Champlain spent the winter with in 1615-16. His journals describe for us the techniques he employed for gathering reliable information that pertained to the unknown regions that were unexplored by the French. He would sit down with knowledgeable native people and ask, ". . . what was his country?" They would respond by drawing upon a piece of bark with a piece of charcoal the area they knew. Champlain would interview several individuals comparing consistent results in order to get credible information. (1.)

What is most interesting about the western portion illustrated on the 1616 map is that of the *Les puans*, who are depicted as occupying a rather general location on the north shore of Lake Superior. What is so intriguing about this is that of all the other ethnic groups illustrated in southern Georgian Bay that are mentioned in his journal covering this trip, this group is not. It is obvious that Champlain had knowledge of the western group at this early date, apparently information supplied to him by the Huron people, who had placed a great deal of trust in him by this time.

Champlain was made aware of the Huron's trade in copper and was told of a "Mine of fine Copper" located somewhere "North," as early as 1603; mines that were located on Isle Royale and particularly the Keweenaw Peninsula. Additionally, they undoubtedly supplied him with the information of the "settlement of Indians" on Sand Point, located in these waters as well. (2.)

(1.) *The Voyages and Exploration of Samuel De Champlain*, Bourne, 1911, Two volumes.

"When we saw that we could do no more we returned to our Pinnace; where we examined the Savages which we had with us, of the end of the River, which I caused them to draw with their hand, and from what part the Head thereof came." Vol. I:199 (1603) "

. . . I gave a hatchet to their chief, who was as much pleased and delighted with it as if I had given him some rich gift. When I asked him what was his country, he indicated it to me with a piece of charcoal on the bark of a tree . . ." Vol. II:67, (1616)

". . . I made them understand, as best I could, that they should show me how the coast lay. After having depicted for them, with a piece of charcoal, the bay and the Island Cape, where we were, they represented for me, with the same crayon, another bay, which they showed as very large. They put six pebbles at equal distances, thus giving me to understand that each of these stood for as many chiefs and tribes." Vol.I:106 (1605)

"We examined two or three Algoumequins to see whether they would agree with those that we had examined touching the end and the begining of the said River of Canada. Vol. I:204. (1603)

"And this assuredly is all which they have told me that they have seen: which differeth very little from the report of the first Savages." Vol. I:206. (1603)

(2.) Ibid.

"I enquired of them [Algonkins], whether they had any knowledge of any Mines? They told us, that there is a Nation which are called, the good Irocois (Hurons), which come to exchange for merchandises, which the French ships do give to the Algoumequins, which say, that there is toward the North a Mine of fine Copper, whereof they shewed us certain Bracelets, which they had received of the said Good Irocois: and that if any of us would go thither, they would bring us to the place which should be appointed for that business." Vol. I:209 (1603)

The Archaeological Report's findings indicate that the Sand Point Site was a location that provided for the industrial working of copper.

In 1610 Champlain sent Etienne Brulé with the Hurons into their country [Georgian Bay] to:

"learn their language, get acquainted with the country, see the great lake [Georgian Bay], observe the rivers, and what people inhabited it; also to explore the mines and rarer things of this place, so that on his return, he could give us information about all these things." Vol. I:228 (1610).

There is no doubt that when Champlain learned of the Puans or the Sea People, it fired his imagination for his search of the passage to the "South Sea." This information was invaluable and had to be kept confidential if he was to protect this opportunity for himself; consequently, it escapes any mention in his journal. It will become evident just how valuable these people were to Champlain later in 1634 when he sent his most trusted Interpreter by the name of Jean Nicolet on an important mission to make contact with this mystical group—a unique journey involving a Chinese robe that was not recorded anywhere until six years after the incident took place and after Champlain died. Strangely, the details of this mission even escape mention by the prominent missionary, Breabuef, who accompanied him to the Huron mission at Ste. Marie in southern Georgian Bay. It was here that Nicolet departed from and returned to before continuing on to Three Rivers, thus completing his historic voyage. (1.)

*The Missionaries*

After having established that the 1616 map of Champlain's did indeed portray Lake Superior, we can now examine DuVal's 1653 map and determine how it became engulfed and overwhelmed with information that totally changed its geography. Whereas, our former Lake Superior, under the engenderment of Champlain, had now been transformed into the waters of Georgian Bay and Green Bay of Lake Michigan! (2.)

It is a simple matter for us to understand the transformation of Lake Superior, relative to Champlain's map, when we know that the missionaries

(1.) *The Voyages and Exploration of Samuel De Champlain*, Bourne, 1911, Two volumes.

In 1603 Champlain established an early theory that the Mer douce contained an "exceeding great Riuer" that would "issue forth" into a "South Sea." This salt sea would then give way to the route to China and Japan. Champlain's "judgement" would mistakenly identify reports from the natives that applied to the Mississippi River and the Gulf of Mexico as the "South Sea." It would appear that when Champlain learned of the Sea People (puans), who were "so called because they came from the coast of a salt sea," who resided in the unknown western region "200 or 300 leagues" from the Huron country [west of Ste. Marie, located in southern Georgian Bay], it perpetuated his theory, culminating in 1634, when Nicolet journeys "300 leagues west of the Huron country" to locate them, accompanied with a Chinese robe. Vol. I:202, 203. (1603) (See Chapter 8.)

The concept of the "exceeding great River" and the "South Sea" theory continued to perpetuate French thinking of the Great Lakes as late as 1658, as this route was still being sought from the west end of Lake Superior. J.R. Vol. 44:247, Dreuillette. (See Chapter 8:102.)

(2.) Ibid.

Champlain's journal for his 1616 journey states that:

"With regard to the regions farther west we cannot really know their extent, inasmuch as the peoples have no knowledge of it beyond 200 or 300 leagues or more toward the west [of the Huron country on Georgian Bay] whence come this great river [St. Lawrence]; which goes, among other places, through a lake extending nearly thirty days journey by canoe, to wit, the one that we named the Fresh Sea [Mer douce] on account of its great extent, which is forty days' journey in the canoes of the savages to whom we have access." Vol.I:117

Because of its "great extent," the Mer douce is described as a "lake extending nearly thirty days journey by canoe." This description implies that it would include that of Lake Superior as Champlain has provided with his 1616 map. The natives, in mentioning the extent they could go to the west on the Fresh Sea, apparently did not emphasize, or even mention, the falls or rapids (Sault) at the St. Mary's River. It was therefore absent from his 1616 map. Vol. I:117 (18.)

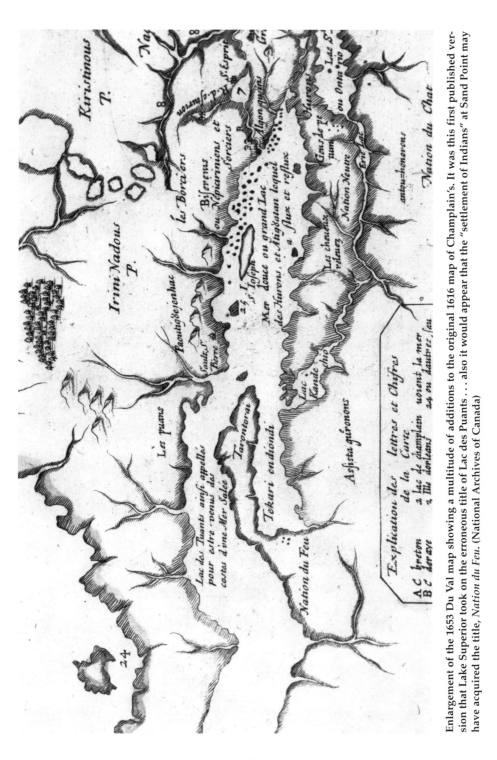

Enlargement of the 1653 Du Val map showing a multitude of additions to the original 1616 map of Champlain's. It was this first published version that Lake Superior took on the erroneous title of Lac des Puants . . . also it would appear that the "settlement of Indians" at Sand Point may have acquired the title, *Nation du Feu*. (National Archives of Canada)

had a very definite influence on Canadian cartography, especially after the death of Champlain. (1.)

When the missionary journals are examined, we can accurately identify pertinent references that would have significance to their missions as they appear on the 1653 published map. Of special significance are the place-names of:

(1.) *St. Joseph Island (I. S. Iofeph)*

(2.) The reference to the *Lac des Puants* . . . (so called because they came from the coast of a salt sea )

These references can be documented from the missionary journals of 1648 and 1649.

When we examine the history of St. Joseph Island, as it so boldly appears on the 1653 map, we learn that it was not established until 1648. Later called Christian Island, it was located just off shore from the mission of Ste. Marie in southern Georgian Bay. Neither of these missions existed after 1649 when the Iroquois overran them and drove the Hurons and the French from their shores. (2.)

The reference to the *Lac des Puants* . . . corresponded to a newly discovered "third Lake" or Green Bay of Lake Michigan, that also occurred and was reported in 1648 by the same missionary, Ragueneau, Superior at Ste. Marie. These two references were added to the 1653 map by the same missionary author, who had knowledge of this information and was accessible for their entry in France. That missionary was none other than Father Paul LeJune. (3.)

We can therefore conclude: the additions by LeJune were made after his return to France sometime after November of 1649 or during 1650 when the map was completed. It was published in 1653.

But how did Lake Superior become associated with the area of Green Bay?

Apparently our missionary cartographer decided that since the Sault of the St. Marys River was not evident on this body of water it had to be what the French considered at the time, the "Gulf" of Georgian Bay, which is present day

---

(1.) *Early Printed Maps of Canada*, Kershaw, 1993:125.

(2.) J.R. Vol. 34:203, (1649), Ragueneau—Ste. Joseph Island—later called Christian Island.

". . . others have taken their stand on an Island which we name St. Joseph Island, where we began nearly a year ago, a new mission." (The Hurons were fleeing the Iroquois in 1649.) Note that the mission of Ste. Marie does not appear until after 1664, showing up on the 1670 map.

(3.) J.R. Vol. 33:61, 140, (1648), Ragueneau.

This is the very first mention in the missionary journals to the "Lac des Puants." LeJune's reference to the Puants in 1640 states verbatim that they were, "so called because they came from the coast of a salt sea . . . ;" thus, complementing the reference as it is stated on the map of 1653. Therefore, the author for this addition was none other than Father Paul LeJune, who was the Superior in Quebec in 1640 when he learned of the information about the Puants from Nicolet (Nicolet drowns in 1642). This is LeJune's signature.

LeJune departed Quebec on Oct. 31, 1649, returned to France and became Procuror of Foreign Missions. LeJune was still in Quebec in 1648 when the "Lac des Puants" is recorded by Ragueneau. LeJune was the most knowledgeable French authority of the New French missions, having been there for 17 years!

Father Paul LeJune is therefore the most probable candidate for the addition of many of the references that we find on the 1653 published map. He dies in 1664, thus, the 1664 state of the map is left without modification to this region. It is not until after 1664 that the additions of "Nation of the Puants . . .", "Nations of Algonouines" and "Ste. Marie" appear on the 1670 map by another author. J.R. Vols. 5:275, 34:61, 37:77, 145.

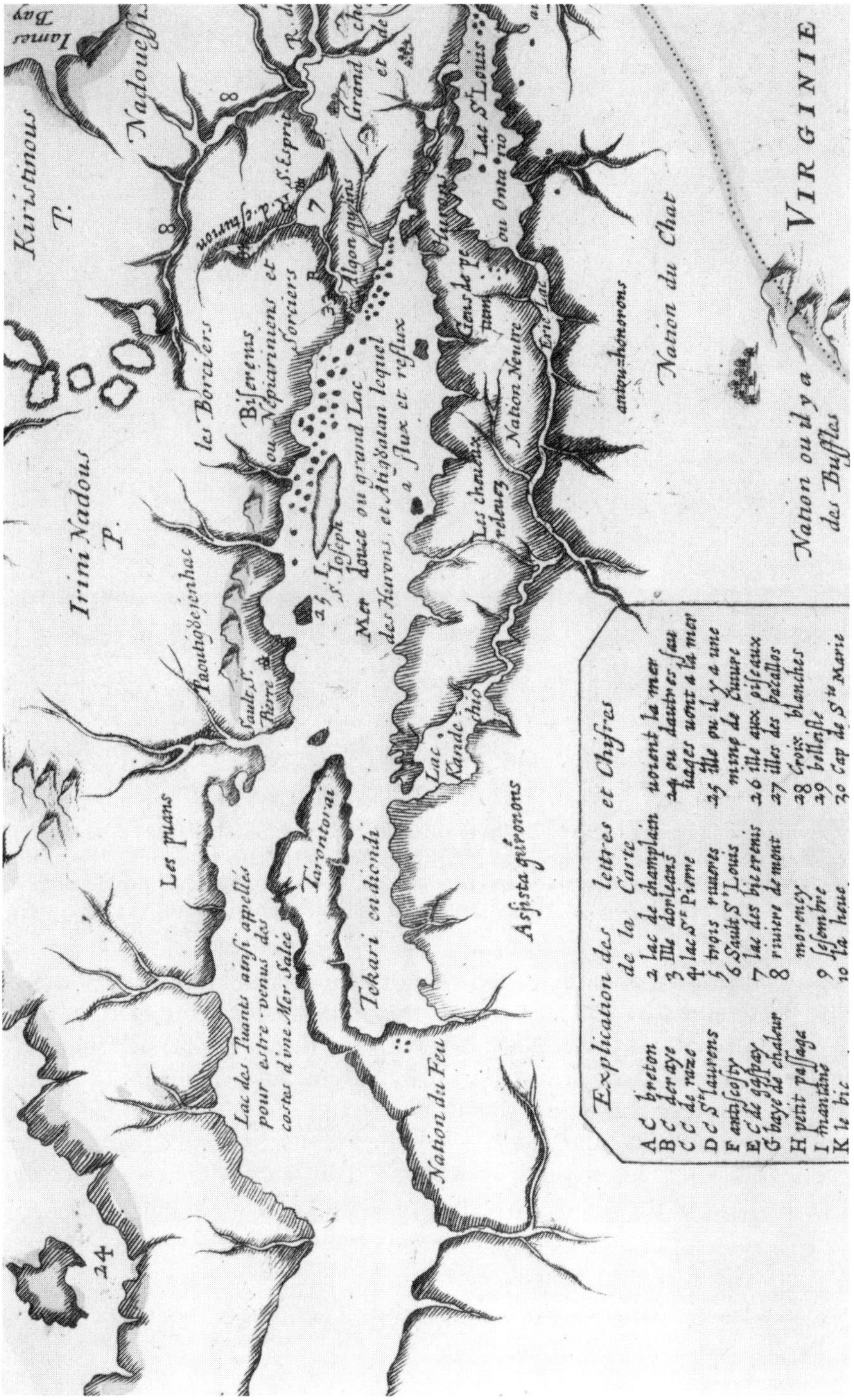

Map labels (reading across the engraving):

James Bay · Nadouessi · Kiristinous P. · Irini Nadous P. · Les puans · Nation du Feu · VIRGINIE · Nation du Chat · Nation ou il y a des Buffles · Nation Neutre · Erie Lac · Lac St Louis ou Onta.rio · R. du St. Esprit · Algonquins · les Borciers · Biserens ou Nipiarniens et sorciers · Taouigoyerithac · Sault St Pierre · Tekari ondiondi · Tarontorai · Asista geronons · Les chastaux relevez · S. Joseph · Mer douce ou grand Lac des Hurons, et St. Joseph auquel a flux et reflux · Lac des Puans ainsi appellés pour estre venus des costes d'vne Mer Salée

Explication des lettres et Chifres de la Carte

A C breton
B C d'raye
C C de raze
D C St Laurens
E C de gaspey
F enchicoly
G baye de chaleur
H petit passage
I musardine
K le bic

2 lac de champlain
3 Ille d'orleans
4 lac St Pierre
5 trois rivieres
6 Sault St Louis
7 lac des hierenis
8 riviere de mont
9 septembre
10 la hue

23 voient la mer
24 ou sauluescent sea tiages vont a la mer
25 ille ou il y a une mine de Cuivre
26 ille aux pisceaux
27 illes des pazallos
28 Croix blanches
29 bellisle
30 cap de Ste Marie

25 S. Joseph

Enlargement of the Du Val 1664 map does not deviate from the 1653. Note how the Island of Saint Joseph (I.S. Ioseph) dwarfs Isle Royale. All of the additions can be identified with the missionary Father Paul LeJune. (William L. Clements Library, University of Michigan)

The very famous rapids on the St. Mary's River referred to as the "Sault." It was called "Sault S. Pierre," and was occupied by native people the French called the "Sauteurs." The Sault would become a well known landmark that was reported as early as 1621, when Brulé made the first journey of any Frenchmen into these waters. (From the Collections of the Marquette County Historical Society)

Green Bay, Wisconsin. After all, the location of the *Les puans* was already chart-ed on the north shore by Champlain and this undoubtedly confused its mis-sionary author, who had to correlate that with the discovery of the "Puants," in Green Bay. This discovery occurred in 1648 with the knowledge that a penin-sula of land separated Lake Superior from the so called "Gulf" of Georgian Bay. At this date, located in the "Gulf," were the Puants, hence the name *Lac des Puants* .... This newly discovered "third Lake" was later called the Bay of the Puants of the Lake of the Illinois, which is present day Lake Michigan. (1.)

(1.) J.R. Vol. 33:149, (1648), Raguenau.
    "A Peninsula, or a rather narrow strip of land, separates that superior Lake [Lake Superior] from a third Lake, which we call the Lake of the Puants, which also flows into our fresh-water sea [Georgian Bay] by a mouth [Straits] on the other side of the Peninsula, about ten leagues farther West than the Sault. This third Lake extends between the West and Southwest, . . . and is almost equal in size to our fresh-water sea."

*(continued on next page)*

**Enlargement of Du Val's 1670 (1669) map. Note the addition of the "Nation des Puants..." west of the river on the south shore of Lake Superior. This is the last and final modification to the Mer douce, indicative of yet another author making his contribution to further confuse the cartographic researcher. (William L. Clements Library, University of Michigan)**

The Sault was placed in an obscure location on the north shore identifying it as the Sault S. Pierre, and the native group of the *Paouhgejenhac*, who resided at the rapids of the St. Marys River and were called by the French, the "Sauteurs." The missionaries made contact with this group in 1641. (1.)

It would therefore appear that the peninsula that was formerly the Keweenaw was then transformed into either the lower peninsula of Michigan or the Bruce Peninsula of Georgian Bay. The (Huron) Iroquois words *Tekari endiondi* and *Tarontorai* that appear refer to either one or the other of these. We should also note that the addition of *Nation des Puants . . .* to the extreme far west was not added until 1670. This would indicate the confusion that existed during the course of reconstructing the location of these people with the absence of Lake Michigan on Champlain's original 1616 map. The emphasis on Georgian Bay is quite obvious on the 1653 map with the insertion of the *I. of St. Joseph*, illustrated at five times its size and placed right smack up against Isle Royale! At any rate, Champlain's 1616 map has entirely lost its original

*(continued from previous page)*

Raguenau portrays for us the fresh understanding of this newly discovered "third Lake," stating that it is "almost equal in size" to Georgian Bay. This typifies the understanding that this body of water, which is present day Green Bay of Wis., was considered merely a "Gulf" to Georgian Bay, as is illustrated by Dablon as late as 1670. The knowledge of the Lake of the Illinois (Lake Mich.) was just coming into being in 1670 and was thought to be smaller than that of Georgian Bay. J.R. Vol 54:199.

This is also the very first recorded reference to Lake Superior as "that superior Lake."

(1.) J.R. Vol. 33:149, (1648).

Raguenau identifies the Paouitagoung as the Nation of the Sault ( Ojibway), which is identified on the 1653 map and residing by "a very large and very rapid river . . . that rolls over a falls" (St. Marys River) that discharges by a "superior Lake," (Lake Superior).

J.R. Vol. 23:225,(1641), Missionary journey to the Sauteurs.

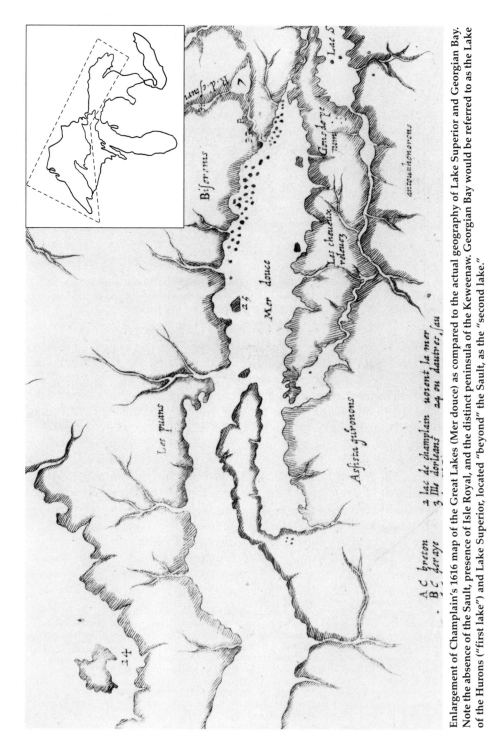

Enlargement of Champlain's 1616 map of the Great Lakes (Mer douce) as compared to the actual geography of Lake Superior and Georgian Bay. Note the absence of the Sault, presence of Isle Royal, and the distinct peninsula of the Keweenaw. Georgian Bay would be referred to as the Lake of the Hurons ("first lake") and Lake Superior, located "beyond" the Sault, as the "second lake."

geography and critical ethnological placement due to the pious editing of the missionaries.

Complementary to the 1653 map is the addition of the words *Nation du Feu*, located next to the "settlement of Indians" on Sand Point. *Nations Algonouines* was added to the 1670 map identifying the southern region of the peninsula (see respective map plates). Since the reference to *Nation du Feu* (Nation of Fire) was added to the 1616 map, we know now that it had absolutely no correlation to the Indian village that is indicated by the four dots. In fact, this reference, also added by our missionary author, is the French equivalent of the Huron (Iroquois) word *Asfista guronons*, already supplied by Champlain on the 1616 map. *Nation Algonouines* also applied to this same large group of combined native tribes located in southern Lower Michigan. They were called the Fire Nation and were a very large group of Algonkin speaking people thought by the missionaries to be larger in number than the Huron, Neutral and Iroquois combined. The Ottawa and Neutral were at war with the Fire Nation when Champlain made the entry on his 1616 map. (1.)

Concluding, we now know that the "settlement of Indians" on Keweenaw Bay was not to be confused with the Fire Nation of southern Michigan. Reexamining Champlain's 1616 map, we can observe that the *only ethnic designation* that applied to this western body of water was that of the *Les puans*. These were the people that his Huron informants had identified residing on Lake Superior with a significant habitation located at Sand Point.

Our search will continue to define the *Les puans* of Lake Superior as we intensify our efforts to examine the journals of the missionaries and research Jean Nicolet's journey to this western native settlement. Without the historical documentation of Nicolet's journey we are at a loss to know which of the Great Lakes he was in in order to make contact with them. The ultimate goal will be to seek explanations that will clarify a great deal of the confusion that has surrounded this ethnic group, that for years has caused so much debate among historians.

---

(1.) J.R. Vol. 27:27.

"This Nation of fire alone is more populous than all the Neutral Nation, all the Hurons and all the Iroquois, enemies of the Huron, put together. It consists of a large number of villages, wherein is spoken the Algonquin language, which prevails still farther on."

*The Voyages and Explorations of Samuel de Champlain*, Bourne, 1911.

"In the first place the [Ottawa] are at war with another tribe of savages called Asistaguerouan which means Fire People, who live ten days journey from them." Vol. II:100.

"They [Neutral] live to the south of the Fresh Sea, [Georgian Bay] and assist the cheveux Releves [Ottawa] against the Fire People." Vol. II:102.

# 8

# THE NICOLET MYTH AND THE REAL JOURNEY

During the course of searching through the local newspaper for information of the Sand Point discovery, it was realized that very few photos were included of this event. So having learned of the owner of the newspaper at the time, I decided to seek out any surviving relatives who might have some photographs in their private collections.

Ms. Karla Menge is the surviving daughter of the owner and, to my disappointment, informed me that I was out of luck as far as photos were concerned. Karla is a native of L'Anse and her family has a long history in the L'Anse area. For the past 30 years she has been involved with the Green Bay area public schools as a librarian and has lived in Green Bay, Wisconsin. Therefore, she was very familiar with the historical events surrounding the area. We talked at length over the phone and discussed the historical information surrounding the Nicolet event. It was at this point that I began to reflect back on a Michigan history class from my high school days some 30 years ago. For some obscure reason I can still remember the Nicolet story and the textbook with the very vivid picture of this Frenchman in his orange robe, standing on the beach, armed with two pistols, among a multitude of Indians. The location of this historic event was to have occurred at Green Bay and Jean Nicolet was to have been the first European to have stepped upon the shores of present day Wisconsin. Nicolet has been but a very vague part of Michigan's history with Wisconsin traditionally harboring what we have accepted to be the location of his final destination.

Karla suggested a couple text books that contained pictures of Nicolet. One such picture was a copy of an original painting that is hanging in the Brown County Public Library in Green Bay. Additionally, Nicolet was also included in a segment of a large wall mural depicting Wisconsin history in the Wisconsin state capital building at Madison. So the story of Nicolet has not only been a major event in the history of Green Bay, but also in the State of Wisconsin.

The proponents of the Nicolet event, as we have traditionally come to know it, were all Wisconsin historians with the most influential being members of the State Historical Society. The most recognized of these early historians are: John Gilmary Shea, C.W. Buttterfield, Ruben Gold Thwaites, Emma Blair and Louise Phelphs Kellogg. They are all authors of historical publications and books covering the Nicolet event and are the principal proponents responsible for our existing knowledge on the subject.

What we must remember is that any recorded history is only as valid as the information from which it was derived. The purpose here is not to discredit these very fine authors and historians. These learned men and women have contributed a great deal to western Great Lakes history and their example is one we should emulate. No one would question the required astronomical amounts of time and energy expended to access and compile the many volumes of historical information that has been so beneficial to us.

The period when these historians were researching dates from the mid-1800's and much of the material they were accessing was from the 1600's, and was fresh and new to them. They were responsible for the English translation and editing of the *Relations* into the existing 73 volume compilation we know as the *Jesuit Relations and Allied Documents*. Old maps and documents covering the Great Lakes were being exposed for the first time after being buried away in dusty corners. Many of these documents would have never been available if some of these historians had not sought to preserve them in their private collections. We are indebted to them for their contributions in providing such a vast amount of information, allowing those of us who follow opportunities to build upon their efforts; otherwise, advanced research would be impossible.

During the recollection of the Michigan history class, I recalled our instructor citing an article in the 1966 publication of the *Michigan History Magazine*, authored by Harry Dever of Cedarville that disputed the claim by the Wisconsin historians on the discovery of Green Bay by Nicolet. Why I should remember something like this from so long ago still baffles me. I did not even like history! It may have been because I identified with Harry Dever for his courage to challenge the authors of Wisconsin, whose interpretation of history we have so unquestioningly accepted. (1.)

Although not in total agreement with Mr. Dever's article, he deserves all due respect, especially since his article was one of the principal motivations for my research. Could there possibly be a connection between his theory of Nicolet's entering Lake Superior and his being responsible for the information that I was trying to validate on the DuVal 1669 map? Initially this possibility seemed remote, but after a great deal of research the investigation began to unfold and to focus on Nicolet. Was Nicolet the French connection between the Sand Point site and the Puans? In the Michigan History publication, Mr. Dever successfully gets us into Lake Superior and then leads us up the north shore to the Montreal River in Canada. There he takes Nicolet into the Cree country near Hudson Bay. He is successful in convincing me of Nicolet's entering Lake Superior but fails to convince me on the latter. He manages to get us into the right church but the wrong pew.

(1.) *Michigan History Magazine*, Dever, 1966, Vol. L. No. 4.

As Mr. Dever states, it is the *Relations* that contain what can be considered the only prime source of Nicolet's journey. The Jesuit records are vague as to exactly which of the Great Lakes Nicolet was on or where his final destination was. In fact, the *Relations*, from which these references are drawn, fails to record the date of this important event. The Nicolet journey has been historically somewhat of an enigma. (1.)

The Wisconsin historians have provided us with the historical interpretation of the *Relations* surrounding the Nicolet event. This account has prevailed for the past 145 years and has been the traditionally accepted theory taught in our schools for many years.

## The Nicolet Myth

The origin of the Green Bay theory first appeared in a publication called *Discovery and Exploration of the Mississippi Valley* (New York: Clinton Hall, 1852, pp. 20-22), authored by John Gilmary Shea. His theory was "the first to advance the claim" that Nicolet had explored Green Bay. Additionally, he claimed that Nicolet ascended the Fox River, eventually making portage and becoming the "first Frenchman to reach the waters of the Mississippi River."

Other Wisconsin authors followed his theory in other publications. Mr. Dever states in his article, "later writers have overestimated the carefulness of Shea's analysis, and have paid too much attention to Shea and his followers and not enough to the *Relations*."

The most adamant follower of Shea's theory was C. W. Butterfield, who, in 1881, published the *History of the Discovery of the Northwest by John Nicolet*. He perpetuates Shea's interpretation with the use of Champlain's 1632 map, agreeing that a mysterious lake that appears is that of Lake Michigan and Green Bay.

Wisconsin historian's claim that it was Green Bay where Nicolet landed was due solely to the misconstruing of this map, since this is the *only* reference that substantiated their conclusion. Butterfield goes into great detail attempting to justify the bizarre location of this mysterious lake north of Lake Superior as that of Lake Michigan (see Champlain's 1632 map). This rationale is based on the fact that at its far end is located the "La Nation des Puans," the name of the tribe Nicolet contacted on his journey. They are convinced that this must be the location of Green Bay that appears on later map references and discredits any conflicting testaments in the *Relations* that may refute it.

Let us begin with the best evidence we have of Nicolet's journey and present the documentation of the testaments themselves. Due to previous histori-

---

(1.) Voyager, Rodesch, 1984:4-8.
 "In 1634 Jean Nicolet, emmissary of Govenor Samuel de Champlain of New France, landed at Red Banks on the the shore of Green Bay about a mile west of here . . . . If not proven, it is a plausible version of the Nicolet voyage. If the facts are uncertain, Nicolet and Red Banks stand at the beginning of the region's history. They are fixed in tradition and eleborated in picture and story . . . . We know comparatively little about the journey that gave him enough significance to be a public memory, to be a part of history . . . . Even so . . . Nicolet is the dominant figure."

Enlargement of Champlain's confusing 1632 map that Butterfield utilized to explain the Nicolet journey. He depicts the "mystery lake" containing *The Nation of the Puans* and the *Isle where there is a mine of copper* (Isle Royale), as Green Bay, stating it was erroneously placed on the wrong side of the Grand Lac (Lake Superior). Also note the major river running into the Grand Lac identified as the *Grand River that flows from the south* (Ontonagon River). (From the Collections of the Marquette County Historical Society)

cal misinterpretation and former pious editing of the references of these two accounts, they are being provided verbatim so the reader may know exactly what they state.

The following are the two accounts from the *Relations* that serve as references for the Nicolet journey. The brackets [ ] and under scored are the author's.

The first account provides the only specific motivations for his voyage.

Vol. 23:277-79 (1642-43) Author: Father Barthélemy Vimont

While in the exercise of this office he [Nicolet] was delegated to make a journey to the nation called People of the sea, and arrange peace between them and the Hurons, from whom they are distant about three hundred leagues Westward. He embarked in the Huron country, with seven Savages; and they passed by many small nations, both going and returning. When they arrived at their destination, they fastened two sticks in the earth, and hung gifts thereon, so as to relieve these tribes from the notion of mistakening them for enemies to be massacred.

When he was two day's journey from that nation, he sent one of those Savages to bear tidings of a peace, which word was especially well received when they heard that it was a European who carried the message; they dispatched several young men to meet the Manitouririnou—that is to say, "the wonderful man." They meet him; they escort him, and carry all his bagage. He wore a grand robe of China damask, all strewn with flowers and birds of many colors. No sooner did they perceive him than the women and children fled, at the sight of a man who carried thunder in both hands—for thus they called the two pistols that he held.

The news of his coming quickly spread to the places round about, and there assembled four or five thousand men. Each of the chief men made a feast for him, and at one of these banquets they served six scores [120] beavers. The peace was concluded; he returned to the Hurons, and some time later to three Rivers, where he continued his employment as Agent and Interpreter, . . . .

The second account gives a sound summary of the tribes of the Upper Great Lakes and the details of the course of his journey, which were provided to our author by Nicolet.

Vol. 18:231-339 (1640) Author: Father Paul LeJune

Let us return now to the fresh-water sea [Georgian Bay of Lake Huron]. This sea is nothing but a large lake which, becoming narrower [St. Mary's River] in the West or West Northwest, forms another smaller lake [Whitefish Bay], or second fresh-water sea [Lake Superior]. Such are the Nations that border these great Lakes or Seas of the North.

I have said that at the entrance to the <u>first of these lakes</u> [Georgian Bay] we find the Hurons. Leaving them, to sail farther up in the lake, we find on the North the Ouasouarini; farther up are the Outchougai and still farther up at the mouth of the River [French] which comes from lake Nipisin, are the Atchiliquoan. Beyond, upon the same shores of this fresh-water sea, [Georgian Bay] are the Amikouai, or the Nation of the beaver. To the South of these is an Island [Manitoulin] in this fresh-water sea about thirty leagues long, inhabited by the Outaouan; [Ottawa] these are people who have come from the Nation of raised hair. After the Amikoua, upon the same shores of the great Lake, are the Oumisaqai, whom we pass while proceeding to Bouichtiquoian, —that is to say, to the Nation of the people of the Sault, for, in fact, there is a Rapid [St. Mary's River], which rushes at this point into the fresh-water sea [Georgian Bay of Lake Huron]. <u>Beyond this rapid</u> we find <u>the little lake</u>, [Whitefish Bay of Lake Superior] upon the shores of which, to the North, are the Roquai; to the North of these are the Mantoue, people who navigate very little, living upon the fruit of the earth. Passing this smaller Lake,<u> we enter the second fresh-water Sea</u>, [Lake Superior] upon the shore of which are the Maroumine; and still farther, <u>upon the same banks, dwell the Ouinipigou</u>, a sedentary people, who are very numerous; some of the French call them the "Nation of Stinkards," because the Algonquin word 'ouinipeg' signifies 'bad smelling water' and they apply this name to the water of the salt sea—so that these people are called Ouinipigou because they come from the shores of a sea about which we have no knowledge; and hence they ought not be called the nation of stinkards, but nation of the Sea. In the neighborhood of this nation are the Naduesia, the Assinipour, the Eriniouai, the Rasaouakoueton, and the Pouutouatami. These are the nations which are beyond the shore of the great river saint Lawerence and of the great Lakes of the Hurons on the North. I will now visit the South shores, I will say, by the way, that sieur Nicolet, interpreter of the Algonquin and Huron languages for the Gentlemen of New France, has given me the names of these Nations, which he himself has visited, for the most part in their own country. All of these people understand Algonquin, except the Hurons, who have a language of their own, as also have the Ouinipegou, or people of the sea.

Before proceeding any further let us make ourselves very familiar with the many references that were applied to the Indian tribe with whom Nicolet was sent to make contact. As we can see from the above, we have such names as the "nation of the Sea" and "people of the sea" that are part of LeJune's text. So that we fully understand the linguistic applications of these references we must identify the source of the application and what meaning it had for them. As an example the word, "Ouinipigou" is an Algonkin word for those tribes to mean salty water or undrinkable water, which is considered smelly or stinky. Anyone ever attempting to drink ocean water can identify with this association. In the course of their relating this description to the French, they interpreted it to mean water that is stinking or smells bad, hence, "Stinkards." And the French word for stinking is, "Puan or Puant." So when the French referred to the "Ouinipigou" they referred to them as the "Nation des Puans." LeJune very explicitly explains the complexities of these references and goes so far as to explain that in actuality they should be properly called, "nation of the Sea, . . . because they come from the shores of a sea about which we have no knowledge." This explanation is reinforced in other locations of the *Relations* by other authors.

In addition to the names given the Ouinipegou in these two cited references, a generic term was also applied to the western Sioux speaking groups, which the Ouinipegou were part of. This Algonkin reference was "Nadouessis," which applied to any groups that were their enemies. Not only did it apply to the Sioux, but also to the Iroquois. This reference appeared on an early French map that identified the occupants of Lake Superior (see pg. 86, Boisseau 1643). From the French spelling, Ouinipegou, (pronounced, Wee-knee-pea-goo), the English version of Winnebago was derived. Even as recently as 1994 this nation has relinquished the latter and is now identified as the Ho-Chunk Nation. (1.)

The name "Ouinipegou" has various spellings as do most of the Indian names we find in the *Relations* and other journals from the early French records. We must understand that native peoples did not possess a written language; therefore, the learned missionaries were doing their best to phonetically spell (in French) these very difficult names as they heard them from the local native peoples. We can be sure that there were variations in the pronunciation of the names between the various clans and tribes as well as between individuals themselves.

At any rate, the Ouinipegou pose for us a great challenge. There probably is not another native American tribe of people who historically have been identified with as many names. With so many references for the same people, it is no wonder that these mysterious people have eluded historians for so long. In fact, this is what makes these people unique in our search for who they were and where they came from.

Now that we know who the Puans are let us get back to Butterfield and his story as he relates for us his version of the Nicolet journey.

Butterfield totally disregards LeJune's reference of the Ouinipegou being located "beyond this rapid," which is the unmistakable rapids or falls (the French word Sault), at the entrance to Lake Superior. He states that the "small lake" visited by Nicolet was Bay de Noquet on the Lake Michigan shore.

While Nicolet was at the Sault, Butterfield states:

Nicolet tarried among 'the People of the Falls' probably, but a brief period. His voyage, after leaving them, must have been to him one of great interest. He

(1.) For some 380 years, this nation was labeled as the Winnebago Tribe. In Nov. 1994, a National Secretarial Election was published, approving the revised Constitution, changing the name to Ho-Chunk (People with the Big Voice).

returned down the strait, passing *it is thought*, through the western 'detour' to Mackinaw. Not very many miles brought him to 'the second fresh-water sea,' Lake Michigan . . . The bold Frenchmen fearlessly threaded his way along its northern shore . . . until the bay of Noquet . . . .

It is true Vimont speaks of the 'small lake' as lying 'beyond the fall'; but his meaning is, nearer the Winnebagos. If taken literally, his words would indicate a lake further up the strait above the Sault Sainte Marie, meaning Lake Superior, which of course, would not answer the description of a small Lake. It must be remembered that the missionary was writing at his home upon the St. Lawrence, and was giving his description from his standpoint. [Italics added] (1.)

Butterfield chooses to disregard the critical and literal meaning of the reference to "beyond the falls" and dismisses this testament because the author was too far removed from the actual location of this event to be geographically knowledgeable of its elements. Ironically this reference is not Vimont's but LeJune's, but we will excuse Butterfield's error as an oversight. It does not end here, as we continue to realize other oversights within his analogy.

Butterfield continues to state that upon reaching Bay de Noquet, "which is in reality, a northern arm of Green Bay . . . four or five thousand people assembled of different tribes." He goes on to explain how Nicolet must have traveled up the Fox River to make contact with the various tribes mentioned.

Butterfield has even greater problems with the interpretation of Champlain's 1632 map of the Great Lakes. According to the map, Butterfield's so-called Lake Michigan also had an island on which there was a copper mine, an island that is indisputably Isle Royale of Lake Superior. The problem is that he already had one Lake Superior on the 1632 map referred to as "Grand Lac." He also thought the large river with islands to the south of it may be that of the Mississippi. This is difficult to ascertain, when according to the map, it specifically states that it "flows from the south." It is hard to imagine how the Mississippi could be running the wrong way into Lake Superior instead of the Gulf of Mexico! Somehow, Shea and Butterfield concluded that the lake, which we shall henceforth call the *mystery lake*, was Lake Michigan, and was erroneously placed north of the Sault when it should have been to the south.

Even prior to Dever's rendition, another historian submitted a brilliant dissertation many years previous. In 1946, Clifford P. Wilson narrated a most concise account using the testaments of the missionaries that relate

(1.) *History of the Discovery of the Northwest by John Nicolet*, Butterfield, 1881:55.

The Wisconsin State Historical Society published a volume titled: *Wisconsin in Three Centuries*, 1634-1905, Copyright 1906. On page 87, is the quote:

"It has been *surmised* that Nicolet, while at the Sault, ascended St. Mary's River far enough to get a view of the end of Lake Superior, but had he in any degree explored Lake Superior, there would surely be some record of the fact, especially as his achievements are set forth, in the chronicles of his time, with not a little particularity." [Italics added]

It is evident that the Wisconsin historians made every attempt to illusively divert Nicolet into the waters of Lake Michigan.

to the only known information of Nicolet's journey. It appeared in the *Minnesota History Magazine*, The Minnesota Historical Society, Vol. 27, Sept. 1946, No. 3.

In an article titled, *Where Did Nicolet Go?*, Mr. Wilson proceeds: (Brackets and italics used are Mr. Wilson's.)

THE THEORY that Jean Nicolet visited Green Bay in 1634 has been accepted as gospel truth for so long—even by leading historians—that any attempt to show he did not will doubtless be greeted with disdain. Considering how extremely flimsy is the evidence upon which the accepted theory is based, however, I may perhaps be pardoned for advancing another one.

First, let us recognize the fact that all reports of Nicolet's journey to the 'People of the Sea' have come down to us second hand. He left no firsthand accounts, but he told of his adventures to some Jesuits, who wrote them into their *Relations* in somewhat garbled form.

The earliest reference to Nicolet's voyage of 1634 is found in Paul LeJune's *Relations* for 1640. 'Let us return now to the fresh-water sea [*Lake Huron*],' it reads. 'The sea is nothing but a large Lake which, becoming narrower in the West, or the West Northwest, forms another *smaller* Lake, which then begins to enlarge into another great Lake or second fresh-water sea.'

Disregarding any previous theories as to where Nicolet went, let us interpret this passage in terms of modern geographical knowledge. The picture we get is of Lake Huron narrowing to the St. Mary's River, then widening into a smaller lake, which in turn enlarges into Lake Superior. The question arises: 'Which is the smaller lake?'

On the next page of LeJune's *Relations* we come to this passage: 'for, in fact, there is a Rapid, which rushes at this point [*Sault de Ste. Marie*] into the fresh-water sea, Beyond [*au del'a*] this rapid we find the *little lake*, upon the shore of which, to the North, are the Roquai. To the North of these are the Mantoue . . . Passing this *smaller lake*, we enter the second fresh-water sea, upon the shore of which are Maroumine; and still farther, upon the same banks, dwell the Ouinipigou . . . In the neighborhood of this nation are the Naduesia, the Assinipour,' and other tribes. For this it is obvious that the 'smaller lake' is beyond the Sault, and that it opens out into another very large lake, which could be none other than Lake Superior. Looking at the map, we see no little lake in this location—only Whitefish Bay, but maps are sometimes misleading.

Imagine yourself in a canoe, setting out westward from the head of St. Mary's rapids, without a map or any knowledge of how the land lies. Since you are looking for a tribe living to the west or northwest, you follow the south shore of the river, and after you pass Point Iroquois, no more land is seen to the north. The south shore leads you on westward, but eventually it turns at a right angle and leads you straight north for about eighteen miles. Not until you pass

Whitefish Point does the land fall away again to the west, and the huge expanse of Lake Superior opens up before your eyes.

To all intents and purposes, then, you have been traveling along the southern and western shores of a lake—quite a large lake, but much smaller than either the fresh-water sea below the Sault or the second fresh-water sea upon which your canoe is now floating. If this explanation seems farfetched, look at a map of the north shore of Lake Erie, and remember that in Galinée *Relations* of the voyage with Dollier de Casson, he referred to Long Point Bay as a 'little lake.'

To continue now with LeJune's *Relation*: 'But I will say, in passing, that it is highly probable one can descend through the second great lake of the Hurons, and through the tribes that we have named, into this sea that he [*an Englishman*] was seeking. Sieur Nicolet, who has advanced farthest into these so distant countries, has assured me that, if he had sailed three day's journey farther upon a great river which issues from this lake, he would have found the sea.' This is the only mention LeJune makes of Nicolet in connection with the voyage under discussion. The 'second great lake of the Hurons' is evidently Lake Superior, and LeJune speaks of a river issuing from that lake. Of course, no river issues from Lake Superior except the St. Mary's. Possibly he misunderstood Nicolet, or possibly he meant that Nicolet's route issued from the lake. Barthelemy Vimont's *Relation* of 1642 describes Nicolet's meeting with the People of the Sea, but gives no indication of his route. For information on this, then, we can depend only on LeJune's account, written six years after the voyage took place.

The question now arises: Why have we been told all these years that Nicolet turned back from the Sault and headed south through the Straits of Mackinac for Green Bay? Simply because the tribes that LeJune indicates Nicolet met lived on the shore of Green Bay *several years later*. But it so happens that these tribes, without exception, were nomadic, and in 1634 they could easily have been living on the shore of Lake Superior, instead of on Lake Michigan.

And Wilson continues by explaining the relocation of the tribes of the Roquai, (Noukek), Mantoue, and the Maroumine (Maloumines or Menominee). Wilson goes on to state:

The Ouinipegou or Winnebago were five hundred leagues from Quebec as the crow flies, in 1623. They were on the shores of the 'second fresh-water sea,' in 1634, beyond the Maroumine, and they were 'called Ouinipegou because they come from the shore of a sea about which we have no knowledge.' In 1657 they were near St. Michel, and 1670, at Baye des Puants, which was named for them. (1.) [This author's footnote.]

The chief reason why Nicolet is said to have visited Green Bay appears to have been because the object of his trip was to visit the People of the Sea, after whom

(1.) St. Michel was located in Green Bay at the Baye des Puants, and the 1657 date is from Dreuillette's *Relation*, information that was gleaned from Radisson and Grosiller's trip to this region. The 1670 date is from Allouez's *Relation*, while at Green Bay. The 1623 reference is from Champlain's journals.

Green Bay was named Baye des Puants. But mention of the bay by this name does not appear in the *Relations* until 1648-49—fourteen years after Nicolet's journey. (1.) [This author's footnote.]

Champlain's map of 1632, it is true, shows a 'Riviere des Puans' flowing into the north channel of Lake Huron out of a lake where there is a mine of red copper on an island. But as no native copper has ever been known north of Lake Huron, the location of the lake and river must have been wrong. A map of 1643 in the *Relations* is copied directly from Champlain's, but even with the added knowledge acquired during the eleven intervening years, there is no indication that Lake Michigan was then known.

The map of 1643 that Wilson is referring to above is that of Jean Boisseau (See pg. 86). It identifies Champlain's Lake Superior or Grand Lac as *Grand Lac of the Nadouassiou* (Sioux), meaning "the enemies" of the Algonkin. (2.) And Wilson continues:

It therefore seems evident that when Nicolet visited the Winnebago they were living on the south shore of Lake Superior, but that some time within the next fourteen years they crossed the Michigan Peninsula and established themselves near Green Bay.

Mr. Wilson sums up his narrative:

It would appear, then, that the only point in favor of the accepted theory is that some of the tribes Nicolet presumably visited were later living near Green Bay; while the only weak spot in the theory now advanced is that Whitefish Bay is not really a little lake. (3.)

(1.) J.R. Vol. 33:61, 149, (1648), Ragueneau.
(2.) J.R. Vol. 23. Map of New France, 1643 by Jean Boisseau.
    (The Ouinipegou were also Sioux speaking people.)
    Historic references to native peoples are especially confusing. If a specific tribe of a similar linguistic group had some significance to the French, they would be distinguished with a special identity, such as the Ouinipegou, who were Sioux or Nadouassiou, were in contact with the Huron traders, and were therefore not considered as Nadouassiou or "our enemy."
    The perfect example is the identity of the Huron. They were of the same linguistic speaking group as were the Iroquois, located south of the St. Lawrence River. However, they were enemies—at war with each other. The French befriended those north of the river, whom Champlain called the "good Irocois." They became known as the Huron, *Quelle hures*, a French reference to specifically identify them from the Iroquois, by the manner in which they wore their hair, resembling that of the "boar."
    The word "Iroquois" is also a French creation. No explanation is given, however. It may be inferred that because Champlain befriended the Chief of the Huron group, whose name was Iroquet, they were called "Iroqu-ois." Champlain sent Brulé, "his lad," with Chief Iroquet to live among the Hurons (1610). Iroquet reciprocated by allowing his son to return to France; after a year, they were returned. This ritual exchange bonded the French and the Hurons in a close alliance until 1649.
    The Algonkin groups allied to the Hurons also called the Iroquois the "Nadousioux," which is an Algonkin word meaning literally, "of the adders" or "our enemies." Thus, the reference of Nadousioux was employed to mean anyone that the Algonkins were at war with or were enemies thereof.
(3.) Mr. Donald Chaput, who was the editor of *Michigan History Magazine* in 1969, wrote an article titled, "Europeans Enter The Lake Superior Country," appearing in *Baraga County Historical Pageant*, 1969. He supported the account of Nicolet entering Lake Superior, visiting the various groups mentioned, "all of whom were located on the shores of Lake Superior." However, "the exact route he followed is not known."

Enlargement of Jean Boisseau 1643 map of New France. An obvious copy of Champlain's 1632 map. Note that Lake Superior is identified as "Grand Lac des Nodouaffiou," or Nadouassiou, who were the enemies of the Algonkin. They were the Sioux, which included the Sioux speaking Puans or Ouinipegou. (M.T.U. Archives and Copper Country Historical Collections, Michigan Technological University)

Mr. Wilson correctly places us in the right church and pew, but is unable to tell us exactly where the Puants were when Nicolet located them in 1634 (only somewhere on the south shore of Lake Superior). Wilson accurately places the tribes that Nicolet locates on the north shore of Superior "beyond the Sault" and offers an explanation as to their relocating on the shores of Lake Michigan, which is a correct evaluation. These were the Noukek and the Menominee. Butterfield takes great issue with these two tribes. They are a key factor in his explanation for plotting Nicolet's course into Lake Michigan's waters, as he directs Nicolet into Green Bay.

Despite the accuracy of Wilson's description of the tribes' relocation between the years of 1634 and 1648, he fails to understand the reason for their relocation. In fact, had he continued his research in the *Relations* on into the 1670's with Allouez, he would have learned that they had relocated due to being nearly decimated by the Illinois some 30 years earlier. The Menominee and Noquet apparently gained access to the Menominee River and Bay de Noquet during the conflict that existed in Green Bay *after* 1634. The remaining survivors of the Puans, who were few, resettled in Green Bay, after which, this area took on the historic identity of the Lake of the Puants, when this "third Lake" was discovered by the French and reported in 1648. With the entire Upper Peninsula no longer occupied by the Ouinipegou, it allowed Algonkin tribes to migrate into this area sometime after 1642, after Nicolet's journey and prior to Radisson's and Grosiller's documenting them at these historic locations in 1657. (1.)

As we continue to critique the findings of the early Wisconsin historians we must at the same time remember that they did the best they could with the resources that were available to them. Butterfield was working with the three bulky volumes of the *Relations* published in 1858 in the French language, and they were not conveniently edited. This may account for the errors in dates with some of Butterfield's references. Shea began his work with the original Cramoisy publications, which were rare. Because of the initiative of the Wisconsin historians in 1898, in particular, the editor Ruben Gold Thwaites and his staff, we have the compilation of the *Jesuit Relations and Allied Documents*, in 73 volumes, which have been edited and translated into English for our reading convenience. (2.)

---

(1.) J.R. Vol. 44:247, (1658), Dreuillette, (information supplied by Radisson).

"The second Nation is composed of the Noukek and Ouinipegouek and Malouminek. These people are but a very short distance from the Village of Saint Michel [Green Bay] . . . . About two hundred Algonquins who used to dwell on the Northern shores of the great Lake or the Fresh-water sea of the Hurons, have taken refuge in this place."

(2.) *The French in North America*, Beers, 1957:97-101.

John Dawson Gilmary Shea worked assiduously on the history of the Catholic Church in the United States. He gave up a career as a priest in 1852, where he joined the Society of Jesus in 1848, spending four years as a novice at Fordham and at St. Mary's College, Montreal, Canada (John Gilmary Shea, Peter K. Guilday, New York, 1926), (Historiography of the American Catholic Church, Cadden).

*(continued on next page)*

These early historians were not privy to the related maps of DuVal that surfaced in subsequent years (1930, 1953, etc.) which provide us with a great deal of information that offers explanation to the otherwise confusing references in the missionary journals.

## The Mystery Lake

What explanation can we render for the *mystery lake* that Butterfield struggled so hard to convince us was Lake Michigan?

The map that Butterfield utilizes to substantiate his argument for the location of the Puans is the Champlain 1632 map. He attempts to correlate this map with later references in the *Relations* that place the location of the Puans at Green Bay in Lake Michigan. He identifies the *mystery lake* with that of Green Bay, and states that Champlain erred when he placed Green Bay on the wrong side of the Grand Lac (Lake Superior), north of it, instead of south.

This *mystery lake* of Champlain's is confusing; however, it does not have to be if we understand the circumstances and events of its inception. We now know the 1632 map is Champlain's second rendition of the Great Lakes, with the 1616 map being the first. Even though he is the author of both, he never had occasion to explore any farther than Georgian Bay of his Mer douce. His initial concept of the "fresh-water seas" was that it was a single large body of water, where at some point, an "exceeding great River would issue" from it, and flow to the "South Sea," where it would access Japan and China. (1.)

When Champlain wintered with the Hurons in 1615-16, the native people provided him with his cartographical interpretation of the Mer douce, which included Georgian Bay and Lake Superior, but was missing the narrow Sault

---

*(continued from previous page)*

Shea's series of Jesuit relations consisted largely of new material, but it included a few reprints from the original Cramoisy series published in Paris. Editorially, the volumes do not exhibit the standards which have come to be regarded as the best practice. They were issued as the documents became available to him and therefore were without chronological order. He failed to indicate regularly the sources of his documents. The texts were not always reproduced with scrupulous accuracy, modernizations and emendation being introduced. Consequently, use should be made, in preference to Shea's series, of the same relations which were again printed from the sources in Thwaites's Jesuit *Relations*, which is amply fortified with bibliographical data.

(1.) *The Voyages and Exploration of Samuel De Champlain*, Bourne, 1911.

Champlain: 1603, Vol. I:202. ". . . said Lake might take his course by other Riuers, which passe within the Lands, either to the South or to the North, whereof ther are many that runne there, the end whereof they see not. Now, in my judgement, if so many Riuers fall into this Lake [Mer douce] hauing so small a course at the said Sault, it must needs of necessitie fall out, that it must haue his issue forth by some exceeding great Riuer. But that which maketh me beleeue that there is no Riuer by which this Lake doth issue forth (considering the number of so many Riuers as fall into it) is this, that the Sauages haue not seene any Riuer, that runneth through the Countries, saue the place where they were. Which maketh me beleeue that this is the South Sea, being salt as they say . . ."

Champlain: 1615, Vol. II:67. "It is very large and is nearly 300 leagues long from east to west and 50 wide and because of its great extent, I named it, The Fresh Sea." [Mer douce]

It is not unlikely that Champlain gives as the length of Lake Huron [Georgian Bay] what the Indians gave as the combined length of Superior and Huron, omitting or not making clear the existence of the St. Mary's River, (Sault). Lake Huron is about 250 miles long and from 50-200 miles wide.

or rapids located at the outlet to Superior at present day, St. Mary's River. Thus, the Mer douce appeared as a single large body of water.

When Champlain left the Huron country to return to Quebec, he left instructions with Brulé and another interpreter named Crenole (also Grenole or Grenoble) to become knowledgeable of this western expanse of the Great Lakes. It was shortly after this that Brulé accessed Lake Superior. He returned with reports of his exploits, but Champlain is still convinced that his "Mer douce" does not have boundaries as does this lake the interpreters had just entered and returned from. It could not have, since they undoubtedly reported the river that separates it from Georgian Bay, called on the map, "River of the Puants, that is coming from a lake where close to it is a mine of copper" (note 33. in the 1632 map legend). From the natives, Champlain learned that there was a rapids that distinguishes Georgian Bay from his Grand Lac, which is also Lake Superior, identifying it as the Rapid of Gaston, (note 34.).

The Recollet Sagard gives us insight into what Champlain knew of Lake Superior from Brulé's journey. After being shown a copper ingot he submitted that:

> The Interpreter Brulé and a number of Indians have assured us that beyond the mer douce [Georgian Bay] there is another lake [Lake Superior], which empties into the former by a waterfall [Sault Ste. Marie], nearly two leagues across.

Also from Brulé he reported:

> . . . about eighty or a hundred leagues from the Hurons there is a mine of copper, an ingot from which was shown me by the interpreter on his return from a journey made in the district.

And from Crenole who:

> . . . had been trading among a nation towards the North, about a hundred leagues from us, getting copper from a mine. He told us on his return that he had seen several girls there with the ends of their nose cut off, according to the customs of their country . . . for having made a breach in their chastity . . . . (1.)

In the course of being supplied with accounts from Sagard, Brulé, Crenole and the natives, Champlain establishes both of these bodies of water in his 1632 rendition.

---

(1.) *The Long Journey to the Country of the Hurons*, Wrong, 1968:135.

 References to this unusual treatment of women identified two groups of western people, the Siouan tribes (Ouinipegou), and the Algonkin-Illinois (Marquette's journey down the Mississippi). Sagard's is the first historically recorded incidence of this behavior, which identify's Brulé and Crenole's presence into western Lake Superior among the Quinipegou and the copper rich region of the Keweenaw Peninsula and Isle Royale.

 Lalemont, in the *Relations* of 1659-60, reported Radisson and Grosiller's return from their journey:

 "They passed the winter on the shore of lake Superior. Continuing their circuit, they were much surprised on visiting the Nadwechiwec, to see women disfigured by having the ends of their noses cut off

*(continued next page)*

When Champlain composed his 1632 map, he was not about to surrender his theory about the Great Lakes accessing the sea, and he accommodates both his own theory and that of Brulé's report of Lake Superior. Hence, the Grand Lac appears on his map without a western boundary with the map's final completion eventually bearing *two* Lake Superiors!

We must also bear in mind that from 1629-1633, Champlain has been in France compiling his journals and the 1632 map to accommodate them. The French have lost possession of the colony at Quebec, and Champlain is probably resentful of Brulé and his role in its capitulation. This may or may not have had an impact on what information Champlain was willing to surrender to his map. Brulé was irresponsible and was known to exaggerate stories about himself. He was the French curse to the colony, according to the missionaries. When Champlain was deported back to France, Brulé stayed behind with the Hurons, who delighted in finally killing him and eating his flesh in a ritual feast. His body was exhumed from a Christian grave, surrendered to the Hurons by the missionaries, and tossed into a mass grave commemorating the "feast of the dead."

Just the same, we have to give credit to these interpreters for Champlain's knowledge of the *mystery lake*. It complements everything about Lake Superior and its relationship with the Puants as it is reported in the missionary journals—knowledge that was first gained by Brulé and Crenole, who would pave the way for Nicolet's journey into Lake Superior in 1634.

These interpreters also have to be given credit for supplying Champlain with his knowledge of the "Grand River that flows from the south" that appears on his 1632 map. It is this river that Butterfield thinks might be the Mississippi. This river shows up vaguely on the 1616 map, but it is specifically identified on the 1632 map, only because someone had to have been there to know that it actually existed and that it flowed south!

Butterfield is under the impression that Champlain gathered very little information from the Indians in his sojourn with them in 1615-16, regarding the nations beyond the great lake ("Mer Douce" i.e., Lake Huron). Unfortunately for these early historians, the 1616 map that was a product of Champlain's winter experience with the Georgian Bay tribes was yet to be discovered! (1.)

(*continued from previous page*)
down to the cartilage; in that part of the face, then, they resembled death's heads. Moreover, they have a round portion on the top of their heads torn away. Making inquiry as to the cause of this ill-treatment, they learned, to their admiration, that it is the law of the country which condemns to this punishment all women guilty of adultery, in order that they may bear, graven on their faces, the penalty and shame of their sin. What renders this custom the more admirable is that, although each man in that country has seven or eight wives, the temptation is, consequently, much stronger among those poor creatures—some of whom are always more cherished than others—yet the law is more strictly executed there than it would be perhaps in the most highly civilized Cities, if it should be established therein."
(1.) *History of Brulé's Discoveries and Explorations*, Butterfield, 1898:104(1.).

Given what we know of Brulé's insatiable appetite for exploration, he no doubt was all over the Lake Superior region in the years that he spent there. He apparently had been into the southern interior, as well as all the way around the lake, in order for the *mystery lake* to appear on the 1632 map, with its shores bounded and containing the "Grand River . . ." as well as Isle Royale.

Butterfield's assumption is that Champlain erroneously placed Lake Michigan on the wrong side of Lake Superior, north, instead of south of it, not something that was characteristically a practice of Champlain's cartographical knowledge and experience. Before we could accept this lake as Lake Michigan it would be more plausible to identify it as Lake Nipigon. Whatever the case, one must really stretch one's imagination to think that the *mystery lake* is Lake Michigan.

Despite our criticism of Shea, there is absolutely no historical evidence anywhere that would support the theory that Green Bay of Lake Michigan was discovered prior to 1647 (recorded in 1648). Since Shea's only argument hinges solely on the suggested erroneous plotting of the *mystery lake* on the 1632 map, it is a very unfounded one. All of the historic evidence that exists supports Nicolet's journey into the "second lake" which was Lake Superior, the same lake that was explored by Brulé and Crenole many years previous—a lake that could only be accessed one way, and that was by following the north shore "beyond this rapid" of the St. Mary's River.

As will be explored in the following documentations, Lake Michigan was yet to be discovered. It would seem strange how this lake could show up on a map that has no historical confirmation leading up to its discovery. If Nicolet was the first European to land at Green Bay, how does the erroneous *mystery lake* of Lake Michigan appear on a map that precedes his journey by two years? If Nicolet was the first to discover this body of water in 1634, how was it that Green Bay does not show up on any maps until 1650?

The Puants were still an enigma to Champlain despite his confining them to the *mystery lake*. They will have to be sought out to settle the war taking place in this region, and because they speak a language that is totally foreign to the Algonkin and Iroquois, they may even be of Asian descent. What was most intriguing to Champlain in his quest for the passage, however, was that they were called the "Sea People, because they come from the coast of a salt sea of which we have no knowledge."

*The Real Journey*

Before proceeding with the details of Nicolet's journey, we should first understand the existing situation in New France. It will give us a greater appreciation of how critical Nicolet's mission really was.

Back home, France was having its own local dispute with England, and the consequences would affect the New World. In 1629 Quebec was captured by the English, and Champlain and his followers were taken prisoner and escorted back to France. When the dispute was resolved, the French would return to Quebec in 1632, with Champlain returning as Governor in 1633. It was during this four year hiatus that he would write his 1632 journal with the 1632 map to accompany it.

When the French returned, the most immediate issue was to reestablish trade. The economic survival of New France depended on it. So the very first thing Champlain did was to provide additional security and greater access to the trading tribes by constructing a fort up river from Quebec at the confluence of the St. Maurice River, calling it Three Rivers. This was in response to the attacks from the Iroquois, who were threatening the trading tribes descending the rivers to engage in trade with the French. It was Jean Nicolet who was employed as Interpreter for the Gentlemen of New France at this new post and was responsible for transacting trade with the arriving native traders.

Of critical importance to the French was the fact that by now local populations of beaver were in short supply, necessitating expansion of trade further into the unexplored regions of the west. Efforts to engage these regions had already been attempted by trading tribes, who were running into difficulties dealing with these western groups, namely the Puans. The region of Green Bay became embroiled in conflict when the French introduced their trade goods to the trading Algonkins of Georgian Bay, who attempted to trade them with the Puans. It was the resistance of the Puans to trade with these former enemies of the Algonkins that caused war to break out among all of the resident groups in the Green Bay area (see Chapter 9:130).

The second most immediate issue was to resolve the wars that existed between these groups in order that trade may be accessed in this new untapped region. Champlain selected Nicolet as emissary for this particular mission, also; but this is not all.

The third issue and likely the most important, at least in Champlain's mind, was discovering the "exceeding great River" that would access the "South Sea" to China and Japan. There is no doubt that Champlain thought that by making contact with the Sea People he would learn of the route to the sea. He imagined these people as the link to the much sought after northwest passage through the Americas, connecting the Atlantic and Pacific Oceans. After all, they were called the "Sea People, . . . because they come from the coast of a sea . . . ." He learned they spoke a language foreign to the Huron and Algonkin, suspecting they were of Asian descent or may have traded with Asian people. Find the Sea People; find the sea. An Asian robe accompanied Champlain's return to New France.

After a thorough examination of LeJune's account of Nicolet's journey, we should by now be confident that he was in Lake Superior. It is his exact point of landing "beyond this rapid" that those who agree with the accuracy of this account give up the trail. This was both Dever and Wilson's problem in rendering their accounts, especially with the accuracy of Wilson's.

If we follow LeJune's account and ascend "beyond this rapid," and proceed north as he instructs us, the Ouinipegou would be located "upon the same banks." But why would you travel the long way around the north shore of Lake Superior to get to Sand Point located on the south shore? When you understand Lake Superior, this becomes very evident.

Travel in Lake Superior by the natives and early explorers from the Sault to the western end was along the northern shore. When one travels westward this shore line offers protection from the worst of storms that can suddenly whip-up from the north and northeast. These are the worst storms that plague even the largest vessels today. But more importantly, to travel by canoe along the south shore of Lake Superior places one in jeopardy, especially along a most treacherous stretch of shoreline extending from present day Grand Marais to Munising, which today is the Pictured Rocks National Lake Shore under the jurisdiction of the National Park Service. (1.)

When Father Claude Dablon journeyed westward to Chequamegon in 1670, he speaks of the north shore and describes Lake Superior:

> It is clear almost throughout and unencumbered with Islands, which are ordinarily found only toward the North shores. This great open space gives force to the winds, and they stir it up with as much violence as the Ocean. (2.)

It was Radisson, however, who recorded the first historic journey along the south shore:

> As we went along we saw banks of sand so high that one of our wildmen went [up] for our curiosity. Being there, [he] did show no more [larger] than a crow. That place is most dangerous when there is any storm, being no landing place so long as the sandy banks are under water, . . . After this we came to a remarkable place. It's a bank of rocks that the wildmen made a sacrifice to. They call it Nauitouchsinagoit, which signifies the likeness of the devil . . . . it is so high and so deep that it's impossible to climb up to the point . . . . We must look to ourselves and take time with our small boats. The coast of rocks is five or six leagues, and there [is] scarce[ly] a place to put a boat in [with] assurance from the waves. (3.)

So travel was common along the north shore, as LeJune indicates with Nicolet's journey. Following the north shore would eventually bring you to the

(1.) *Dangerous Coast: Pictured Rocks Shipwrecks*, Stonehouse, 1997:9.
(2.) J.R. Vol. 54:149.
(3.) *The Explorations of Pierre Esprit Radisson*, Adams, 1961:122,123.

Keweenaw Peninsula on its south shore. If you followed it far enough, you would return to your point of beginning at the Sault, still on the same banks! But the real answer to this paradox is in Champlain's 1616 map. When Champlain charted the "puans" on this early map, long before Nicolet's journey, he plotted them on the north shore of Lake Superior, "on the same banks." Ironically, the "puans" were the only ethnicity identified with this vast body of water to the west.

When Nicolet and his seven Huron companions left the Huron country, which was located at the southern end of Georgian Bay, they went north into Superior, followed the north shore around to the western end, eventually circled around to its south shore and to the Keweenaw Peninsula.

By traveling the recorded "300 leagues" from Ste. Marie, located at the southern end of Georgian Bay, and following the route just described, you would arrive at the door step of Sand Point. However, the same cannot be said if you were to run the course, as advocated by Butterfield, to the Sault and then to Green Bay along the Lake Michigan shore. Instead, you would have traversed only *half* the distance! (1.)

Interestingly, the Wisconsin historians have argued endlessly over the years as to exactly where Nicolet may have touched shore in Green Bay. As a result of the uncertainty among them they have formed individual factions, who have supported various theories that identify several locations for this possibility, places such as: Red Banks, Menasha, Doty Island and the Fox River. One of these locations even sports a bronze statue of Nicolet and another a monument with a plaque.

For us to become more aware of the actual events of Nicolet's contact with the Sea People, once he arrived at his destination, we have to refer to Vimont's account. This narrative was told to him by Nicolet himself. We will take this narrative apart and examine its details so that they will provide us with some geographical association with the already known location of Sand Point. It will be a matter of examining the phraseology of the narrative in order to establish meaning and a greater understanding of these otherwise confusing references as they were reported by the missionaries.

As we get into the details of this account, we should first know that the trip of Nicolet's was well planned and the Hurons that were accompanying him knew exactly where they were going. They had been on this route many times

---

(1.) One league = approximately 3 miles. Approximately 900 miles.

before on ventures to trade tobacco for copper, and they knew the occupation of the Sea People well. (1.)

In recent years trade with the Algonkins had caused war among the Sea People and a "union" of Algonkin tribes, who had migrated into the region of Green Bay from lower Michigan. The situation in the west was very fervid and it is for this reason that Hurons, rather than Algonkins, accompanied Nicolet to secure a peace. Since the Sea People were even warring among themselves, the initial contacts by the Hurons could be fatal despite previous trading activity between them. (2.)

When we examine Vimont's account of the journey, we can understand many pertinent facts that were played out prior to Nicolet making his grand entry on the beach at Sand Point.

The record states:

When they arrived at their destination, they fastened two sticks in the earth and hung gifts thereon, so as to relieve these tribes from the notion of mistaking them for enemies to be massacred.

When he was two days journey from that nation, he sent one of those Savages to bear tidings of the peace, which word was especially well received when they heard that it was a European who carried the message; . . . .

These two references follow in order and may seem confusing to us. We should not be confused with the terms used to distinguish "their destination" and the location of "that nation." They were *two* different locations.

What actually took place was that when they were "two days journey from this nation . . . they fastened the two sticks in the earth and hung gifts thereon." And it was after they "relieve these tribes from the notion of mistaking them for enemies to be massacred . . . ." they then, "sent one of those Savages to bear the tidings of the peace," to a location which was yet, "two days journey" away. It means that they still had another two days of travel before they were to arrive at their destination, where the central settlement of the Puants was located, and the actual meeting would take place between Nicolet and the

---

(1.) *The Voyages and Exploration of Samuel De Champlain*, Bourne,1911, Vol. I:209.
   "I inquired of them, whether they had any knowledge of any Mines? They told us, that there is a Nation which are called, the good Irocois [Hurons], which come to exchange for merchandises, which the French ships doiqiue to the Algoumequins, which say, that there is toward the North a Mine of fine Copper, whereof they shewed us certain Bracelets, which they had received of the said Good Irocois; and that if any of us would go thither, they would bring them to the place, which should be appointed for that business." [1603]

(2.) Vimont states the peace that was made was between the Hurons and the Puans. This is not exactly the case. The peace was to resolve the conflict between the "union" of the Fire Nation tribes and the Puans. This was brought on by Algonkin traders (Outaouaks) who were killed by the Puans. War even broke out among the Puans themselves! The Hurons were the last peaceful traders that had dealt with them and it was hopeful that they could make inital contact with these fearsome people without provocation. This situation was very tense, the mission very important (see Chapter 9:130).

central leaders. It would be here that gifts would be presented in order to secure the peace.

When we understand this we can also interpret the fact that in order for Nicolet to have "arrived at their destination," would imply that they intended to arrive at a particular place in order to conduct their experiment with the hanging of the gifts. The question is, where was this place that was "two days journey" from Sand Point? Knowing that Sand Point was the meeting place, we only have to back track the distance and we come up with a most ideal location, which is none other than the confluence of the distinguished river on Champlain's 1632 map, the Ontonagon River. A two day journey for the natives was equivalent to approximately 120 miles. This water route can easily be traced from the northern route around Lake Superior, coming from the west, "continuing on the same banks" eventually approaching the mouth of this "Grand River that flows from the south."

It would be the Ontonagon River that would be the most likely place to confront a small element of the Puants who may have been residing on the river or, who may have been fishing the river when Nicolet was making his way into the area. Judging from the strategy intended by Nicolet, it appears that he did not want to confront the main assembly, but instead chose to confront a fringe element of only a few members to demonstrate initially their peaceful intentions. The Ontonagon River would be an ideal location for this. We will elaborate more on the significance of this "Grand River . . ." later. (1.)

A two day journey from the Ontonagon River consisted of travel up the shore of Lake Superior to the famous "Portage" that today is called the Portage Entry or Keweenaw Waterway. After carrying their vessels across an area approximately a mile in distance, they would access the waterway that bisects the Keweenaw Peninsula for which it is named. This waterway empties into Keweenaw Bay just to the north of Sand Point, a distance of approximately 120 miles—a two day journey by canoe. It would be to Sand Point that Nicolet would send the messenger, who would inform the headsmen of their presence in their country so they would be granted safe passage the rest of the way.

The situation at the Ontonagon River was likely very tense for Nicolet and his seven companions. It would be here that they would make their initial contact with the fearsome Puants by the hanging of the gifts. Like most of the traders he carried a pair of pistols, which Champlain explained was necessary since you, "never approach these people without being armed."

---

(1.) This was Nicolet's second peace effort. The first was with the Iroquois when 400 Algonkin warriors accompanied him. This mission was more sensitive despite the fact that only seven warriors were present. Nicolet knew that attempting to approach the fearsome Puans with a large contingent of warriors would intimidate and incite them into battle. The Hurons accompanied him as insurance to an initial non-violent contact, since they previously engaged them in trade. The seven Hurons would act as guides and provide the additional man-power required to transport the French trade goods that were necessary as gifts in order to secure the peace.

At Sand Point, his entourage would be greeted by the expectant Sea People, who were excited by the arrival of a European. They would be eager recipients of the much-sought-after trade goods they had already been exposed to by earlier exploits of the Hurons, Brulé and Crenole, as well as the Outaouacks (Algonkin traders).

As Nicolet's canoe noses up on the beach at Sand Point "they meet him, they escort him, and carry all his bagage." He steps from his vessel garbed in the "grand robe of China damask, all strewn with flowers and birds of many colors." To the Sea People, they were indeed observing a "Manitouririnou" not just a "wonderful man," but a God! A Manitou! A man-god. All of this was done not because he thought he was in China or that they were Chinese, but in order to fulfill the waiting crowd's expectation for something great and grand—in their eyes a Manitou. To cap off their expectations, Nicolet apparently discharged his pistols to demonstrate his powerful medicine as he "holds thunder in both hands" and "sends the women and children running." Nicolet was an experienced trader and was very familiar with the customs and beliefs of the native people. He knew exactly what he was doing by staging this display of grandeur, being *dressed to impress* by wearing this flamboyant apparel. This demonstration would be essential in favorably posturing himself to seal the peace agreement with these people, who were known to "kill strangers without reason." (1.)

The most significant piece of evidence secured by the archaeologist at Sand Point was a musket ball and gun flint that Mr. Moore reported. These pieces are especially significant because they are the *only* historic artifacts that were discovered in the entire dig that may date to or around the 17th century period. These historic pieces at the time did not appear to hold much significance since this was to be a project that primarily entailed the excavation of a prehistory native culture. Most of the emphasis was placed on the importance of the prehistoric artifacts. With the present existence of all the historical evidence identifying Sand Point as the location of Nicolet's landing, the mere presence of the musket ball and gun flint are more than just coincidence. This would highly suggest that there is a strong probability that it may have been the very round that was fired from the hand of Nicolet himself! It is especially significant that the round ball and gun flint would both be found in the same area, indicating that the musket ball was fired and not dropped by some historic intruder. The flint could have come loose from the firing mechanism of the pistol, either in the course of discharging it, or become entangled

(1.) Initial exposure to guns for the native people was horrifying, thinking that the possessor held the power of the greatest of Manitous—the Thunderbird. This divinity was perceived to be a large bird that caused lightning flashes by winking its eye and thunder by flapping its wings. The report of the firearm was more revered than the actual fear of being shot. Guns and gun powder were very powerful forces for French traders who imposed their magic on the unsuspecting native people.

in his clothing. Remember, he was wearing a loose fitting Asian robe that was to complement the purpose of his mission. (1.)

During Nicolet's stay with the Sea People he would learn of the other nations who were "in the neighborhood." They would "come from round about" where during this time there would be gathered "4 or 5 thousand men." At one of these feasts, they would be served 120 beaver by one of these headsmen.

The peace having been made, Nicolet made his way back to the Huron mission on Georgian Bay, and from there to Quebec to meet with Champlain to discuss the details of his trip. They would include the success of the peace that was made and the news of being able to access the sea by a "great river." (2.)

## The Great River to the Sea.

When Nicolet returned he had apparently learned from the Sea People that had he "sailed three days journey farther upon a *great river* . . . he would have found the sea." This reference alone has perplexed many historians, and those of Wisconsin have chosen to interpret this river to be the Fox River of Green Bay. Rather than dwell on the problems with this theory, as many of these historians have done, we will instead go directly to the missionary record and other historic evidence that overwhelmingly supports the fact that this "great river" was the Ontonagon River, and not the Fox. (3.)

The following reference to the "great river" is a continuation of LeJune's account of Nicolet's journey that we cited earlier in the chapter. LeJune first

(1.) Mr. Moore stated that the beach area was not designated as a dig site since it was considered disturbed with the presence of too much human activity, i.e. footprints etc. Archaeologists located pieces of pottery sherds scattered throughout the beach area and even out in the water. Mr. Moore found the musket ball one day and the gun flint a couple days later, about 10 yards apart. He reported that the musket ball was in good condition and about the size of a marble.

Historic evidence: Mr. Moore reported that he located modern day bottle caps in an upper strata of one of the mounds that was excavated. He learned from Dr. Guy that they had used the mound as a loading ramp to load a bulldozer on a trailer some eight or nine years previous.

(2.) *Wisconsin Historical Collections*, Vol. 8. 1877:192, (Notes on Jean Nicolet) Benjamin Sulte. Sulte does a remarkable job of researching the church register to establish the date of Nicolet's departure as July of 1634, disproving Shea's theory of 1639. Sulte thinks that he returned in July of 1635. It may have been as late as August when Champlain continued his commission as Interpreter of the Three Rivers post. We are informed that he returned first to the Huron country and then sometime later to Three Rivers. Nicolet's name does not appear in the church register until Dec. 9th of 1635. During the same month it appears three other times, the 21st, 27th and 29th. Champlain has been critically ill and bed ridden for the preceding three months and dies on Dec. 25th. He was 68 years old.

(3.) The reference to sailing three days farther upon a river is a perplexing one. If Nicolet thought that he was that close to the sea, why did he not continue on to confirm that it was actually there? It was only three days away! Quite possibly, due to the intensity of this mission among this fearsome tribe, he spent only enough time to consummate the peace, which required meeting in council with the 4-5 thousand men. If this were the case, he would not have spent the winter among them, but instead, spent it at Ste. Marie, which may have been implied when the record stated that "sometime later he returned to three Rivers." As important as finding the passage was to the French, should compel us to think that he would surely have taken a mere three days to find it, unless, this mission was so risky that he did not want to press his luck by venturing into the interior, via a river, that may have had other unknown warring groups "in the neighborhood." That being the case, he probably spent the winter at Ste. Marie. After the peace was completed it would have been more important for Nicolet to return to Quebec than chance being eaten, knowing the unpredictable temperament of the Sea People.

**Winston Moore locating the musket ball on the beach of the Sand Point. A gun flint was recovered two days later approximately ten yards from where the musket ball was located.**

explains how he made contact with an English wilderness adventurer (the Englishman that Wilson mentions), who explained how he had journeyed for two years to seek a route to the "sea of the North." LeJune says this good man related wonderful things to us about new Mexico. "I have learned, said he, that one can sail to that country through *seas* that are North of it." The route that this English adventurer had heard about was none other than the Mississippi River and its route north to access the Great Lakes, or seas, that were reported north of the Gulf of Mexico. What follows is a reference that is the most convincing of all the historical data in the *Relations* that unequivocally places Nicolet in Lake Superior.

LeJune continues by stating:

> But I will say, in passing, that it is highly probable one can descend through <u>the second great lake</u> of the Hurons [Lake Superior], and through the tribes that we have named, into this sea [South Sea—Pacific Ocean] that he [the Englishman] was seeking. Sieur Nicolet, who had advanced farthest into these so distant countries, has assured me that, if he had sailed three days' journey farther <u>upon a great river that issues from this lake</u> [second great lake—Lake Superior], he would have found the sea [South Sea—Pacific Ocean]. Now I have strong suspicions that this is the sea [fresh-water sea—Lake Superior] which answers to that North of new Mexico, and that from this sea [Lake Superior] there would be an outlet towards Japan and China. Nevertheless, as we do not know whither this great lake [Lake Superior] tends, or this fresh-water sea, it would be a bold undertaking to go and explore those countries. Our Fathers who are among

Aerial view of the Sand Point beach area where the musket ball and gun flint were found. This is where Nicolet made his landing in 1634 among the Ouinipegou of Lake Superior. Shoreline has been altered due to dredging & filling. Note Pequaming Point in the upper right of photo.

the Hurons, invited by some Algonquins [Sauteurs], are about to extend their labors to the *people of the other sea* [second great lake—Lake Superior] of which I have spoken above. (1.)

Note the importance of the remarks of the Englishman having knowledge about sailing from Mexico (Gulf) to the sea, or Lake Superior, that was suspected north of it. This undoubtedly implies the accessing of the Mississippi River.

LeJune states, ". . . it is highly probable one can descend through the *second great lake* of the Hurons . . . ," to the sea the Englishman was seeking. And this "second great lake" was the lake that Nicolet had journeyed on to locate the Puants. It was upon "a great river" which *issues* from this "second lake" that he would have found the South sea, had he sailed three days further.

LeJune expresses the general impression shared by the French that a water course existed which flowed from this "second great lake" to the South Sea, connecting China and Japan. These very references by LeJune are repetitious of those used by Champlain in his understanding of the geography of the "Mer douce." Whereas, Champlain was convinced in his "judgment" that:

(1.) J.R.,Vol. 18:237, 1640—LeJune. Italics, underscore and [ ] 's added.

this Lake [Mer douce] . . . it must need of necessity fall out, that it must have his issue forth by some exceeding great River . . . . Which maketh me believe that this is the South Sea, being salt as they say . . . . (1.)

The most important reference by LeJune is to the "second great lake of the Hurons" where we again reiterate that it was this lake that Nicolet was in to complete his journey to the Puans. This lake was Lake Superior, not Lake Michigan! This is the same lake that Sagard described as lying "beyond the Mer douce . . . which empties into the former by a waterfall . . . ."

This "second great lake" was also where the missionaries intended to extend their labors to the "people of the other sea . . . ." These were the native groups that LeJune mentioned in his account. They were the groups that Nicolet explained resided *beyond* the Sault in the "second lake," or Lake Superior. They were the Roquai, Mantoue, Maroumine, Ouinipegou, Naduesia, Assinipour, Eriniouai, Rasaouakoueton, and Pouutouatami. They are the people LeJune described who "are the nations which are beyond the shore of the great river saint Lawrence and of the great Lakes of the Hurons on the North." These were the people who the "Fathers" were about to extend their labors to by invitation of the Algonkins (Sauteurs), who were located at the "waterfall" that separated Lake Superior from Georgian Bay.

We continue our analysis by following where the "Fathers" actually went and what their intentions were after arriving and meeting with the Sauteurs the following year in 1641. We can further establish that the "second great lake" was indeed Lake Superior and that the "people of the other sea" mentioned could only be accessed by commencing above the Sault and traversing Lake Superior, where they were "situated to the Northwest or West of the Sault, eighteen days journey . . . ."

This entry is Father Jerome Lalemont's writing of the missionary "Fathers," Charles Raymbault and Isaac Joques, who made the journey to the Sault and mentioned how to access the *people of the other sea* that LeJune mentions in his account.

> They started from our house of Ste. Marie about the end of September, and after 17 days of navigation on the great Lake or fresh-water sea that baths the land of the Hurons [Georgian Bay], they reach the Sault [present day Sault Ste. Marie], when they find about two thousand souls, and obtain information about a great many other sendentary Nations, the Nadouessis, situated to the Northwest or West of the Sault, eighteen days journey further away. The first nine days are occupied crossing another great lake [Lake Superior] that commences *above* the Sault; during the last nine days one has to *ascend* a River [Ontonagon] that traver those lands. These people till the soil in the manner of our Hurons, and harvest indian corn and tobacco. Their villages are larger and in better state of defence,

(1.) *The Voyages and Exploration of Samuel De Champlain*, Bourne, 1911, Vol. I:202.

owing to their continueal war with the Kiristinons [Algonkin-Cree], the Irinions [Algonkin-Illinios], and other great Nations who inhabit the same Country. Their language [Sioux-Nadouessis] differs from the Algonkin and Huron [Iroquois] tongues. (1.)

The location of the "second lake" or "another great lake" is located *above* the Sault which is Lake Superior. The exact same Sault that Nicolet traveled *beyond* in LeJune's account. We now have two references to confirm that Nicolet's "second lake," was indeed Lake Superior. It also continues to describe the location of the enemies (Nadouessis) of the Algonkin who are to the west in Lake Superior and it requires that one *ascend* for nine days up a "River that traver those lands," that "River" being the Ontonagon!

We conclude that Nicolet was in Lake Superior in order to have been in the "second lake" that was referred to in LeJune's account. The *great river* that LeJune reports, which was to have *issued* from this lake, was the Ontonagon. Nicolet *assured* LeJune that had he descended it for three days he would have reached the sea. Since there is no such river that affords this luxury, we may suggest that either LeJune misunderstood Nicolet, or Nicolet misunderstood the natives. We might prefer to think the latter, since his knowledge of such a river was due to information received from the Ouinipegou, who spoke an unfamiliar language. Since his journey took him as far as the Keweenaw, where he returned by the same northern route, he left much of Lake Superior unexplored.

LeJune explains that "as we do not know whither this great lake [Superior] tends, . . . it would be a bold undertaking to go and explore those countries." It is obvious that Nicolet had not circumnavigated Lake Superior. It would require ventures by other Frenchmen to explore and report the magnitude of this lake, which would lead to the discovery of another lake that existed to the south, the "third Lake."

To further emphasize Lake Superior's importance in the search for the passage leading to Japan and China, we note Dreuillette's entry as late as 1658, long after the discovery of the "third Lake." He confirms the fact that the route sought was from the end of Lake Superior.

This lake [Lake Superior] which is more than eighty leagues by forty wide in certain places, is studded with islands picturesquely distributed along its shores . . . . But there are riches of another nature. The Savages <u>dwelling about that end of the lake . . . touching the route to Japan and China, for which so much search has been made.</u> For we learn from these people that they find the Sea on three sides, towards the South, toward the West . . . . Now we know that, proceeding Southward for about 300 leagues <u>from the end of lake Superior,</u> of which I have

(1.) J.R., Vol. 23:225-7. Editors explain the correlation of these two references of LeJune and Lalemont. Italics, underscore and [ ] 's added.

just spoken, we come to the bay of St. Esprit . . . in the Gulf of Mexico on the Coast of Florida . . . . (1.)

Dreuillette had acquired his information from Radisson and Grosiller, who were very knowledgeable of the region of Green Bay ("third Lake" or "Lake of the Puants"), which was not discovered until 1647. During this time the "third Lake" was still considered a "Gulf" of Georgian Bay. They had yet to understand the magnitude of Lake Michigan, as yet to be identified as the Lake of the Illinois. Dreuillette's knowledge of the Gulf of Mexico is a result of Radisson's journey to Green Bay where he accessed the Mississippi River and learned this information from the native groups located there. This entry firmly establishes the southward accessing of the Gulf of Mexico from the "end of lake Superior" where much search had been made for the route to Japan and China. (2.)

We continue to identify the *great river* that LeJune refers to that supposedly was to lead Nicolet to the sea. By referring to Raymbault and Joques' journey to the Sault, Lalemont points out a "River" that can be ascended after crossing Lake Superior that will lead to the Nadouessis (which means in Algonkin—"our enemies," who were the Sioux speaking tribes). The "River" that had to be *ascended* rather than *descended* was the Ontonagon. (3.)

The Ontonagon River system accesses the Wisconsin River at its headwater—Lake Vieux Desert. Although it also requires portage, as would the Fox, there is no doubt that this is the river that was being referred to. (To confirm this claim we refer to Henry Schoolcraft's journal where he reported ascending a portion of the river with the assistance of an Indian guide.)

He says:

---

(1.) J.R., Vol. 44:247, Underscore and [ ] 's added.

(2.) *The Explorations of Pierre Esprit Radisson*, Adams, 1961.

Adams mentions that Radisson wintered with a group of Sauteurs located five days journey from the Sault. He contends that this location was on Lake Superior, likely where Radisson constructed a fort at Chequamegon on his Superior voyage. It was from here that Radisson made a snowshoe trek south to access the Mississippi. Radisson was apparently familiar with the area south of Lake Superior and west of Green Bay, but was not aware of the magnitude of Lake Michigan outside of the Door Peninsula. There is no doubt that Radisson was looking for the passage as his purpose was to "discover the great lakes . . . which was upon the border of the sea."

(3.) The French interpretation of Champlain's 1632 map reference, "Grande River qui vient du Midy," meaning, "Grand River that flows from the south."

The Ontonagon River is the largest river system of the Upper Peninsula. Located west of the Keweenaw Peninsula and flowing into Lake Superior. This river is extremely muddy year around which makes it unique to all the other rivers on this shoreline, making it easy to locate along the Superior shore.

Champlain's map of 1632 very vividly illustrates this river, identifying it as "Grand River that flows from the south." His map also shows the presence of islands at its confluence to the "Grand Lac," which are no longer present today, but did exist then.

*The Pioneer Letters*, (1846), Anonymous, 1994:18.

"The Ontonagon was one of the largest streams emptying into the lake. It is about 100 yards wide at the mouth but much wider inside and divided by a long narrow island."

> This lake [Vieux Desert] has also an outlet into the Menomie river of Green Bay, and another into the Chippewa river of the Mississippi by means of which the country is traversed in canoes by the traders and Indians. (1.)

Schoolcraft was not personally aware of the exact source of the Ontonagon and therefore did not know that it was not at Vieux Desert. The south branch, however, heads out only two miles from the lake and apparently this was portaged by the tribes (Ojibway) using this route at the time. Despite the fact that Schoolcraft's account is much later than the period we are researching, these river routes and trail systems would still be put to service by whatever tribe was occupying the region at the time. The following is the key entry that provides us with a clue to Nicolet's reference to the "three days journey" that would have allowed him access to the sea.

Schoolcraft continues:

> Indians say they generally walk to its head in three or four days, but on account of numerous rapids, it is only ascended in canoes about thirty-six miles, and a portage then made to its source, which is in a small lake called, *Vieux Desert*.

What is more important for us to know is that Lake Vieux Desert is the origin (headwaters) of the Wisconsin River. This major water course flows the entire length of Wisconsin into the Mississippi, eventually leading to the sea at the Gulf of Mexico. (2.)

The location of Schoolcraft's Lake Vieux Desert is truly a remarkable junction, and for this reason a nearby town is called Watersmeet. We have two primary river systems that originate there. The Wisconsin that flows south and the Ontonagon that flows north. *This* is our highway to the sea. It was a *3 days journey* from the mouth of the Ontonagon to its junction, before one could *descend* it to the sea. LeJune's entry should more aptly have read— *had he journed three days upon a river he could have descended it to the sea.*

We can not over emphasize the importance of this "Great River" (Ontonagon), not only to Champlain, but to the Hurons. Not only was the river a principal transportation route, but upon its banks was located a major source of the copper that was finding its way to the French colony. The Hurons had

---

(1.) *Narrative Journals of Travels from Detroit Northwest through the Great Lakes Chain of American Lakes to the Source of the Mississippi River in the year 1820.* Schoolcraft, 1821:171.
(2.) *Narrative Journals of Travels from Detroit Northwest through the Great Lakes Chain of American Lakes to the Source of the Mississippi River in the year 1820.* Williams, 1953:421.
    James Duane Doty, who was the appointed journalist to the expedition to keep the official diary and serve as public relations agent recorded:
    "A short distance above the copper rock [Ontonagon boulder], the Ntenagon [river] is divided into 2 forks of equal size, one coming from the country towards the Mississippi, and perhaps interlocking with the Chipeway [river], the other from Green Bay and interlocking with the Menomine river . . . It is 160 yards wide at its mouth and continues about the same width 9 miles up . . . . The Indian who acted as guide told us he would point out a small piece of copper on the banks of the river near the lake . . . ."
The Ontonagon boulder is presently displayed at the Smithsonian Institute, Washington D.C.

been trading with the Puants long before the French had set foot on their America and were very knowledgeable as to where these copper reserves could be located.

Champlain's journal cites a reference where he came in contact with an Algonkin chief, who presented him with his first observation of native copper. The chief produced this piece of copper from a sack where he said there were "large quantities on the bank of a river near a lake." Although, at the time, these travelers were quite distant from Lake Superior, there is no question as to their source for the copper. The river that was ascended was likely none other than the Ontonagon.

The peace that Nicolet so dutifully negotiated with the Puants was short-lived, lasting only a year. It would not be until Nicolas Perrot accessed Green Bay in 1665 that any European would learn of the fateful series of events that embroiled the lives of this once populous and fearsome nation. The missionary journals would not mention anything of their fate until 1670. A nation that once boasted 20,000 people was now reduced to no more than 300.

It is only from the historical records provided by the mission bound servants of France that we can acquire any knowledgeable account of Nicolet's journey to the Puants. It was in Lake Superior that he located them, only by traveling *north*, *beyond* and *above* the rapids.

## INCORRECT IDENTIFICATION OF THE PUANS

The *Relations* are the pivotal source for defining the Nicolet event. Our success in tracing his journey, as well as many of the events in these historic journals, depends on how well we understand the many references that the missionaries applied to these native groups. Attempting to accurately identify many of the references can be a difficult and arduous task, if at times, even possible.

The very first reference of the Puans mentioned in the *Relations* is found in Vol. 10:83. The editors of the *Relations* have mislead us into thinking that this reference applied to the Nipissing tribe from Lake Nipissing, Ontario, rather than the Ouinipegou of the western Great Lakes. The following is an attempt to clarify the rationale that the Wisconsin historians used to mistakenly associate the Puans with the Nipissings.

We begin by citing the reference in the *Relations* that is in dispute. It applies to the peace agreement that was broken by the Puans, made by Nicolet only the year before. The victims were the Beaver Nation located at the mouth of the Spanish River in northern Georgian Bay. Father Jean Breabuef reports from the Huron Mission in southern Georgian Bay in 1636:

On the eight of June, the Captain of the Naiz percez, or Nation of the Beaver [Amikouan] which is three days journey from us, come to request one of our Frenchmen to spend the Summer with them, in a fort they had made from fear of the Aweatsewaenrrhonon, or stinking tribe [Puans] who have broken the treaty of peace, and have killed two of their men, of whom they made a feast. (1.)

This is an important reference for anyone researching the history of the Puans. It informs us of the short duration of the peace that was made by Nicolet, broken already the following year.

There is no recorded evidence that the Nipissing and Amikoua were at war or that a peace was ever made by the Nipissing. The record does identify the friction that existed between the Nipissings and the Allumette's.

Before we begin this analysis, it is pertinent that we understand that the French reference to the Ouinipegou as the "Puans" is central to the problem of interpreting the events of these people. This word meaning, "stinking" has not only misled the editors, but it was even confusing to the later missionaries and traders. This became more evident in the succeeding years after the death of Nicolet, or deaths and departure of the earlier missionaries from New France.

The reference to the Puans as the "Aweatsewaenrrhonon" must have greatly confused the editors. Breabuef, who had lived among the Hurons for eleven years and was considered an expert in the Iroquois language by LeJune, leaves us with no explanation for its meaning. We have to rely on another reference in the *Relations* to understand that it applies to those who live by the sea or Sea People. (2.)

Now, let us analyze how the editors may have mistakenly identified the Puans with the Nipissings. These historians undoubtedly played on a reference cited by Father Gabriel Dreuillette recorded in 1658. It is a testament recording the account of the travels of a Nipissirien Indian named Awatanik. His journey describes departing from the:

> . . . lake of the Ouinipegouek, which is strictly only a large bay in lake Huron. It is called by others 'the lake of the stinkards' not because it is salt, like the water of the Sea—which the Savages call Ouinipeg, or 'stinking water'—but because it is surrounded by sulfurous soil, whence issue several springs which convey

---

(1.) J.R. Vol. 10:83.
(2.) J.R. Vol. 30:113, Pijart & Gareau.
  ". . . the Aoueatsiouaenronnon—that is to say, "who inhabit the coasts of the Sea . . . ."
  Even with Nicolet's contact with them in 1634, it would not be until 1640 that LeJune would enlighten us with the fact that the Ouinipegou were the "stinkards" or Puans, and should be properly called, "Sea People, because they come from the coast of a sea which we have no knowledge." Vol. 18:231.
  Strangely, the editors disagreed with Butterfield, who correctly identified Breabuef's reference of the Puants with the Winnebago. His 1881 publication preceded that of the 1889-1901 publication of the *Jesuit Relations and Allied Documents*. See History of the *Discovery of the Northwest by Jean Nicolet*, Butterfield, 1881:45-6.

into the lake the impurities absorbed by their waters in the places of their origin. (1.)

Awatanik was a baptised Nipissirien, and the editors presumed that he departed on his journey from his home country, Lake Nipissing. They also identified Lake Nipissing as the lake that was "surrounded by sulfurous soil," which has sulfurous springs running into it. An editorial footnote to Breabuef's reference attempts to explain this:

> The French term 'gen puants' was also applied to the Winnebago tribe. The confusion thus arising in the identity of these tribes may have been occasioned from the fact that numerous places were marked on the early maps as 'puants' presumably meaning 'alkaline.'

Dreuillette's reference is very misleading as it incorrectly identifies the proper meaning for the Ouinipegou or Puants. Accordingly, the editors were also misled in their interpretation and associated the meaning of "puants" with "sulfurous" to mean "alkaline." The correct meaning of Ouinipegou is very clearly explained by LeJune from Nicolet's contact with them. Because they were eventually located on Green Bay in 1647, they became associated with the peculiarities of its murky waters. The editors were not alone in failing to understand the real meaning of "Ouinipeg" as it is illustrated in Dreuillette's entry; other Frenchmen would do the same.

Dreuillette received his information from Radisson or Grosiller, who had just returned from Green Bay. The body of water referred to is Green Bay. It was these two explorers to whom we can give the ignoble credit for mis-identifying the Puans or Ouinipegouek, with water being "surrounded by sulfurous soil," due to "several springs which convey into the lake the impurities absorbed by their waters . . . ." It was Green Bay, not Lake Nipissing, that was considered "only a large bay in lake Huron." (2.)

---

(1.) J.R. Vol. 44:247.

Dreuillette provides a very lengthy account of the status of the refugee tribes that were distributed in the region surrounding Green Bay (St. Michel). Information that he acquired from Radisson or Grosiller, who had just returned from a voyage to this area. Atwatanik was one of these refugees who was part of the large contingency fleeing the Iroquois.

(2.) J.R. Vol. 54:199, (1670). Dablon accompanied Allouez to Green Bay.

"On the fourth, toward noon, we doubled the Cape which forms the detour, and is the beginning of the Strait or the Gulf of Lake Huron [Green Bay], which is well known, and of the Lake of the Illinois— which up to the present time is unknown, and is much smaller than Lake Huron."

Dablon refers to Green Bay as a "Gulf of Lake Huron" [Georgian Bay] the same as Dreuillette refers to it as a "large bay of lake Huron." Dreuillette's "lake of the Ouinipegouek" of 1658, is the same "lake of the Puans" of Raganeau of 1648, which made this "Gulf" or "large bay of lake Huron" so well known by 1670, as stated by Dablon.

J.R. Vol. 73:69, Index. Under the listing of "Lakes" the editors erroneously list: "Ouinipegouek," as that of Lake Nipisin, the lake of the Nipissiriniens.

Dreuillette and Radisson's pronunciation and spelling are uniquely similar: "Ouinipegouek" and "Ouinipigousek," respectively. This is Radisson's signature. Also compare DeQueen's entry of 1656, also information acquired from Radisson's previous journey to Green Bay. J.R. Vol. 42:219.

Wе only have to read the succeeding chronicles of those following Radisson and Grosiller into Green Bay to understand how the references to the Puans began to take on new meaning.

Perrot follows their lead in 1665, suspecting that because it is called a:

... salt-water bay ... careful search ... be made to ascertain ... some salt-water springs ....,

He claims the name (Baye des Puans) was given to the bay:

on account of the ... mud and mire ... from which continually arise unwholesome vapors ....

Even later, when Marquette arrives in Green Bay, the "sulfur" notion is still being perpetuated as he commences to search for "salt-springs." Before Marquette, Allouez extends this misconception when he identifies the Puans with the waters of Green Bay. Consequently, these waters had become notorious for their so-called "alkaline" appearance, as Allouez referred to the bay as "stagnant ditch-water."

## ANALYSIS AND EVIDENTIARY SUMMARY:
### (Basis for determining the destination of the Nicolet event.)

*Evidentiary basis:*

(1.) Presence of a "settlement of Indians" located at Sand Point in Lake Superior appears on a map drafted by Samuel de Champlain in 1616.

(2.) The only Indian tribe identified with the western expanse of Lake Superior on 1616 map is that of the "puans," who are located on the north shore or "banks."

(3.) In accordance with the explanation of the missionary journals, the "Puans" are also the "Ouinipegou" or, more properly, the "Sea People."

(4.) The missionary journals also document (per testament of Nicolet), that the Ouinipegou were located *above* and *beyond* the Sault of the Ste. Mary's River in Lake Superior, the "second lake." They could be found "north on the same banks." This "second lake" is the lake that is identified by Sagard, "which empties into the former (Georgian Bay) by a waterfalls."

(5.) Nicolet journeyed 300 leagues west of the Huron country, with the distance to Green Bay, Wisconsin, being only half that!

(6.) When Nicolet was "two days journey" from his destination he made contact with the Ouinipegou. The location was the confluence of the Ontonagon River appearing on Champlain's map of 1632 as the "Grand River that flows from the south." A river that was explored by Brulé & Crenole who observed "Indians *removing* copper from a mine."

(7.) In 1970 archaeologists discover and confirm a former "settlement of Indians" located on Sand Point—a significant location that contained 20 burial mounds and was occupied during the late Mississippian period. It was also confirmed that this site was the focus of a copper industry and provided an integral link in the copper connection between central Wisconsin and the Straits of Michigan.

(8.) The Huron (good Irocois) were acquiring copper from mines to the "North" trading with the Ouinipegou, who were copper industrialists.

(9.) Champlain directs Nicolet, who is guided by seven Hurons into the "second lake" (Lake Superior) to locate the Nation of the Puans or the Ouinipegou, in order to "make a peace."

(10.) Nicolet reaches his destination, advances the "Sea People" wearing a Chinese robe and discharges his pistols, causing the women and children to run.

(11.) Archaeologists confirm the location of a "settlement of Indians" at Sand Point and locate a musket ball and gun flint on the beach during their excavation of the site.

## CONCLUSION:

The historical evidence, as provided in the missionary journals, overwhelmingly supports the fact that Lake Michigan was not known until the discovery of the so-called "Lake of the Puants" reported in 1648. A well documented observation that established the Puants at Green Bay at that point in time. Lake Superior, however, was very well known prior to this date, since it was from its western end "for which so much search has been made" for the passage.

The "Lake of the Puants" was also called the "third Lake" obviously due to the order in which is was discovered. The earliest depiction of Green Bay on any of the early maps does not appear until 1650 (Sanson, See Chapter 9:146). The "second lake" is obviously Lake Superior, the lake on which Nicolet located the Puants; therefore, Nicolet could not possibly have been anywhere in Lake Michigan in 1634! The evidence overwhelmingly identifies his journey occurring in Lake Superior with his final destination at Sand Point, located on the Keweenaw Peninsula.

# THE ROBE
## THE SEARCH FOR THE PASSAGE

In most modern circles of Michigan history, very few people, if any, are even familiar with the name Jean Nicolet, let alone the details of his journey to the Great Lakes. The educators who briefly touch on his exploits make him out to be an awkward adventurer who thought he was in China when he arrived among so-called "peaceful" Winnebago Indians. This characterization is due to history's vividly portraying him wearing the famous Asian robe, as well as most historians' lack of knowledge regarding the actual documentation of this event. It might serve us better to explain the circumstances surrounding this event in order to put to rest this unfortunate myth that inaccurately identifies Jean Nicolet, as well as the Winnebago.

There is no question that the robe was to be instrumental in Champlain's quest for the much sought after northwest passage and that Nicolet was to be a key player in his plan. Did Champlain think that the Sea People were residing on or near the Pacific Ocean? Did Nicolet think he was in China when he set foot on the beach of Sand Point? If not, then why was he wearing the Chinese robe?

Since Champlain is the principal proponent advancing this journey, the answers to this question lie primarily in his and Gabriel Sagard's journals. The sole historic source of it ever taking place, however, is recorded only in a single entry of a missionary journal. We can make a determination regarding the *motive* behind this Frenchmen's staging such a grand event on the beach of Sand Point by comparing information from these sources.

The one thing that is clear is that Champlain actually thought the Pacific Ocean or "South Sea" was not far removed from the Great Lakes or was just bordering on them. He believed that the "salt Sea" was 1200 miles from the LaChine (China) Rapids, located on the St. Lawrence River. No one knew just how much land mass separated the two coastal seas that bordered North America's east and west shores. Our first conclusion is that Champlain believed the Pacific Ocean to be just beyond the fringes of the Great Lakes. In his "judgment" he also believed that an "exceeding great River" would "issue" from these Great Lakes adjoining the sea to Japan and China.

Regardless of how close Champlain thought the ocean was to the Great Lakes, there was no way that Nicolet was going to continue his journey to China or Japan in the vessel or vessels that were part of this mission. He may have thought that the Pacific Ocean was within convenient accessibility via canoe, but to think that Nicolet was going to end up in China on this trip is ludicrous! Additionally, the missionary journals tell us that this was not the sole purpose of the trip and that he was seeking out the Sea People in order to settle a war that was very disruptive to trade and exploration in these very important western waters.

Before we get into the specifics, there is one important and disturbing fact that raises an objectionable point regarding our argument, and it concerns Champlain's 1632 map. On his map he has added the *mystery lake* (Lake Superior) and identifies the Sea People (puans) as residents to this restricted body of water. This would lead us to believe that the Sea People should no longer be part of Champlain's "South Sea" equation. It should be noted, however, that the *mystery lake* is a supplement to his former concept of the "Mer douce" previously portrayed on his 1616 map. He maintains the existence of this great body of water to the south of the *mystery lake*, calling it the "Grand Lac," which in reality is also Lake Superior. If this appears to be confusing, it undoubtedly was to Champlain, who never had been in these waters himself and was trying to decipher information from a variety of sources: Brulé, Crenole, Sagard, and many of the native people.

There is no doubt that Champlain has every intention of protecting his former perception of the Great Lakes by retaining the Grand Lac and leaving its western boundary open and uncharted. He still believes that the Pacific Ocean is just beyond its reaches. It is not enough, however, that he be convinced of this, more importantly, the Cardinal and King must be convinced also. At this point he has not been successful in locating the route to the sea, and his supporters in France may be getting somewhat skeptical of his abilities. If *he* is to return to New France in 1633 in order to make a final attempt to locate the northwest passage, he has to emphasize how important it is to these officials that they should not give up now. Regardless of which lake he has portrayed the Sea People, if the passage cannot be found on one of them, it can be found on another!

> All this is only to show how much honor, <u>if this passage</u>, which was so greatly desired, had been found, would have come to him who lighted upon it; and how much advantage to the state or realm which would have possessed it. Since, then, it is our own opinion that <u>this enterprise is of such value, it should not be despised now, and that which cannot be done in one place can be accomplished in another</u>, in time, provided His Majesty be pleased to assist the undertaker of so praise worth a project. (Champlain's journals of 1632)

Up to the time of 1632, at least as it is reflected in Champlain's journals and maps, the most western known native group are still the Sea People or Puans. It is not until Nicolet returns from his journey in 1635 do we learn of other groups that "are in the neighborhood." So, up to this point in time, the Sea People are Champlain's *only hope* for any connection in his search for the northwest passage.

We might think that from Brulé and Crenole's extensive exploits into Lake Superior, it would have exhausted any further attempts to locate a sea route from its western limits. Especially as the *mystery lake*, with its boundaries, finds its way onto Champlain's 1632 map.

When we examine the missionary records of this event they only reveal that Nicolet's purpose for contacting the Puans was "to make a peace." Nothing is mentioned of Nicolet's intent or purpose for locating the northwest passage. Interestingly, we would never have known of Nicolet's Asian robe if it had not been divulged by the missionary Vimont. This is the *only* record of it ever happening! Was this Champlain and Nicolet's personal little secret?

The missionary Breabuef, who accompanied Nicolet up the Ottawa River and was at Ste. Marie, where Nicolet departed from and returned, made no mention of Nicolet's journey whatsoever. He knew the details of his journey, as he reported the breaking of the peace with the Puans in his journal the following year. The robe incident does not appear in any other records, except that of Vimont's, eight years after the event. Interestingly, Vimont knew about it previous to 1642 because he mentioned this event simultaneous to eulogizing Nicolet's death. It is apparent that during this period information relative to the search for the "South Sea" stayed out of the missionary records. It is with great difficulty that we attempt to reconstruct these exploratory activities.

The most convincing evidence in determining the real purpose of Nicolet's Asian robe is found in Gabriel Sagard's journal. Sagard only spent one year in Canada (1623-24) but reported what appears to be a very logical explanation for the robe.

Sagard and Champlain must have been comparing notes since their journals complement many references, and it is probably no coincidence that their journals were both published in 1632. Sagard enables us to understand the most recent thinking regarding the Ouinipegou, with Champlain's return to Quebec in 1633 and Nicolet's journey in 1634.

The French had gathered information from the Nipissings (Epicerinys) who wintered in the Huron country near Georgian Bay. Sagard explains:

> The Epicerinys talked to us several times about <u>a certain nation</u> to whom they go once every year for trading, . . . which is a month's or six week's journey . . . To the same nation also come for trade <u>a certain people who reach the place by sea</u>, in great wooden boats or ships laden with different kinds of merchandise, such as axes shaped like the tail of a partridge, leggings with the shoes attached but as flexible as a glove, and many other things . . . <u>They told us also that these persons have no hair, neither beard nor hair on the head</u> . . . and they assured us that these people had said that from the description of us given them they would be glad to see us. <u>This made us conjecture that they might be some civilized race and nation living in the direction of the Chinese sea, which bounds this country on the west.</u> (1.)

---

(1.) *The Long Journey to the Country of the Hurons*, Sagard, Wrong, 1968:87.

The French interpreted this reference to mean that "a certain nation" that was trading with the Nipissing (who were thought to be the Puans or Sea People), were trading with the Chinese who were accessing "this country on the west" and that this "civilized race . . . would be glad to see them." An exciting bit of information that would surely allude to establishing trading opportunities with the Chinese through the Sea People!

However misunderstood this may have been, this truly offers an explanation for the presence of the Chinese robe of Nicolet's journey. Unknown to the French at this time was that the Nipissings were actually running a trading circuit into Lake Superior, north to Hudson Bay, and returning south via the river systems that flowed into the St. Lawrence. The "certain nation" they were referring to was the Cree on Hudson Bay. Just the same, the French apparently "conjectured" that the Nipissings were trading with the Puans, instead of the Cree.

One very disturbing problem faced Champlain when he returned in 1633. The Puans were at war and had been since Brulé and Crenole's journey to Lake Superior. Any possibilities of making connections with the Asians or the western sea were hopeless unless a peace could be made with the Sea People, and that may be a very difficult and extremely dangerous mission. Contrary to former perceptions, the Sea People were a very fearsome tribe, as later historical accounts would document.

Understanding this, we can review Vimont's account of Nicolet's journey and more greatly appreciate his strategy for hanging trade goods from two sticks, as well as wearing the Chinese robe. They were both measures he took so that he "would not be mistaken for enemies" for "fear of being massacred." With the Puans identified as the trading middlemen with the Chinese, an Asian robe would serve to masquerade as an Asian trader who could slip into the waters of the Sea People without fear of being attacked and killed.

"Two days journey" from his destination Nicolet made initial contact with the Puans, probably a small group still some distance from the main settlement, where he performed the hanging of the gifts. Once this peaceful contact was made the Puans sent messengers to the main settlement ("their destination") on Keweenaw Bay. They would travel ahead to announce the arrival of a European. Nicolet and his seven companions had to travel for two more days before arriving at Sand Point.

We could question the necessity of wearing the Chinese robe at this point, since it would appear that Nicolet had broken the tension that he was anticipating, especially once the Puans knew he was a European and were waiting his arrival with great expectation. Apparently Nicolet reconsidered his strategy as he was traveling with his escorts who are directing him to the location of the chiefs and headsmen. He must have contemplated how he was going to meet the expectation of a God (Manitou) that the Sea People were so eagerly awaiting. The "grand robe of China damask" that was decorated with "birds and flowers" would play an important role in how he was perceived by these people, despite any former thought as to their Chinese trading connections.

The robe was essential to making nonviolent contact with the fearsome Sea People, with Nicolet's mission focused on making a peace. He knew he was not in China, nor did he think the Puans were Chinese. After the initial contact he probably also realized that they had never engaged in Asian trade. The robe's purpose was to keep Nicolet from getting himself killed while engaging the warring Sea People.

Nicolet successfully pulls off the peace mission; however, he does not find any direct route to Champlain's South Sea. He learned, most likely from the Sea People, that a sea route did exist via a river that had to be navigated for three days. Had he followed it, he would have found the sea.

If Nicolet thought that he was only three days journey from the sea via this river, as the missionary journal states, why did he not continue on it to confirm that it really would access the sea? Instead, he returned and reported this mysterious river route. This route from the western waters of Lake Superior would continue to perpetuate French thinking as they continued to search for it until 1658!

We can only assume that Nicolet's peace mission was of paramount importance at the moment, and he may have been a little anxious about spending any more time than absolutely necessary with these extremely temperamental people. He may not have wanted to press his luck by penetrating the interior via an unknown river, especially since learning of other unknown groups that were "in the neighborhood." Possibly, any further attempts to penetrate beyond the country of the Sea People may have been threatening for him by these very people. Trade among the native groups was guarded with a great deal of jealousy, and these people had already proved that by crossing the Ottawa. After all, that is what the peace mission was all about. It was important that he return with the success of his mission and make another journey to locate the "exceeding great River" that Champlain had instilled in everyone's mind.

Unfortunately, neither Champlain or Nicolet would live long enough to realize the disappointing truth regarding their search for the northwest passage. Champlain would die on Christmas day of 1635, and Nicolet would succumb to drowning on the St. Lawrence River in 1642.

The search for the northwest passage via the Great Lakes would continue, however, as others would follow, perpetuating the myth created by Champlain in order to locate the "South Sea" leading to China and Japan.

*Nicolet and the Nipissing Myth*

The history of the Nipissing myth (trading with the Sea People) originated long before Sagard's entry in 1623, which climaxes with Nicolet's journey in 1634. It began with the Interpreter, Nicolas Vignaud, who preceded Nicolet.

We are introduced to a group occupying an island in the midst of the Ottawa River, called the Allumettes. They were important in the trading scheme since they occupied an island that required passage in order to portage a set of rapids. The one-eyed chief took advantage of this situation by extorting trade goods from anyone using his island. Champlain realized the importance of the old chief and even admired him. He sent Nicolas Vignaud to live among the Allumettes in order to learn their language as well as to maintain desirable relations with them.

Nicolas Vignaud would eventually learn of the Nipissings' trade route to the "North Sea" of Hudson Bay. How he secured this information is uncertain; however, it nearly got him killed! He convinced Champlain that he had learned the route to the sea and expected great fame and fortune for his efforts. Champlain, not wanting to be left out of the great discovery, accompanied Vignaud up the river in 1613. When they reached the Allumettes, the old one-eyed chief accused Vignaud of lying, and only under great protest was Champlain able to save his life. Telling a lie of his own, the chief succeeded in discouraging Champlain from continuing his journey to the Nipissings, informing him that they were at war and would surely kill him. In order to maintain friendly relations with the Allumettes, Champlain and Vignaud returned to Quebec. The next journey up the Ottawa River for Champlain would have to wait until 1615 and would be his last. Nicolas Vignaud was sent back to France.

With Sagard's entry more details were learned about the Nipissings and their trading activities. It was suspected that they were trading with the Puans, who were trading with the Chinese. Here enters Jean Nicolet, who had arrived in 1620. He, like Vignaud, was also sent to live among the Allumettes for one year. He was then assigned to the Nipissings, where he spent the winters until 1628. This would imply that Nicolet had a definite purpose for his assignment among the Nipissings. The purpose among the Allumettes was to learn the Algonkin language as well as establish friendly relations with them. Once having learned the language (the Nipissings were also Algonkin), he would attempt to secure not only their trade but also to infiltrate their ranks in hopes of learning their routes and with whom they were making contact. (1.)

(1.) The Nipissings wintered only twelve miles from the Hurons on Georgian Bay where they would have been conveniently accessible to the mission of Ste. Marie. The missionaries report that Nicolet only wintered among the Nipissing and must have spent an equal amount of time among the Hurons since he was also fluent in their language.

Despite the many years spent among the Nipissings, they never revealed their trading secrets to Nicolet. This was made obvious, since he was still ignorant of their activities in 1634, when the Chinese robe became part of a peace strategy that was used to approach the warring Puans. (1.)

Since the information the French received from various trading groups was guarded with such secrecy, much of it was vague and forced them to make presumptive conclusions. Such was the case of the Puans and the Chinese. Who would more aptly fit the description of the middlemen than the Puans, or more appropriately the Sea People, who were so called "because they come from the coast of a salt sea, which we have no knowledge." Hence, we find Nicolet's use of the Chinese robe instrumental in portraying the French impression of the boundaries of the western Great Lakes as lying on the "border of the sea." (2.)

(1.) *The Long Journey to the Country of the Hurons*, Sagard, Wrong, 1968: 87.
(2.) *The Explorations of Pierre Esprit Radisson*, Adams, 1961:79.

# 9

# THE OUINIPEGOU

## IDENTITY AND TRANSFORMATION OF THE 'SEA PEOPLE'

The French called them the *puans*; the Hurons called them the *Aweatsewaenrrhonon*; the Algonkin called them the *Ouinipegou*, from which the present and more common name *Winnebago* is derived. All of these references mean *Sea People*. The missionaries clarify this for us to mean they were, "so called because they came from the coast of a salt sea." The Siouan people, however, were also identified by the Algonkin as the *Nadouassiou* or "our enemy" (of the adder). It is from this reference that the name *Sioux* is derived and it remains as a principal designation for all these related ethnicities. It was the Ouinipegou, however, who claimed they "had come from the shore of a *far distant sea* towards the North."(1.)

Champlain's records provide us with the first recorded reference to these people. He first learned of them through his contacts with the Algonkin and Huron groups in 1616. The reference of *Sea People* was applied by both of these groups. Brulé, who was Champlain's interpreter, would have knowledge of both languages, having lived principally among the Hurons, but also exposed to the Algonkin groups of the Cheveux Releves and the Nippissing (both Algonkin speakers), who wintered with the Hurons.

The very first recorded reference to the Sea People in the missionary journals does not appear until 1636 by Father Breabuef. He was very fluent in the Huron language and uses the Iroquois word, *Aweatsewaenrrhonon*. He does not elaborate beyond this and we must find the meaning of this reference in a later entry of the missionary journals. (2.)

(1.) J.R. Vol. 33:149, (1648-49), Ragueneau describes the Puants located on Green Bay.
"These people are called Puants, not because of any bad odor that is peculiar to them; but, because they say that they come from the shore of a far distant sea toward the North, the water of which is salt, they are called "the people of the stinking water."
Information that identified the Ouinipegou's claims to their origin was secured by the French donné journey in 1647 that discovered the "third Lake," which found them located in Green Bay, calling it the Lake of the Puans.

(2.) J.R. Vol. 10:83, Breabuef, "Aweatsewaenrrhonon," (has several deviant spellings).
J.R. 30:113, (1646-47), Claude Pijart & Leonard Gareau.
The "Aoueatsiouanenronnon" that is to say, "who inhabit the coast of the Sea." This Huron reference, by this writer, was used to describe the Algonkin Cree on Hudson Bay.

Later historic references to the Ouinipegou, by later trader journals, state that that they were referred to as the "People of the parent speech." Also Fish-eating Dakotas, (Dakota is another corruption of the word Sioux or Nadousioux). Alas, only two years ago, this group was destined to further identify themselves as the Ho Chunk Nation. This nation continues to mystify us with the addition of another historical dimension to their lives. (1.)

## EVALUATION OF THE ARCHAEOLOGICAL REPORT

Historically, the Winnebago people have been confined geographically to the region surrounding Green Bay, Wisconsin. Anthropologists and ethnohistorians have established that the Lake Winnebago Focus had a very early and lengthy tenure in this state. With this as a basis we will reexamine the information of the Archaeological Report, compare it with the historical information, and determine how it impacts the location of Sand Point.

*Biological intersite comparison:*

Probably the most confusing and contradictory aspect of the archaeology report was for the various anthropologists who attempted to identify the similarities of the Sand Point people with those of surrounding cultures. This was done by noting similarities of ceramic design, mound construction, burial customs, lithics, and by the physical comparison (T-score) to 30 other Woodland Cultures in the region.

Lawrence Dorothy noted that the majority of the pottery had closest affinities with certain types in Wisconsin classified as Madison Ware of the Effigy Mound Tradition. He suggests a possible manifestation of the Effigy Mound Tradition at Sand Point. Triangular projectile points, typical among Effigy Mound Traditions were also found at Sand Point, would further support this inclusion. It would place Sand Point in the "Late Effigy Mound" period that extended into the historic period (A.D. 300-A.D. 1642). (2.)

The report also concludes that the physical anthropology analysis identified that the Sand Point people were most closely related physically to peoples living in Wisconsin (Addington and Wyckoff). This was reinforced by ceramic and mound construction similarities as suggested by Dorothy and Dr. Cremin. (3.)

Dr. Cremin further states the Sand Point site was associated with sites of the "Lakes Phase," a Late Woodland manifestation (A.D. 600-1400) in the Lakes District of north central Wisconsin. Also, the ceramics appeared to fall within the Effigy Mound Tradition. The lithage assemblage consisted principally of small triangular points also typical of the Effigy Mound Tradition. He also

---

(1.) Siouan name: Ho-tcan'-ga-ra, or Ochungra, or Otchagra.

(2.) *The Michigan Archaeologist*, Dorothy, Vol. 26, Nos. 3-4, 1980:68, 69.

(3.) Ibid. Editor, (personal communication 1972). Vol. 27, Nos. 1-2, 1981:3.

mentioned the Robinson site (Lakes Phase site) which exhibited burial mounds in groups of conical, linear and tapering linear forms, with both the burial procedures and details of mound construction showing marked similarity with those observed at the Sand Point site. (1.)

However, when Larry Wyckoff published the physical comparisons in his report, he identified the Sand Point people with those of Manitoulin Island, Ontario (Old Birch Island Ojibway) and the Fletcher site of Lower Michigan, both determined to be Algonkin. He thus concludes:

> In all probability the Sand Point and Robinson people represent an Algonquin population due to their similarity to the Old Birch Island Ojibwa. This conclusion is also supported by the close similarity of the Sand Point to the historical Fletcher site population in Bay City, Michigan, determined to be an Algonquin occupation. (2.)

From the T-score results, Wyckoff chose to ignore the close similarity of the Winnebago Focus, which was more similar than the Fletcher site. Nor is the similarity of the Orr Focus of Iowa and Minnesota even mentioned. He implicates the Robinson site as an Algonkin speaking people along with the Old Birch Island Ojibway. The irony of the comparisons is that the Old Birch, Winnebago and Robinson sites had very comparable probabilities and correlation coefficients. It is a confusing comparison when we attempt to classify the linguistics of these people by physical comparisons, when we know the historic Winnebago to be Siouan speakers (see Chapter 10:176).

Because of this confusion it would appear that physical anthropology results may be inadequate to establish linguistic classifications which conflict with our ability to decipher other archaeological data collected. It is especially enlightening to know that the Sand Point people were a historic group that spoke what we know as the Siouan language. However, that still does not explain the close physical similarities to Algonkin sites, raising questions about whether physical comparisons should be the determining factor in deciding classification of ethnology. (3.)

The real confusion is in the physical comparisons that existed between the Sand Point people and the Effigy Mound Tradition. This critical contradiction indicates that of the other 30 site comparisons the Sand Point people were most dissimilar to the Effigy Mound Tradition! This is in spite of references in the report that the Sand Point people were most closely related physically to peoples living in Wisconsin. Despite this contradiction, Dorothy identifies cultur-

(1.) *The Michigan Archaeologist*, Cremin, Vol. 26, Nos. 3-4, 1980:15.

(2.) Ibid. Wyckoff, Vol. 27, Nos. 1-2, 1981:24.

(3.) *Aspects of Upper Great Lakes Anthropology*, Johnson, (Ossenberg), No. 11., 1974:38.
   Inferences about linguistic identity of Woodland populations on the basis of genetic affinities are highly speculative. Other studies have shown that because of such processes as migration, assimilation, and cultural diffusion there is often little correlation between glottochronological and biological estimates of distance. (Spuhler, 1972; Dolgikh, 1965).

al similarities with what he calls a manifestation of the Effigy Mound Tradition. Cremin supports this by stating that the ceramics, lithage, and burial mound construction and procedures showed marked similarity to this tradition. (1.)

Were the Sand Point people or Ouinipegou (Sea People) similar to the Effigy Mound Tradition who spoke the Siouan language? What was the linguistic correlation of the so-called Winnebago Focus to that of the Effigy Mound Tradition, or any other contemporary occupations of Wisconsin and Upper Michigan?

Dorothy mentions the Juntunen site of Bois Blanc Island on the east end of the Upper Peninsula near the straits. He mentions the similarity in pottery types with that of Sand Point and the fact that this location was also the site of a copper related culture. Unexplainable is why 61% of the Juntunen ware collected at Sand Point show up in the habitation area. Only one of the total 18 vessels was recovered from the burial mounds with the remaining vessels collected from the beach area. (2.)

A simple explanation for this enigma is that the people of Bois Blanc Island, probably consanguine, were driven out of the straits by encroaching Algonkins arriving from the east battling for the food rich fishery of the St. Mary's River. With the remainder fleeing to the west, which may have been few, some may have taken up residence among the Sand Point people. Because their pottery only shows up in the two areas, one may infer that an occurrence took place more near the historic period, demonstrated by the lack of vessels within the burial mounds.

At any rate, possibly language categorization is not the most ideological method for identification of these early primitive populations, for we find in the historical documents evidence that these groups lived in a constant world of cultural interaction with each other, either through trade or war. (3.)

The historical records reported Algonkin and Sioux groups occupying the same habitations around the Green Bay region even prior to the advent of the Iroquois war. Algonkin refugees began to pour into this Siouan region from Lower Michigan as early as 1620 or before. Strangely, they chose the area

---

(1.) *The Michigan Archaeologist*, Wyckoff, Vol. 27, Nos. 1-2, 1981:17-19. Addington and Wyckoff, Vol. 27., Nos. 1-2, 1981:3, Cremin, Vol. 26., Nos 3-4, 1980:15.

(2.) Ibid. Wyckoff, Vol. 26, Nos. 3-4, 1980:44, 60, 61.

(3.) *The Middle Ground*, White, 1991:16

White cites the refugee experience occurring in Green Bay after 1649. "The ethnological detail concerning these peoples have to be examined with care. The refugees ranged from hunting bands such as the various Ojibwas group to the Maimis, who initially may have verged on being a chiefdom. Structurally, they ran the gamut from remnants of eastern confederations like the Huron-Petuns, who were matrilineal, and the Ojibwas and Ottawas, who seem to have originally lacked clans, they were all patrilineal village peoples who were organized into exogamous clans which often had ritual functions. Such clans were sometimes grouped into paired moieties and sometimes organized into many phratries. The accounts of early ethnologists who studied these tribes and codified them are full of internal contradictions because they sought to freeze and codify what was, in fact, a world in flux."

Charles Callender, *Social Organization of the Central Algonkian Indians*, Milwaukee Public Museum, Publications in Anthropology 7 (Milwaukee: Milwaukee Public Museum, 1962): 19-28, 34-35, 38-41, 65, 70, 82-83.

around Lake Winnebago and Green Bay to find asylum from the warring tribes of the Algonkin on Georgian Bay and Neutral in Ontario. They gathered here rather than flee south, where the region was virtually void of human occupation. It almost appears as though there may have been some prior interrelation between various groups of these two major linguistic classifications as the physical anthropology may indicate. This activity in the region of Wisconsin may be an indication of earlier fluxing that had been perpetuated long before any historical observations.

*Environmental and Subsistence:*

The historical record may provide us with an explanation for many of the uncertainties that were mentioned in the Archaeological Report relative to the foods that were gathered by the Ouinipegou at Sand Point. Many potential sources were mentioned. Mysteriously, the foods thought to be most available were not evidenced in the archaeological collection.

Food such as acorns were very abundant and a principal botanical food source, along with other principal foods such as beaver, waterfowl, and fish scarcely showed any archaeological evidence of consumption. The report also states that this was unusual, especially with the evidence supporting a large population, indicated by the multitude of hunting points and pottery recovered. The listing of potential foods by the report attempts to cover almost every species of wildlife possibly indigenous to the region. We will key on those that would have been principal foods and give other possible reasons for their lack of evidence.

Fish, acorns, beaver, and waterfowl were the most utilized foods. Acorns would obviously organically decay, especially in the highly acidic soil of the Sand Point site; however, the remains of bones from fish and mammals should have had more representation.

The fall represented a period of great activity, the harvesting of large amounts of acorns as well as huge amounts of game in order to "winter in," especially in this region of severe cold, heavy snowfall, and long winters. Large quantities of fish in the fall would be smoked or dried for winter use. There is no doubt that fish topped the list of available foods. The Ouinipegou's ability to harvest wholesale quantities is evidenced by the use of nets that were also discovered at the site. The most immediate source of fish would be the lake trout and white fish accessible at their doorstep in Lake Superior. Lake trout would be readily available to the Sand Point site even in the midst of winter. These predacious fish could be easily caught on hand lines with barbs through the ice. Many of the freshly caught fish could be put on the ice once a school was located.

The use of nets greatly enhanced the ability of hunter-gathering people to capture fish and animals successfully. The large spawning lake trout would cruise the shallows, nosing along the shoreline, making them especially vulnerable to off-shore fishing with short gangs of nets. It would not be unusual for these fish to run in excess of twenty pounds apiece. In the spring, large runs of suckers, pike, walleyes and especially sturgeon would congregate in the rivers. They could either be seined out with nets, or gaffed with the use of weirs. The net was even instrumental in catching beaver attempting to escape their lodges. A single lodge produced an average of five or six beaver.

Not only would their nets serve to gather large numbers of large spawning fish, but they would also take waterfowl in these very same devices. "Clouds" of migrating waterfowl would be available and could be taken simultaneously. When waterfowl were the principal target, nets would be laid flat in the shallow bays. The principal waterfowl harvested was the diver species: canvasback, scaup, goldeneye, bufflehead, ringneck, scoters and mergansers. These particular species would congregate in large rafts in the shallow bays and would feed by diving down and securing food from the bottom. None of the diver species is mentioned in the report. (1.)

Another device for the wholesale harvesting of fish was the weir. One design was placed in the river in such a manner so as to allow the fishermen to gaff from its construction. This device was reportedly employed in the Ontonagon River by the Ojibwa fishing for spawning sturgeon. A barrier was constructed at an angle in shallow water with an opening at the upstream end. By standing on the weir, fish were gaffed in the muddy river by resting a long handled gaff hook on the bottom. When the large fish rubbed against the shaft they were snagged and brought to the surface. However, the real harvest took place when the fish returned down stream to reenter Lake Superior. They would be trapped as they descended, congregated in a thick school in the down stream crotch of the weir. It was reported that in a very short period of time enough sturgeon could be collected to feed an entire regiment (1400) — with most of these fish running three feet long.

Another weir device was reportedly used in the Fox River of Green Bay. It consisted of poles constructed at an angle from midstream to the shore where fish would be diverted into a pot or holding cage to be dipped out at the convenience of the user. They were reported to have bells affixed to alert the fisherman when fish were in the pot.

W hy were the foods consumed by these people not more represented in the archaeological collection at Sand Point? We only have to cite the historical records to understand the cultural practices of many of the native people and how they processed and disposed of food remains.

---

(1.) The Indians of the Western Great Lakes, Kinietz, 1965:381.
    "They catch ducks with nets spread flat on the water." (Sauk of Green Bay).
J.R. Vol. 54:215. Allouez
    "The Savages set snares [nets] for them [ducks] at the head of the bay [Green Bay], where they catch as many as fifty in one night . . . ."

The handling of food remains, when they existed, were universal to most native groups with certain variations. Many revered bone remains with extreme superstition. This applied to human bones as well. Bones possessed the life spirit that represented regeneration. Not disposing of the bones properly would jeopardize the continued availability of the food source. It meant that the bones of a beaver would have to be returned to the water where the spirit could be regenerated into other beavers. The same would hold true with fish. (1.)

Champlain cites a classic example of handling food among the Hurons. He distrusted the natives to cook his food for him; instead, he chose to pick out a fish and prepare it himself. It is likely there were many times that it was not quite cooked to completion to satisfy Champlain's palate. He was criticized for roasting a beaver and allowing the renderings to drip into the fire. He was informed that he would not find any more beaver to eat. Most of their food was boiled in water for this obvious reason. Although some cultures did dispose of bones in the fire, rarely would they be tossed to dogs to scavenge on! The dog, although valuable and an immediate food source, was considered the most deplorable of creatures. The greatest insult to a native male was to call him a "dog," or worse, "a woman."

One has to live in this region to appreciate the voracity of the many predacious and scavenging creatures that exist here. Processing fish on the beach of Sand Point would immediately draw horrendous flocks of gulls, making even the most accidental droppings disappear without a trace. The same is true for the remains of wild creatures anywhere in the wilds. Ravens and crows can locate and devour the gut-pile of a deer in minutes. Wolves, coyotes, fishers, raccoons, and martins would dispose of bones, and Canada Jays or camp robbers would snatch up just about anything left laying around. It is unlikely that evidence of fish remains at Sand Point were concealed due to high water levels, as was indicated in the Archaeological Report.

There was no archaeological evidence that would support the cultivation of domestic plants, such as corn, squash and beans at Sand Point. This raises the question of whether in fact such cultivation was even possible in this northern climate.

There are select areas along the Lake Superior shore that are within the 120 day frost free zones necessary for growing such foods as corn, squash and beans. Due to the uncertainty of the climate in this region, there would be years of crop failures. It must be remembered, however, that these foods would be supplemental to other principal food sources such as fish, acorns, etc.

Corn was not always allowed to mature prior to harvest in order to be utilized as a food source. Seed for the following year would need to be collected

(1.) J.R. Vols. 6:209, 211, 219; 10:167, 169; 44:301, 303.

from mature plants. Holding seed in reserve from year to year would safeguard against the loss due to frost. Trading seed from their southern cousins would also safeguard against this dependency. One such location that renders evidence of prehistoric cultivation is located directly across Keweenaw Bay from Sand Point, called Pequaming Point.

Pequaming is unique because it is surrounded by water where it is protected from the seasonal threat of late spring and early fall frost. Even today, not only is corn grown here, but gardens of tomatoes are successful where they are not anywhere else. It also contains rich fertile top soil that occurs naturally.

It is possible that the present day point was surrounded by water, even as late as the arrival of Father Menard in 1659. It is believed that Menard wintered at Pequaming with a group of fleeing Ottawa. There is evidence that this location had been long utilized by aboriginal groups, even prior to this historic observation. (1.)

As late as 1922, remains of cultivated garden beds at Pequaming could still be observed that were likely products of an earlier occupation, preceding the Ottawa and Ojibwa. Evidence to support this was the presence of cairns that were also located here and obviously not indigenous to either of these cultures. (2.)

It was recorded in Johnston's journals in 1803 that Indians on the Keweenaw Peninsula were growing corn and utilized many other foods indigenous to the peninsula. (3.)

*Copper Assemblage:*

The report identifies the location of Sand Point as a "workshop," for a modest copper industry, with the emphasis on the use of float copper, rather than

---

(1.) This group of Algonkin peoples were called the Keinouche or the 'Pickerel' clan. [*Archaeological Report*, Algonquin Subtribes and Clans of Ontario, Ontario Ministries, 1922:30.]

Our best confirmation that this location was visited by Menard is by observing an early map of Keweenaw Bay that included a 'mysterious island' that was identified as the 'Isle de Saint Francois Xavier.' The island was apparently identified with 'Pequa-quaming' and Menard, who according to the *Relations*, was identified with the Saint; both martyred. J.R. Vol. 42:115. [map of *Cartes des lac du Canada*, by Bellin, Paris 1744, appears in the book of Charlevoix, *Journal d'un Voyage.* ] [Pequa-quaming: Algonkin; meaning a narrow neck of land almost surrounded by water.]

(2.) John Jonston, trader, 1792-1807. Entry of 1803:

"The mountains from behind the Huron River bend back towards the south as if to make way for two bays, and then wheeling around to the north for the tongue of land called by the French L'Anse and the Indians 'Keewaynan,' here the Indians have a summer village and cultivate some maize." [*Superior Heartland*, Rydholm, Vol. 1., 1989:89 ]

According to the legends of the Ojibwa, who occupied this point during the historic period, it is believed that it was under cultivation hundreds of years before their occupation. In 1922, "Traces of the old Indian cultivation can still be seen in some places." [*The history of L'Anse Township*, American History Class of L'Anse High School.]

(3.) *Transactions*, Perry, 1877:178, 179.

"Keweenaw point . . . here the soil is sandy loam, and never freezes, being protected by six feet of snow, and is very fertile—the long days of summer (nineteen hours of daylight at the solstice) seeming to force the growth of every plant adapted to the locality . . . here is the very paradise of the strawberry, red rasberry, service-berry, wild cherry, gooseberry, and huckleberries of four distinct varieties . . . ."

copper extraction from mines or pits. The report mentions the mining of copper on Isle Royale, but fails to recognize any of the hundreds of mine pits located along the Ontonagon River from Rockland to Lake Linden, mine pits that were virtually located in their back yard! The type of mining the report stated would require a "greater amount of time and labor and a specialized extractive technology."

The topic of prehistoric copper mining in this region has been a long disputed subject. Although little exploration or study has been initiated on the mainland mines, there is ample evidence of how they were worked. Pits contained hundreds of hammer stones utilized in the extraction process. Evidence of the use of cribbing to elevate large masses of copper has also been located in one pit that was 26 feet deep. It is believed that these pits are from a later period due to the modification in the hammerstones found in comparison to those on Isle Royale (see Chapter 10:158). (1.)

Twenty-eight tools were recovered from Sand Point. Most of these were awls and barbs (fishhooks). One of the most common as well as important tools to complement the needs of these native people was the awl. This device was instrumental in working holes in wood, stone, copper and leather items. It was the basic tool for leather work. Lacing was accomplished with its use, as well as body piercing (the nose and ears) and the universal art of tattooing. Many of these very pointed copper instruments are eight to nine inches long. Despite the presence of few skilled copper artifacts in the collection, the awl was one that was produced here.

Also collected were 204 non-utilitarian copper ornaments worn for personal adornment, items that were also locally produced in their industry and a product of trade. Pendants were popular among the western lakes Siouan groups, as witnessed during the historic period by Radisson. Ornaments hung from pierced ears in the shape of stars and half moons (crescents). Such ornaments were found at Sand Point. (2.)

Only one copper projectile point was recovered from Sand Point. This is unusual since they are frequently located in the immediate and surrounding area by relic hunters using metal detectors to locate float copper. Copper projectile points are also very common in areas of Wisconsin.

During the early historic period reports of unworked copper appeared in locations distant from the copper range, indicating that copper was traded in this state. It probably was worked into form by the securing parties, producing items which contained their own local expressions.

(1.) *Miskwabik—Red Metal*, Halsey. pg. 2.
    "Most of the copper prehistoric Indians used was forcibly extracted from the ancient bedrock of the Keweenaw Peninsula and Isle Royal using the most elementary of tools, human muscle and a touch of physics."
(2.) *Voyages of Peter Esprit Radisson*, Scull 1858:212.
    "Their ears are pierced in 5 places; the holes are so bigg that the little finger might pass through. They have yellow waire that they make with copper, made like a star or a half moone and there hang it." Nation of Nadoneferonons (Nadouessi)—"Nation of the Beefe"(Buffalo) or Sioux. pg. 207.

*Bone Deformation and Preburial*

There was evidence of bone deformation at the Sand Point site. The report makes a futile attempt to give explanation to this otherwise peculiar practice that appears to be associated with the burial ritual. There was also evidence that preburial was practiced, which would explain the ossuary/bone bundle presence within the mound structures.

Despite the vague references in the report, it may be that the evidence associated with preburial for the Sand Point group is more comparable to the historical evidence cited by the missionaries of the Neutral tribe of Ontario.

Interestingly, the Neutrals were much like the Hurons, who were related to the Iroquois. Unlike the Hurons, their preburial practice was quite different. The missionaries witnessed the Huron ritual that was referred to as the "feast of the Dead." This event climaxed with the movement of the group to a new location, which occurred every ten or twelve years. The corpses would be excavated from the temporary burial locations, and the event would culminate in a grand celebration that entailed the redepositing of the remains into an elaborate mass grave.

The missionaries compared this practice to that of the Neutrals, who were considered more affectionate toward their dead:

> Our Hurons immediately after death carry the bodies to the burying ground and take them away from it only for the feast of the Dead. Those of the Neutral Nation carry the bodies to the burying ground only at the very latest moment possible when decomposition has rendered them insupportable: for this reason, the dead bodies often remain during the entire winter in their cabins; and, having once put them outside upon a scaffold that they may decay, they take away the bones as soon as is possible, and expose them to view, arranged here and there in their cabins, until the feast of the Dead. These objects which they have before their eyes, renewing continually the feeling of their losses, cause them frequently to cry out and to make most lugubrious lamentations, the whole in song. But this is done only by the women. (1.)

This practice may have been more probable among the Sand Point people. The deceased were likely placed somewhere to decompose; it may have been in a tree or on a scaffold to reduce the incidence of scavengers making off with the entire remains. This may explain why some bones are missing from the bundles. Once the flesh had been removed, the bones were collected and became a part of the personal belongings of the deceased survivors. They may have had a special place or were stored, bundled in birch bark or an animal skin (beaver). If they were "arranged here and there in their cabins" they would also be subject to loss from children playing with them or camp dogs running off with them. When the time came to celebrate the special burial

(1.) J.R. Vol. 21:199.

event, the remaining bones would be placed among others of the group in ossuary fashion.

The question of bone deformation is one that puzzles and intrigues anthropologists. Holes present in various locations of certain bones have mystified researchers attempting to understand their purpose. Most of the holes, among the Sand Point people, were produced after the death of the victims (postmortem, those of the long bones, pelvic, etc.). The reason for these bone intrusions is what is so intriguing. Spiritual association has been attributed to the disposition of bones, not only human, but with all creatures that native people disposed of. Could there be more to the act of bone deformation than what meets the eye?

The most deplorable act of aboriginal people that modern researchers find abhorrent is that of cannibalism. The practice of consuming human flesh was one that nearly all the Great Lakes tribes indulged in. Humans did not escape becoming part of the food chain in the natural world of survival for native people. The ritual was not without ceremony. Human flesh, hearts, and brains were all consumed. Many victims were subject to formal tortures to test their strength and courage before being consumed. Hence, the reason for the ritual consumption was to inherit these desirable characteristics spiritually. (1.)

When we examine the Sand Point bone deformations, particularly the long bones, it is obvious that it was important that the bone not be broken. This was evidenced by the location of the hole near the ends of the bone where a blunt instrument could crush the cortex without breaking the bone in half. The hole was carefully constructed with an opening just large enough so the marrow could have been removed. This would become easier with advanced stages of decay, the marrow then being consumed by the partaker. The hole could serve a multipurpose; to allow spiritual escape as well as passage of the characteristics onto its consumer, not to mention its nutritional benefit.

In cases of starvation, corpses had even been dug out of their graves and utilized as food despite the relationship to the deceased; ". . . the teeth of the starving man make no distinction in food, and do not recognize in the dead body him who a little before was called, until he died, father son or brother . . . not only brother to brothers, but even children to their mothers and the parents to their own children . . . even the dung of man or beast is not spared." (2.)

What about the cranial intrusion at the base of the skull? What purpose would it have in a preburial ritual? A likely answer might suggest a purpose for the living, rather than the dead. The mere location of such an intrusion would be the most convincing evidence. The hole was located in the rear and at the base of the skull, where the vertebrae and the cranium meet, the nerve center of the spinal cord and brain, an extremely lethal point on the human body. To puncture this location would mean instant and painless death! This

(1.) J.R. Vol. 22:263, 255.
(2.) J.R. Vol. 35:21.

may have been a means to end terminal illness, injury due to paralysis, coma, etc.—a form of euthanasia. Native people were not beyond killing their own relatives in cases involving survival, terminal illness or injury. (1.)

The size of the holes in the cranium correspond very well with a device that was very common among this copper culture; the awl. These very pointed needle like tools could also serve as very lethal weapons. The diameter of the holes compare very well with the diameter of a large awl.

The spiritual respect for bones is well demonstrated in historical collections. A general myth among many of the cultures advocated that the Great Master created man from the left over spirits of the animals. Consequently, animals were identified as spiritual guides (Manitous), which were revealed through every youngster's visionary quest, growing up in a native culture. The spiritual respect for bones of all creatures was universal, but the various cultures observed separate rituals that could be as diverse as the animals, plants, and the various elements in the forces of nature, that served each individual's need for spiritual guidance.

## OUINIPEGOU HISTORY

Archaeologists and ethnohistorians have established that the Lake Winnebago Focus has had a very early and lengthy tenure in the state of Wisconsin. These Siouan groups have been categorized into "Lakes Phase" occupational sites typifying the locations that were most inhabited by them.

The French trader, Nicolas Perrot, provides us with the historical documentation of the Ouinipegou or Winnebago. He does not elaborate so much on how essential residing along river and lake bodies were for their subsistence, but describes how being scattered out over a wide region provided for their security. As an example he describes how their enemies were unable to conquer the Sioux, because this nation was not confined to a single large sedentary village complex. Rather, they were dispersed among the many lakes that provided food for them. It made it impossible for their enemies to attack all of these groups simultaneously. When one of the settlements was attacked, runners summoned support from adjacent habitations, who would rally to assist the immediate victims. The Oglala Dakota fared much better than did the

---

(1.) While LeJune wintered among the Montanagis, elderly parents, who were unable to make the seasonal migration, were clubbed to death. The wife of the medicine man became terminally ill and mysteriously disappeared. Another incident involved an individual who had fallen into the fire and was severely burned, was also mercifully killed due to his burden to the others.

Ouinipegou, since their occupation of this region extended well into the 18th century. (1.)

It is important for us to understand the demographics of the Ouinipegou of the western Great Lakes, who numbered 20,00 or more, and who inhabited many individual smaller village complexes which were scattered over a region that extended from the shores of Lake Superior to southern Wisconsin. By understanding this system we may be able to explain why Sand Point appeared to have been mysteriously vacated without a single clue. But if this was such a secure system, then how do we account for the near total destruction of this large nation?

*Sequence of Events of the Near Demise of the Ouinipegou*

What happened to this far western group during the early history of French occupation prior to, and after, Nicolet's contact with them in 1634?

Our principal source for the history of the Ouinipegou is contained in the journals of the French trader, Nicolas Perrot, who traded with the many tribes of the Green Bay area beginning in 1665. He was a prominent figure in the history of New France whose tenure covered a period of some 30 years among the native people. (2.)

The missionary journals provide us with a very limited amount of information regarding the once very large population of the Ouinipegou and failed to articulate the problems existing that made this historic group so important to the French, particularly Champlain. (3.)

Although Perrot's occupation follows on the heels of Radisson's exploration of Green Bay, it is Perrot who was witness to the accounts of the Ouinipegou, undoubtedly acquired directly from them or resident groups who were survivors of these events. His account is somewhat general in nature, but it provides us with a complete overview of the history of the Ouinipegou prior to and after the Nicolet event. His account may not be in perfect chronological order or be specific as to the exact locations, but it allows us an explanation to the otherwise mysterious series of events that would otherwise be missing

(1.) *The Indian Tribes of the Upper Mississippi Valley & Region of the Great Lakes.* Blair, 1996, Vol. I:189.
   *The Story of the American Indian*, Radin, 1927:296, 307, 309, 311.
      Radin mentions the Oglala Dakota habitating northern Michigan and Wisconsin as late as the 18th century. It is uncertain how these Sioux may have been associated with the Winnebago as Radin attempts to explain his southern migration theory of the Sioux onto the western plains. He explains they were the latest arrivals to the "great adventure" and that the Oglala were unique from other plains Sioux since they lacked neither clans, dual organizations, agriculture nor sacred bundles, possessing only religious fraternities. It is from the Oglala that the infamous "Sun Dance" originated, a custom "subordinated to the two great obsessions that the tribes of the [Sioux] developed—the supplication to the deities for power, and war . . . ." Radin explains how the Oglala Dakota were individualists par excellence with a particular emphasis on "vision-experiences" for entering a number of "mystery-societies"; all these societies having a supernatural origin. "Almost any individual could found a society, and that is why among these people societies arose and disappeared with such rapidity."
(2.) Ibid. Blair, 1911.
      Emma Blair was also the assistant editor to Ruben Thwaites compilation of the *Jesuit Relations and Allied Documents.*
(3.) J.R. Vols. 55:183, 54:205, 237. Allouez, 1671.

from the pages of history. He does a superb job of laying this out, and many historians have quoted from his journal, but no one has attempted to arrange it in any chronology that would make it historically coherent. We cite the actual references in Perrot's journal so that you may not be prejudiced by any pious editing or variation from the original text.

His journal states:

In former times, the Puans [Ouinipegou] were the masters of this bay, [Green Bay] and of a great extent of adjoining country. This nation was a populous one, very redoubtable, and spared no one; they violated all the laws of nature; they were sodomites, and even had intercourse with beast. If any stranger come among them, he was cooked in their kettles. The Malhominis [Menominee] were the only tribe who maintained relations with them, [and] they did not dare even to complain of their tyranny. Those tribes believed themselves the most powerful in the universe; they declared war on all nations whom they could discover, although they had only stone knives and hatchets. They did not desire to have commerce with the French. The Outaouaks, [Algonkin traders] notwithstanding, sent to them envoys, whom they had the cruelty to eat. This crime incensed all the nations, who formed a union with the Outaouaks, on account of the protection accorded to them by the later under the auspices of the French, from whom they received weapons and all sorts of merchandise. They made frequent expeditions against the Puans, who were giving them much trouble; and then followed civil wars among the Puans—who reproached one another for their ill-fortune, brought upon them by the perfidy of those who had slain the envoys, since the later had brought them knives, bodkins, and many other useful articles, of which they had had no previous knowledge. When they [Puans] found that they were being vigorously attacked, they were compelled to unite all their forces in one village, where they numbered four or five thousand men; but maladies wrought among them more devastation than even the war did, and the exhalations from the rotting corpses caused great mortality. They could not bury the dead, and were soon reduced to fifteen hundred men. Despite all these misfortunes, they sent a party of five hundred warriors against the Outagamis [Fox], who dwelt on the other shore of the lake; but all those men perished, while making that journey, by a tempest which arouse. Their enemies were moved by this disaster, and said that the gods ought to be satisfied with so many punishments; so they ceased making war on those who remained. All these scourges, which ought to have gone home to their consciences, seemed only to increase their iniquities . . . the frequent raids of their enemies had even dispersed the game; and famine was the last scourge that attacked them.

The Islinois [Illinois], touched with compassion for these unfortunates, sent five hundred men, among whom were fifty of the most prominent persons in their nation, to carry them a liberal supply of provisions. Those man-eaters received them at first with the utmost gratitude; but at the same time they mediated taking revenge for their loss by the sacrifice which they meant to make of the Islinois to the shades of their dead. Accordingly, they erected a great cabin in which to lodge these new guests. As it is a custom among the savages to provide dances and public games on splendid occasions, the Puans made ready for a dance expressly for their guests. While the Islinois were engaged in dancing, the Puans cut their bow-strings, and immediately flung themselves upon the Islinois, massacred them, not sparing one man, and made a general feast of their flesh; the enclosure of that cabin, and the melencholy remains of the victims, may still be seen. The Puans rightly judged that all the nations would league themselves together to take vengence for the massacre of the Islinois and for their own cruel ingratitude toward that people, and resolved to abandon the place which they were occupying. But, before they took that final step, each reproached himself for that crime; some dreamed at night that their families were being carried away, and others thought that they saw on every side frightful spectres, who threatened them. They took refuge in an island, which has since been swept away by the ice-floes.

The Islinoi, finding that their people did not return, sent out some men to bring news of them. They arrived at the Puans village, which they found abandoned; but from it they descried the smoke from the one which had just been established in that island. The Islinois saw only the ruins of the cabins, and the bones of many human beings which, they concluded, were those of their own people. When they carried back to their country, this sad news, only weeping and lamentation were heard; they sent word of their loss to their allies, who offered to assist them. The Puans, who knew that the islinois did not use canoes, were sure that in that island they were safe from all affronts. The Islinois were every day consoled by those who had learned of their disaster; and from every side they received presents which wiped away their tears. They consulted together whether they should immediately attempt hostilities against their enemies. Their wisest men said that they ought, in accordance with the custom of their ancestors, to spend one year, or even more, in mourning, to move the Great Spirit; that he had chastised them because they had not offered enough sacrifices to him; that he would, notwithstanding, have pity on them if they were not impatient; and that he would chastise the Puans for so black a deed. They deferred hostilities until the second year, when they assembled a large body of men from all the nations who were interested in the undertaking; and they set out in the winter season, in order not to fail therein. Having reached the island over the ice, they found only the cabins, in which still remained some fire; the puans had gone to their hunt on the day before, and were traveling in a body, that they might not, in any emergency, be surprised by the Islinois. The army of the latter followed these hunters, and on the sixth day descried their village, to which they laid seige. So vigorous was their attack that they killed, wounded, or made prisoners all the Puans, except a few who escaped, and who reached the Malhominis village, but severely wounded by arrows.

The Islinois returned to their country, well avenged; they had, however, the generosity to spare the lives of many women and children, part of who remained among them, while others had liberty to go whither they pleased. A few years ago, the [the Puans] numbered possibly one hundred and fifty warriors. These savages have no mutual fellow-feeling; they have caused their own ruin, and have been obliged to divide their forces. They are naturally very impatient of

control, and very irascible; a little matter excites them; and they are great brag-
garts. They are, however, well built, and are brave soldiers, who do not know
what danger is; and they are subtle and crafty in war. Although they are convinced that their ancestors drew upon themselves the enmity of all the surrounding nations, they cannot be humble; on the contrary, they are the first to
affront those who are with them. Their women are extremely laborious; they are
neat in their houses, but very disgusting about their food. These people are very
fond of the French, who always protect them; without that support, they would
have been long ago utterly destroyed, for none of their neighbors could endure
them on account of their behavior and their insupportable haughtiness. Some
years ago, the Outagamis, Maskoutechs, Kikabous, Sakis, and Miamis were
almost defeated by them; they have [now] become somewhat more tractable.
Some of the Pouteouatemis, Sakis, and Outagamis have taken wives among
them, and have given them their own daughters. (1.)

Perrot has compiled a composite of events that extended over a period of
time from about 1620, to 1642. He apparently acquired information from the
various tribes that were involved and witness to these events, who were still
located at Green Bay in 1665. So let us carefully examine this lengthy dissertation, then identify and place the missing pieces into the Sand Point puzzle.

We first must recognize the enormity of the populations of the Puans which
originally extended over an area larger than that of Green Bay. In fact, it
extended all the way to Lake Superior to include Champlain's Grand Lac, particularly the site at Sand Point. Now let us attempt to chronologize these events
from other knowledge we have of confirmed events and dates recorded in
other references. A good starting point is the journey of Nicolet in 1634, of
which Perrot makes no mention. Somewhere in this lengthy account of his we
must be able to insert this important peace effort. (2.)

The missionary journals quote Nicolet stating that "in the neighborhood"
of the Puans dwell the Potowatomi and the Muskoutens. Our contentions are
that Nicolet is at Sand Point in Lake Superior, and the "neighborhood"

(1.) *The Indian Tribes of the Upper Mississippi Valley & Region of the Great Lakes*, Blair, 1911, Vol. I:293-301.
(2.) *The Winnebago Tribe*, Radin, 1990:5-7.
　　Radin quotes P.V. Lawson, (Wisconsin Archaeologist, vol. 6, no. 3, Milwaukee, 1907:20)
　　Wisconsin historians have debated Nicolet's journey to the Puans as it corresponds to the crushing
defeat by the Illinois. The established date for the near destruction of the Puans was 1640. (Allouez
would record this event 30 years after it occurred). John gilmary Shea and P.V. Lawson made feeble
attempts to give explanation to the chronology of these two events. Shea's thoughts were that if the
destruction of the Puans happened at all, it occurred prior to the making of the peace by Nicolet. He rein-
forces this doubt by stating that Nicolet, "found them prosperous, and we can hardly suppose a tribe
almost annihilated and then restored to its former number in 30 years." Shea also calculated that Perrot's
estimate of 150 men was comparable to the former warrior strength when Nicolet visited them. This was
an obvious error on Shea's part, since the 150 men Perrot documents was a far cry from the four to five
thousand that Nicolet reported. Lawson states the destruction of the Puans, "did not take place after the
coming of Nicolet, as he was followed by other white men in such short periods as to make it impossible for the occurrence of these stirring events to go unrecorded by others."
　　Perrot fails to mention Nicolet's contact and short-lived peace mission with the Ouinipegou in his
journal. Possibly, the failed effort by the French to maintain peace with this tribe precluded Perrot's
recording it in his journal, or he may not have had knowledge of the event through French sources. With
so few survivors of the Ouinipegou remaining, it is possible that none of them would have knowledge

*(continued on next page)*

132

includes the region of Green Bay and vicinity. And he includes the Nadousessis, the Algonkin word for *our enemy*, which are the foreign speakers of the Sioux. This may confuse us since the Ouinipegou are Sioux. It should be noted that an early map of Lake Superior identified this body of water as the "Grand Lake of the Nadouassiou." And that the Ouinipegou were also enemies of the Algonkin groups and were considered Nadousioux and part of the general Siouan group. (1.)

The distinction of the Ouinipegou from other Sioux groups was due to the trading tribes' contact with them. They were the most western group of native people the allied traders had contact with. Champlain is made aware of them as early as 1616, and at that time were distinguished from the other Sioux as the "puans" or Ouinipegou by the Algonkin. We do not learn the elaborate details of why they are called such until Nicolet shares his information with the missionaries. The discovery and evolutionary progressions of the French identification of these early native groups are what make understanding these confusing names so difficult.

The point to be made with Nicolet's statements is that the Algonkin groups that he describes were in Green Bay prior to his accessing Lake Superior and landing at Sand Point. Nicolet only mentions two of the Fire Nation groups, but since he was not in Green Bay the information he was securing about this region was apparently from either the Ouinipegou or his Huron companions acting as his interpreters—implying that the other groups were there without his knowledge, or were soon to follow, since they were being driven out of southern Lower Michigan into the region of Green Bay. According to Champlain's journals, this was as early as 1620 or before. The other Fire Nation groups were the Sauk, Outagamis, Miami and Kickapoo, which Perrot so aptly describes in his journal. If Nicolet had been in Green Bay, he would have had direct knowledge of all of these groups and would have identified them.

Just how intrusive was the imposing migration of the Algonkin Fire Nation into the Green Bay area of the Ouinipegou? According to Perrot the problems do not appear to develop until the Algonkin traders from Georgian Bay attempted to trade the newly introduced goods of the French, however, the mere encroachment into the Ouinipegou territory of Green Bay may in itself have caused friction among the tribes. The issue of trade may have instigated the escalation of the tension into actual bloodshed.

---

*(continued from previous page)*
of it either. The peace was of such short duration that the event itself was likely considered insignificant and quickly forgotten in time.

Only through the missionaries do we learn of this brief encounter and of the peculiar circumstances that surrounded it. The next white men would not enter these western waters until the mid-1640's (see Chapter 9:148. *Discovery of the 'third Lake'*).

(1.) Map of New France, 1643 by Jean Boisseau, *Jesuit Relations and Allied Documents*, Vol. 23.
Lake Superior was called, "Grand Lac des Nadouaffiou." (see map plate, p. 86)
(A map that is an obvious copy of Champlain's of 1632.)

Perrot's journal could mislead us if we did not realize the political implications of the French conquest as it is reflected in his account. He emphasizes the necessity of the tribes to form alliances with them by according them protection under the auspices of the French. This was promised to any native group that was part of a peace agreement that would insure trade.

Perrot's condescension may be in part due to the Ouinipegou's failure to keep the peace that was initiated by Nicolet, which he fails to even mention. Consequently, he portrays the impression that they were deserving of the treatment of the Illinois because they resisted trade with French alliances. Speaking of the Ouinipegou, he concludes:

> These people are very fond of the French, who always protect them; without that support, they would have been long ago utterly destroyed, for none of their neighbors could endure them on account of their behavior and their insupportable haughtiness.

We could endlessly debate the issue behind the motivations for war by these tribes over trade. Native groups formed alliances among themselves through trade, not so much as a means to advance their economic interest, but out of necessity for protection from their enemies. The French understood this perfectly and used it to their advantage when engaging tribes in a peace settlement. They promised to protect them as long as they were peacefully engaged in trade, an assurance that was too freely given, never enforced.

The conflict in Green Bay formed alliances between the Fire Nation and the Outaouaks against the Ouinipegou. It caused the groups of the "union" to stage raids on their scattered villages. The issue of trade even caused division among the Ouinipegou and they attacked each other! War appeared to be inevitable. (1.)

The ineffectiveness of the Algonkin traders to engage peacefully in trade with this large western populus hindered the French objectives of continued expansion into these waters, which was having an impact on the economy of the new colony. It was of special concern to Champlain, who was continually strapped for financial resources.

But the French had more pressing problems of their own. They lost possession of Quebec to the English and were forced back to France and returned only after their differences were resolved in 1632. The French immediately tended to the unfinished business that awaited their return: settling the dispute that continued to exist in these western waters. It is at this point that the French interceded with the journey of Nicolet to conclude a peace. This peace was made on the shore of Lake Superior, where the Puans were isolated from the neighboring Fire Nation groups. The Hurons were certainly not going to lead Nicolet directly into the eye of the storm at Green Bay. His journal is explicit as

(1.) *The Wars of the Iroquois*, Hunt, 1940.
   *The French in North America*, Eccles, 1998:49.

to how sensitive this situation was when he describes the precautionary measures he took, so as not to be "mistaken as enemies to be massacred."

After reading Perrot's account, we can understand why the peace of Nicolet's never had a chance, and it was broken the very next year when the Outaouaks again attempted to engage the Puans in trade. Like the others before them, we are informed of the feast that was made of the two Amikoua who were killed by the Puans in 1636, breaking the peace. The incident causes the Amikouan to even fear an all-out attack by this fearsome tribe. (1.)

It would be the killing of the two Amikoua that would undoubtedly encourage the "union" of the Fire Nation (Outagamis, Maskoutech, Kikabous, Sakis and Miami), to engage in all-out war against the Puans. It was this union that the Puans nearly defeated previously. The Potowatomi were not included.

The survival of the Puans is dependent on their unity against the union of the neighboring tribes when they are unable to defeat them. They must now rally their forces from the surrounding regions and take the defensive. They "unite all their forces in one village where they numbered four or five thousand men." (This is exactly the same number of "men" or warriors that "came from round about," when Nicolet describes his gathering with the Puans in 1634.) Perrot continues to inform us that while confined in this situation against their attackers, they suffer more from the diseases that break out among them. When they are unable to bury their dead, due to their siege, it causes even more death, and only fifteen hundred warriors survive. This does not deter this tribe who "believed themselves the most powerful in the universe" from seeking revenge. As soon as the opportunity presents itself, they send five hundred of their warriors against the notorious Outagamis (Fox). They all drown when a huge wind storm emerges while they are attempting to cross the "lake."

Many early historians have toiled greatly attempting to fathom which body of water this "lake" was since Perrot states the Fox, "dwelt on the other shore of the lake." Some believed this to be Lake Michigan, placing the Fox in lower Michigan. Others thought it was Green Bay and that they drowned while crossing to the Red Banks, where it was believed the Fox resided because they were called the red earth people. Most confusing is the Algonkin word itself, "Outagamis" meaning, "people of the other shore." (2.)

(1.) J.R. Vol. 10:83, Breabuef.
"On the eight of June, the Captain of the Naiz percez, or Nation of the Beaver [Amikouan] which is three days journey from us, come to request one of our Frenchmen to spend the Summer with them, in a fort they had made from fear of the *Aweatsewaenrrhonon* [Sea People], or stinking tribe, [Puans] who have broken the treaty of peace, and have killed two of their men, of whom they made a feast."
(2.) When the Foxes returned to southeastern Lower Michigan, near the fort at Detroit, it is recorded in the French journals that they claimed this region to be their traditional homelands. That being the case, they were likely called "people of the other shore" by the Ottawa and Neutral, who Champlain informs us were at war against the Fire Nation tribes, which the Fox was included. The "other shore" being that of Lower Michigan across Georgian Bay and the Detroit River from Ontario, hence, the origin of this enigma.
Charlevoix interjects the "Lake Michigan crossing" with a dubious account in 1720.

When Perrot uses this reference, it is a literal application and we should not try to read something into it. It is mere coincidence that the Algonkin meaning just happened to coincide with Perrot's reference to where the Fox were located in relationship to the Puans. The literal meaning was therefore to apply to the large lake called Lake Winnebago. There should not be any mystery in this statement when we realize the Fox were located about the lake according to early maps of this period. The Puans would merely access this lake by ascending the Fox River. (1.)

The continual attacks by the enemies of the Puans made it difficult for them to gather food since these "frequent raids . . . had even dispersed the game; famine was the last scourge that attacked them."

Now the story takes an interesting turn as we learn that the Illinois apparently feel sorry for their traditional neighbors to the north and want to show compassion on them by sending an envoy of five hundred warriors that include some headsmen and a large supply of food and clothing. This is heralded as a special occasion with a traditional grand feast with much dancing and the usual games. This is where the Puans so "craftily" conspire to kill everyone of them while they are totally consumed in ritual dance. This is really difficult to rationalize. In fact, nearly impossible. Why would the Puans want to invoke the retaliation of 20,000 warriors of the Illinois confederation! It does not make sense. Of course Perrot is trying in every way to tell us that these people were very different, unlike any of the other tribes he had dealt with. He tells us that they were self-destructive, being without conscience, lacking in self control, irritable and do not know what danger is.

As we should expect, the Illinois oblige the Puans by declaring war on them. Because it is their custom to wait a year, a year passes before they attack. It gives the Illinois ample opportunity to rally the large confederacy while the Puans must await the inevitable. Expecting their arrival the Puans do a remarkable thing. They move out to an island in the bay where the Illinois

---

(1.) Franqualin map of 1688, 'Payes du Outagamis' located to the west of Lake Winnebago.

It appears difficult for historians to understand how native warriors could conceivable drown in an inland lake. Lalemant describes an account that took place on Nov. 16th on the St. Lawrence River that cost a native his life and nearly the Frenchmen's:

"About this time one Joachim, a Christian savage, and the son of Jean Guion, while passing the long point were surprised by a gust of wind from the Northeast, and came near upsetting. They jumped into the water but covered with ice, and the savage clothed more lightly than the frenchmen, the savage died on reaching shore, and the frenchmen had a narrow escape." J.R. Vol. 28:243.

The above account cites a very identical situation that could have befelled the 500 warriors in the process of crossing Lake Winnebago. The canoe was very vulnerable to "upsetting" in sudden wind gust. The written record is repeat of incidents of how scanty the native people clothed themselves despite the time of year. In summer the men were entirely naked.

The record states that 500 Puan warriors suddenly drown when sudden strong winds overcame them, conditions typical of unpredictable weather in either spring or fall when the water or air would be near freezing. If they had been on the war path during these times, their plight would have been very similar to the account described above. Especially if the war party were garbed in traditional war dress covering their bodies, which may have consisted of nothing more than paint and tattoos. Having left the usual war feast of several days preparation, they would have entered the lake feeling invincible. The record states that they drowned when actually they would have succumbed to hypothermia.

would not be able to attack them since they lacked canoes. It apparently never occurred to them that the bay would eventually freeze, come winter, allowing access by foot. The Illinois had planned to attack during winter to ensure their success. Snow would provide the tell-tale evidence of their escape when they arrived at the island. Following their tracks for six days they were found attempting to gather food. The rest is history. The few that escaped were wounded with all the rest, either killed or captured.

This event is documented by Allouez in 1670 while at Green Bay among the Puans. He states that he was informed that this had occurred thirty years previously. Allouez adds that the remnant was eventually released by the Illinois where he located them on the shores of Green Bay. (1.)

Perrot informs us that a few years previous, the fighting strength of the Puans was numbered at one hundred and fifty men. He also states that most of the survivors were women and children. It is mere conjecture to estimate the actual number of surviving male warriors from this event, but it may have been as few as 50. One report of the *Relations* documented that about ten years after the incident 100 fighting men existed. These 100 were a combination of Puans and Potowatomi. (2.) Another account seven years after the event reported that the Potowatomi were considered part of the Nation of the Puants. (3.) The total number given in these statistics may be more represented by Potowatomi, as well as the Sauk and Fox, who Perrot reported were taking the Puan women for wives. It would be a fair estimate to place the total population of the Puans at no more than 300 after this incident, of which most were women and children. This may be a high estimate since it was reported that the total combined population (including men, women and children) among the Fox, Sauk, Potowatomi and Puans in 1670, was 600! (4.)

---

(1.) J.R. Vol. 55:187, Vol. 54:205, 237.
(2.) J.R. Vol. 38:181, 294, 1653.
  "100 Aweatsiwaen'ronnons [Ouinipegou] and people from the Nation of A'chawi' . . . ." A'chawi' was the Captain of the Nation of the Ondatonati [Potowatomi], 400 men, and was head of the entire 1000 man force, consisting of Ottawa, Ojibway and Algonkin clans from north Georgian Bay, who were gathered at Green Bay as a result of fleeing the Iroquois.
(3.) J.R. Vol. 33:151, 1648.
  ". . . the Ondatouatandy [Potowatomi] and the Ouinipegong, who are part of the Nation of the Puants."
  J.R. Vol. 54:237, 1670.
  "I visited them in their cabins [Ouinipegouk] and instructed them, doing the same to the Pouteouatamis who live with them . . . ."
  Allouez also states that there is a total of 600 souls among the Fox, Sauk, Potowatomi and Puans residing at Green Bay.
(4.) J.R. Vol. 44:245.
  "In this Village are computed to be about seven hundred men; that is to say, three thousand souls, since to one man there are at least three or four other persons, namely women and children."

Since the Potowatomi were not listed by Perrot as part of the "union" of the Fire Nation that warred against the Puans, how do we account for them during all this turmoil? Once we identify a date for the near destruction of the Puans by the Illinois, we can associate an event that has been previously misunderstood by early historians. This is the migration of a group of Potowatomi who mysteriously show up at the Sault during this period. Previous historians claim that they had crossed the six mile expanse of the straits in the course of fleeing the Ottawa and Neutral in Lower Michigan, where they previously resided. The event occurred in 1641 and directly coincides with the events transpiring in Green Bay. It is more likely that the Potowatomi were allied with the Puans, and rather than become embroiled in the war with the Illinois, they decided to leave. Hence, they departed and followed the shore to Mackinaw at the straits where they took up residence with the Sauteurs. With the fate of the Puans occurring in the winter of 1641-42, the Potowatomi apparently left in 1641. The Puans knew in advance (one year) that they were to be warred on and moved to the island for protection from the canoeless Illinois. (1.)

In the end, Perrot and Allouez's observation provide us with the cultural fluxing that occurred between the Puans, and the Potowatomis, Sakis, and Outagamis, who have "taken wives among them and have given them their own daughters." Ethnic assimilation was not unique among aboriginal peoples and appears to have coexisted long before any historical observations; however, it was especially evident during the historical period responding to the refugee experience of the Iroquois war. Boundaries between the various tribes were not always clear. Perrot, in a prepared speech to the Fire Nation, emphasized the consequences of the refugee experience and wide spread intermarriages in Green Bay:

> Thou Pouteouatimais, thy tribe is half Sakis (Sauk); thou Sakis are part Renards (Fox); thy cousins are thy brother-in-law are Renards and Sakis,

Similarly, the Winnebagos, according to Perrot were composed largely of adoptees and intermarried peoples. (2.)

The "unclear boundaries" between the various tribes, despite linguistics, may be attributing factors leading to the confusing and contradictory result of archaeological intersite comparison.

This confusion becomes noticeable while attempting to delineate between the Ouinipegou (Sioux) and tribes of the Fire Nation, ( i.e. the Sauk, Fox and

---

(1.) J.R. Vol 23:225, 1641.

> ". . . we learned that a more remote Nation whom they call Pouteatomi had abandoned their own Country and taken refuge with the Inhabitants of the Sault, in order to remove from some other hostile Nation who persecuted them with endless war."

(2.) *The Middle Ground*, White, 1991:19.

other Algonkin speaking people); especially in the course of segregating them through physical anthropological examination.

Prior to this cultural integration, the Ouinipegou (Sioux or Dakota) lacked divisions into families, or what is referred to as a totemic system. Those that do claim totems are descendants of the integrated Algonkin, who have in former times intermarried with them. The system among the subsequent Winnebago, that somewhat resembles family divisions, has been borrowed or derived from the Algic's during their long intercourse with them while residing about Green Bay and other portions of the present state of Wisconsin. (1.)

## Sand Point Ouinipegou

Without Perrot's observation of the Siouan cultural lifestyle in the region we would be at a loss to determine what caused the disappearance of the people at Sand Point. Archaeologists established that they were sedentary and peaceful. No evidence was uncovered that would indicate hostilities contributing to their disappearance at this site. However, they were anything but peaceful. The Ouinipegou, a sedentary people like their Sioux counterparts to the west, were scattered or dispersed in small villages about the lakes. As Perrot states, it made it difficult for their enemies to destroy them, since as soon as one village was attacked, the surrounding villages rallied to their assistance to meet the assailants. These were unlike the large settlements of the Huron, which were vulnerable to large initial losses due to the total population being in a single habitation, facing annihilation due to siege.

The Sand Point site was just one of these scattered locations, although a major one, probably consisting of approximately 500-800 occupants. This figure is somewhat arbitrary, but an estimate that may even be conservative. There were twenty burial mounds located here, one containing approximately 200 remains that were buried over a period of years. The location could support a large population just on the fisheries resource alone.

If Champlain's map is of any significance to us, it depicts the location at Sand Point by identifying the settlement with four very distinctive dots. If we use the criteria he mentions in his journal, then it may indicate there were "four chiefs, and as many tribes" composing the population at this site. That being the case, our estimates may be very conservative. However, this would correlate well with the four youths that were recovered from the remains of the funeral pyre by archaeologists. Indications suggesting that the four were symbolic of some ritual representing four tribes, subtribes, or clans.

(1.) *The History of the Ojibway* People, Warren, 1885:43.

Perrot relates how the escalation of the war eventually caused the Ouinipegou to rally their forces within a single large compound. It would have been at this stage of the conflict that the Sand Point site would have been vacated—when the Lake Superior Ouinipegou rallied to support their fellow clansmen in Green Bay. As the record reflects, this was a critical event that caused major losses as the Algonkin "union" lay siege to this large village. From this juncture the situation only deteriorated for them. For Sand Point, it marked the last time any of the Ouinipegou would enjoy the life that Keweenaw Bay and the surrounding area had to offer. From Sand Point they would gather up their most prized possessions and join the settlement in Green Bay, consequently, leaving behind not so much as even a single complete pot for archaeologists to recover. No historical evidence would be produced from the archaeological dig except the musket ball and gun flint that belonged to Jean Nicolet, who, clad in a Chinese robe, only a few years earlier had advanced these people on their beach. These two items would be the *only* remaining historic evidence to witness the final departure of a people who would later become known as the—*Mystery People of the Cove*.

## Historic Summary

Sand Point played a key role in the French attempt to resolve the wars in which the Ouinipegou were embroiled. This location was singled out to organize these people into gathering from "round about" where Nicolet eventually met with the four to five thousand warriors who comprised this large nation. It was at this location, in 1634, where the French could selectively isolate the Ouinipegou from the neighboring groups in Green Bay that were disputing over trade with the Outaouaks and the Algonkin Fire Nation. Because the French were aware of the tenacity of the Ouinipegou, Nicolet arranged a location and strategy that would not "mistake them for enemies to be massacred."

Sand Point would provide the location for Nicolet to negotiate the much needed peace that was critical to the expansion of the French in the western Great Lakes. The present war was impeding trade and, even more importantly, exploration for the western route to the Sea of Japan and China. It was the enigma of the Sea People, and the unknown sea they had come from, that inspired Champlain to think that a western route was accessible from Lake Superior.

War with the Ouinipegou erupted again shortly following Nicolet's peace effort impeding trade among the native allies of the French. War in the west, along with the escalating problems of the Iroquois that simultaneously mounted along the St. Lawrence, disrupted exploration for the passage. Nicolet's journey, however, did not thwart the hope of locating the sea, and the French would follow Nicolet's experience into Lake Superior.

The French would continue their exploits into Lake Superior by providing garrison escorts for the missionaries and their donnés up the river to Georgian Bay. From here, adventurous donnés would continue to search where Nicolet left off, only after the Ouinipegou threat had been totally removed from the region. These explorers would eventually locate the remnant Ouinipegou residing on Green Bay. It would take the efforts of Perrot and Allouez, many years later, to provide us with the fateful details.

The Ouinipegou or more aptly, the Sea People, were a significant aspect of the early history of the Great Lakes. Champlain was compelled to think that they were pivotal in locating the Pacific Ocean.

The Sea People left little as a testament of their role in providing the beginning pages of Great Lake history. They were caught up in the traditional experiences that typically composed the lifestyles of aboriginal cultures. Is it possible that the bold intervention of European influence may have overwhelmed their ability to become acclimated? Technology that could only be consecrated by Gods? Manitous pledged "support" and "protection" from their enemies that provided a false sense of security, which may have compelled them to act irrationally.

The fate of the Ouinipegou is similar to that of many other native cultures. A process that was part of the aboriginal experience occurring long before the historic intervention of Europeans. Whether the advance of European culture escalated the process is a matter of historic interpretation. The Ouinipegou, however, hold a special place in the annals of Great Lakes history despite their near self-destruction. Those that resided at Sand Point will only be recognized because they have been resurrected, breathing new life into the historical records that once formerly suppressed their existence. No longer will they be deprived of their rightful place in history, and therefore, will no longer remain the enigmatic people that once lived in the cove.

# CHRONOLOGY OF THE PUANS
## OF THE WESTERN GREAT LAKES AND THEIR
## GEOGRAPHICAL EXPLORATION BY THE FRENCH

1603      Champlain is seeking knowledge of mines. He is told that the Hurons come to exchange merchandise and that there is to the "... North, a Mine of fine Copper, whereof they shewed us Bracelets, ... and that if any of us would go thither, they would bring them to the place, which would be appointed for that business." The Hurons are on favorable trading terms with the western group of the Puans.

1610      Etienne Brulé is sent to live with the Hurons on Georgian Bay. This interpreter has been instructed by Champlain to, "... learn their language, get acquainted with the country, see the great lake (Mer douce), observe the rivers, and what people inhabited it; also to explore the *mines* and rarer things of this place, so that on his return, he could give us information about all these things."

1615      Champlain accompanies the Hurons to their country on Georgian Bay via the Ottawa River. Makes contact with the Nipiserins and the Cheveux Releves. He is wounded in a war against the Iroquois and is forced to spend the winter among the Hurons. Writes account in journal and compiles map of 1616 with the aid of the Indian tribes. He learns of the "puans" in Lake Superior and plots the location of "Indian settlement" on Sand Point of Keweenaw Bay. Champlain apparently directs Brulé to accompany the Hurons into these waters to learn of the "mines" which is the stated mission of his interpreters.

Champlain has learned of the Fire Nation tribes to the west of the Huron country. They are at war with the Neutral and Ottawa, therefore little is known of them or their country. They are the: Muscouten, Miami, Kickapoo, Potowatomi, Sauk and Fox. These groups are fleeing southern Lower Michigan and filtering into the area of Green Bay taking up occupancy within the region of the Puans.

1618-1621      Sagard reports that Brulé and Crenole had ventured north and made an attempt to report their observations. They report that they observed "copper being removed from a mine" and "women with their noses cut off." They had apparently been traveling with Huron traders who took them to the mines of the "North," where they were promised if any "of us would go thither, they would bring them to the place, which would be appointed for that business." The location was the Ontonagon River in Lake Superior and it was the Puans who were mining copper. The vague river that Champlain portrayed on his 1616 map, west of the peninsula, was later elaborated on his 1632 map with the reference "Grand River that flows from the south." Information provided by Brulé and Crenole.

After the return of Brulé and Crenole, war broke out among the Puans and the Algonkin Fire Nation tribes around Green Bay. Algonkin traders of northern Georgian Bay (called Ottawa) were attempting to engage in trade with the Green Bay tribes. Attempting to trade French trade goods, they were unsuccessful as their envoys were killed and eaten by the Puans.

Jean Nicolet arrives in New France.

*OTTAWA—(Outaouas or Outaouaks.) This Algonkin reference can be very con-fusing depending on when it was used. Early in the French occupation it was a gener-ic term that meant "to trade" or "traders." Prior to 1649 it was principally applied to those Algonkin groups that were part of the trading network outside of the Huron country. Many of these groups resided on the north and east shores of Georgian Bay. ( . . ."more than thirty different tribes which are found in those countries." Dablon 1670). Some of these groups were identified as proto-Ojibwa tribes.*

*The French had formed a close alliance with the Hurons and were the principal trading group prior to 1649. The outbreak of the Iroquois war broke off trade between Huron and French, driving the Hurons from their home lands and former sedentary life styles. It was not until after the war that the Chevuex Releves took over as princi-pal traders and were thereafter referred to as Ottawa. The former River of the Prairies was changed to reflect this being called the Ottawa (traders) River.*

*When Perrot explains the conflict in Green Bay between the Fire Nation groups as having originated with the Outaouaks attempting to engage in trade with the Puans, he was not referring exclusively to the Cheveux Releves of Manitoulin Island, nor was he referring to the Hurons, but also to other Algonkin groups on Georgian Bay. One of these principal Algonkin groups was the Amikouai or beaver clan.*

*Just prior to the French occupation, there is evidence that this clan was the domi-nant group of the Algonkins in the region. They would be included in the so-called proto-Ojibway tribe.*

*It would appear that it was this group of Algonkin traders that was most responsi-ble for the conflict with the Puans as is recorded by Perrot. These two groups had a long history of being ancestral enemies (Ojibway vs. Sioux). This would also be explained by the missionary Breabuef's reference in 1636 of the Puans breaking the peace with the Amikouai that had been concluded by Nicolet only the year before.*

1629-1632 Quebec surrenders to the English. Champlain is deported back to France.

Champlain compiles his journal of 1632 and published map of the same year. On this map Lake Superior of the Mer douce now becomes the Grand Lac. He attempts to summarize all the information that he has accumulated up to this point in this map, resulting in a very confusing state of the western Great Lakes. An unknown or *mystery lake* appears, duplicating the geography of the already existing Grand Lac. Since he has not personally seen this region he must rely on the reports of the many Indians he has questioned as well as what he can learn from Brulé. It appears that Champlain continued to adhere to his theory of the Grand Lac accessing the sea and was not yet to concede that it had boundaries as it was apparently reported to him by Brulé. So *two* Lake Superiors appear on the 1632 map.

Unrest between the Fire Nation groups and the Puans in the western Great Lakes continues. Even the Hurons are reluctant to approach the Puans. When the French return in 1632, the conflict not only impedes trade but also exploration of the region.

1633 Champlain returns to New France. He immediately has three objectives:

(1.) Provide security and greater access for the trading tribes along the St. Lawrence by constructing a post at the confluence of the St. Maurice River—Three Rivers.

(2.) Expand trade to the western Great Lakes by making peace among the warring tribes of which the Puants is the principal player.

(3.) Find the route to the South Sea that will open the way to the sea of China, thereby connecting the Atlantic and Pacific Oceans.

It is Jean Nicolet that Champlain has chosen to fulfill his expectations for accomplishing all of these objectives. He is designated to be the Interpreter for the Gentlemen of New France for the new trading center at Three Rivers. He is also to be the French emissary to journey to the "second lake" to conclude the peace among the Puants or the Sea People. It is this important journey that Champlain will confide in Nicolet to discover the "exceeding great river that issues forth" from the Grand Lac, thinking that the Sea People are the link to the Asian world. Nicolet includes the Chinese robe among his apparel that Champlain has brought all the way from France for this journey.

Now too old to continue any exploration for himself, he must confide in his most faithful Interpreter. In fact, Champlain by now is quite aged and may not be in the best of health, for upon the return of Nicolet, Champlain becomes bed ridden for four months and dies. Yet his health does not deter him from returning to New France as Governor to make his last effort to learn of the discovery of the passage to the sea.

1634     Jean Nicolet is sent on mission to contact the Sea People, completes the peace, and attempts to learn of the route to the South Sea.

1635     Nicolet returns. Champlain dies on Dec. 25th.

Nicolet is apparently informed by the Puans that had he followed a river (Mississippi) for three days he could have descended it to the sea. The hope of a South Sea route from Lake Superior is still much alive in the minds of the French.

1636     Nicolet's peace with the Puans is broken!

1636-41     War resumes with the Puans and the neighboring Fire Nation tribes in Green Bay.

Puants lose 500 warriors to drowning crossing Lake Winnebago to attack the Fox. Disease also takes its toll on the besieged Puans. They kill a peace envoy of 500 warriors of the Illinois!

1640     Nicolet event is recorded by missionary LeJune. He records his journey into the "second lake" located *beyond* the Sault or rapids. He notes that missionaries will be sent to the *people of the other sea* (second lake).

1641     Missionaries arrive at the Sault and record information from Sauteurs of the *people of the other sea* (Lake Superior). They may be found by traversing the lake *above* the Sault and *ascending* a "River" (Ontonagon) that accesses other great nations.

Potowatomi flee conflict in Green Bay and arrive at the Sault.

1642          Illinois tribe nearly destroys the Puans, which ends the conflict. The remnant take up residence in Green Bay sometime later.

Jean Nicolet drowns in St. Lawrence River.

1648          Ragueneau records the location of the "third Lake" and the knowledge of the land area (Upper Peninsula) that separates it from that of the "second lake" (Lake Superior), calling it the Lake of the Puans. This is the very first recorded reference to Green Bay as the Lake of the Puans, which was to be later called Baye of the Puans. The first map to show the Lake of the Puans is the Map of Sanson's in 1650. Drueillette -1658, refers to Green Bay as "strictly only a large bay in lake Huron (Georgian Bay). Dablon-1670, refers to Green Bay as a "Gulf" of Georgian Bay, which by then was well known. The knowledge of the Lake of the Illinois (Lake Michigan) was just coming into being and was considered smaller than Lake Huron (Georgian Bay). (J.R. 44:247, 54:199 )

Sanson's map of 1650, the first map of the Great Lakes to identify Green Bay, as the Lac des Puans. Located by the donné's journey into the western lakes region in 1647, by crossing the "Peninsula" and discovering the "third Lake." This map was published the same year DuVal's map of 1653 was completed, with the assistance of the missionaries. (Courtesy of *Michigan History Magazine*)

## SEQUENCE OF DISCOVERY

Ragueneau assists us in understanding the sequence of discovery of the three Great Lakes: Lake Huron, Lake Superior and Lake Michigan.

(1.) The Lake of the Hurons being Georgian Bay—Lake Huron, was the first lake. (CHAMPLAIN'S "Mer douce" 1616.), (LEJUNE—"first of these lakes." J.R. Vol. 18:231-339, 1640.)

(2.) The lake that was above and beyond the Sault was the second lake, that of Lake Superior or the Grand Lac. The lake that Nicolet entered to locate the Puans in 1634. (LEJUNE—J.R. 18:231-339, 1640.)

The Recollet Gabriel Sagard provides us with the details of the early exploits of Brulé, who along with a number of Indians, "assured us that beyond the Mer douce there is another lake (Lake Superior) which implies into the former by a waterfall [Sault]." Brulé merely paved the way for Nicolet into Lake Superior, supporting the fact that the second lake was more commonly known than historically suspected.

3.) The third Lake, or Green Bay, that was not reported until 1648, after the Puans were defeated by the Illinois. This bay becomes the Lake of the Puans and was thought to be a "Gulf" of Georgian Bay. Eventually called the Baye of the Puans, it was part of the Lake of the Illinois, now present day Lake Michigan. (RAGUENEAU—J.R. Vol. 33:61, 149, 1648.), (ALLOUEZ—J.R. Vol. 54:199, 1670.)

# DISCOVERY OF THE "THIRD LAKE"
## (The Lake of the Puants)

### THE BENTZEN STONE

The reference of Father Paul Ragueneau to the discovery of the "third Lake" and the "Peninsula" of Upper Michigan correlates very well with a stone that was found in 1902 by a L'Anse resident who owned a small farm on the edge of town. His farm was located on a bluff overlooking Keweenaw Bay directly opposite the site at Sand Point. Mr. Charles P. Bentzen owned the farm and was in the process of working up one of his fields for spring planting when he happened upon this unique artifact. The stone was actually a native stone tool (pestle) used for milling food. It has two flat surfaces that contained very distinguished engraving on both. It displays two sets of initials along with a date of 1647. Who could have engraved this unique stone? What was their purpose here and why was it found at this particular location?

What is of special significance is that the year of the stone correlates so perfectly with Ragueneau's comprehensive description of this region in his *Relations* of 1648—information that could only have been acquired by a Frenchman, who departed from the Sault and traversed the "Peninsula" in order to ascertain that it separated the two lakes of Lake Superior and Michigan. Such a journey to confirm this fact would necessitate following the shores of the "Peninsula," bisecting it at some point, and then returning down the opposite shore to the Sault where their journey began. In the course of doing so, Ragueneau would then be able to describe this "Peninsula" as separating the "superior Lake" from the "third Lake" or the "Lac du Puants," located at Green Bay, Wisconsin. (1.)

Most historical references maintain that after Nicolet's journey and particularly Champlain's death, exploration of the Great Lakes was not resumed for another 20 years; however, the historic evidence suggests otherwise.

*The "River" and the "three days journey" to the sea*

> Sieur Nicolet, who had advanced farthest into these so distant countries, has assured me that, if he had sailed three days' journey farther upon a great river which issues from this lake, he would have found the sea. . . . Nevertheless, as we do not know whither this great lake [Lake Superior] tends . . . it would be a bold undertaking to go and explore those countries. (2.)

(1.) J.R. Vol. 33:149
(2.) J.R. Vol. 18:237

It is obvious from LeJune's quote that when Nicolet returned, despite his unsuccessful attempt to locate the Pacific Ocean, he sustained the impression that he had not been far from it.

How he acquired this impression is uncertain. It was likely due to the language difference of the Puants that he misunderstood their reference as to how to access the Mississippi River from Lake Superior. What we can be certain about is that the "great river" in question was, instead, the Ontonagon. The fact that it was to have "issued" from Lake Superior was more likely a misconception of Nicolet's rather than LeJune's. What is most important, if we are to learn anything from this reference, is that Nicolet's journey still inspired the hope of finding the passage from the western end of Lake Superior. In fact, he makes it certain! LeJune states this with *assurance* from Nicolet. This being the case, the French would have jumped at the first opportunity to get back into these waters and explore this "great river." Nothing was as important to the French occupation of North America as locating the passage.

Locating the passage is basically what the French tried to do from the mission at Ste. Marie after 1642. From here they would almost immediately know the fate of the Puants from reports of the Potowatomi returning to Green Bay. This information would be revealed to the French by native traders traveling back and forth between the Sault and Ste. Marie. It was the Sauteurs who also informed the missionaries in 1641 of a "River" that extended into the country of many other nations via western Lake Superior, a "River" they would have to *ascend* rather than *descend*. (1.)

Exploration by the French of the western Great Lakes as provided by the missionary journals appears to leave us with a historic hiatus from 1642 to 1648. What had happened during this period that led up to the sudden discovery of the "third Lake" or Green Bay of Lake Michigan?

The records are very vague as to any specific exploratory activity in the western Great Lakes during this six year span. We can be certain, however, that this area was being explored by some French adventurers due to the circumstances that presently existed, especially now that the Puants were no longer a threat to exploration of this region. But who were these explorers that made Ragueneau aware of this new lake "we call the Lake of the Puants"?

The historic records appear to be void of any formal exploratory activity since Nicolet's journey in 1634. Exploration of the western Great Lakes ceased, commencing with the breaking of the peace by the Puants soon after in 1636.

(1.) Allouez states that the Puans were nearly decimated 30 years previous to 1670. The date of 1642 is arrived at by the missionaries witness to the arrival of the Potowatomi at the Sault in 1641. Perrot documents the Illinois attack against the Puans being delayed one year. If the Potowatomi arrived at the Sault in 1641 they apparently fled the Green Bay area knowing that the Puans would be attacked that fall or winter. Perrot cites the attack occurring in the winter, which involved crossing the ice on Green Bay to access an island that the Puans had taken refuge on knowing the attack was coming in advance. This being the case, the attack would probably have occurred in the months of Jan., Feb. or Mar. of 1642, when Green Bay would most likely have been frozen over.

Hostilities in the region would endure until 1642, after which this region would be open to exploration. The problem was that in 1641 the French had their hands full at Quebec and Three Rivers with the Iroquois exerting pressure on their ability to make passage up the St. Lawrence River. The river was blocked off by continual Iroquois attacks, and Nicolet was faced with negotiating two French prisoners for guns, a preclusion to the critical situation that would soon escalate into the outbreak of the Iroquois War in 1649. So critical was the situation that from 1641-1644 Breabuef had been unable to get back to Ste. Marie and was only able to do so with an escort from the French garrison. (In 1645 Ragueneau became the superior at Ste. Marie.) (1.)

Interestingly, in 1646, the missionary records provide us with information that may reveal who some of these Frenchmen may have been that provided Ragueneau with the discovery of the "third Lake" that would have occurred in 1647.

From the newly constructed fort at Ste. Marie, seven Frenchmen arrived at Quebec in 1646, where they had been for three years, and reportedly returned. Some of these were donnés, while others may simply have been engaged in assisting the missionaries with the general affairs of the Huron mission on Georgian Bay. They were:

| | | | |
|---|---|---|---|
| Pierrot Cochan | Daniel Carteron | Medart Chouart (des Grosillers) | |
| Gilles Bacon | Jean le Mercier | Etienne Racine | Eustache Lambert |

What leads us to believe that some of these individuals were involved in Great Lakes exploration is that Gilles Bacon was reported to have been searching for "Mines" and returned with samples of "Copper" and suspected gold. This mission was sanctioned by Monsieur the Chevalier de Montmagny, the Governor of New France. It is very possible that Bacon had just returned from Lake Superior, where Nicolet had last reported the "River" accessing the sea— a location, that by now, was becoming very well known as a major source of copper. (2.)

The records also indicate that along on this journey to ". . . reconnoitre the alledged mines . . ." was a Huron convert by the name of Armand. (3.)

When examining the others that returned with Bacon, we find that some of them were later to become explorers and traders, the most noted was des Grosillers, whose sister married Pierre Esprit Radisson.

(1.) J.R. Vol. 28:39, 47; 23:269; 24:271-297; 26:71.
  Not only are the two Frenchmen captured in 1641, but so is Father Joques and Bressani with other Frenchmen in 1642. (Nicolet also drowns in 1642.)
(2.) J.R. Vol. 28:227, 229. *Journals of the Jesuits*, 1646, Lalemont.
  "Arriving at 3 rivers, I found Gilles Bacon, who Straightway came to find Monsieur the governor at Quebek, by order of Monsieur de la Poterie, so as to give information of the Mines of gold and copper that he had found, of which he brought some ores. He was sent back, and they found that it was nothing of value."
(3.) J.R. Vol. 28:24.

We also know that Eustache Lambert served as an interpreter and became a commander of Canada's first militia. He carried on an extensive trading business and became a citizen of considerable wealth and influence.

Pierrot Cochan returned and was "clothed and had 50 livres."

However, a real likely candidate for this excursion may have been Etienne Racine. According to the parish register of Three Rivers, he attended Nicolet's wedding on October 23, 1637. It would appear that he must have known him quite well, since his name appears as a matter of formal record. This suggests that Etienne would have known of the details of Nicolet's journey only three years before and prior to his enlistment to Ste. Marie.

If Bacon's entourage went into Lake Superior to seek out Nicolet's reported river that was supposed to flow out of it, they would have coursed the entire shore of Lake Superior, eventually returning to the Sault knowing that none existed. It would require a second journey if they were to explore the "River" (Ontonagon) that had to be ascended, as reported to them by the Sauteurs—a river that could be ascended in three days before it would descend to the sea.

Ste. Marie had been completely cut off from the St. Lawrence during the season of 1647. Who were the French explorers that returned to Lake Superior in order that Ragueneau would be provided the information of the "third Lake?" Whoever they were may have continued their exploits into the Lake Superior region, followed the south shore of Lake Superior en route to the Ontonagon River, where they retreated into Keweenaw Bay to wait out bad weather. During that time, some in the party occupied themselves by doodling upon the pestle stone.

The pestle stone was engraved both front and back. On one side, in addition to the year of 1647, the initials A.B. appear, along with a face. The reverse also has a face that may be that of a woman and the initials M.A. The two faces and the initials are very intriguing. Who they belong to is subject to much speculation. There are, however, some interesting characteristics that allow us to establish some possibilities.

To begin with, we must acknowledge that the pestle was a native women's tool. In fact, if we examine the stone carefully it appears that the two images were engraved by different people. The front is deeply cut into the stone, whereas, the reverse is only etched into the surface, rendering the appearance that one side may have been done by a man and the other by a woman. The reverse figure even appears to be a woman. Who was this woman with the initials M.A. and this man with the initials, A.B.?

It is possible that A.B. may have been Gillis Bacon, who was also referred to by the missionaries in formal documents as Aegidius Bacon. The native woman may have been one of several with the initials M.A. and it is pure spec-

Bentzen Stone, obverse, with the face and date of 1647. The initials A.B. may belong to Aegidius Bacon. Found across from Sand Point on Keweenaw Bay. Engraving on this side of stone is very deep, probably made with an awl. (photo, In the Mind's Eye, L'Anse)

Stone showing reverse with initials M.A. and female appearing face. This stone artifact is a pestle, a device used by a native woman. The woman pictured may be a Huron convert, Marie Aonetta. (photo, In the Mind's Eye, L'Anse)

ulation as to whom they belonged. In theory, however, based on the abundance of information for one particular woman, they may have been those of Marie Aonetta. The real mystery is why does Gillis's initials appear on the obverse of a native woman's pestle with hers on the reverse. Only more research will determine the true identity of who they were. What is certain is that they were party to a voyage that was to cross the Upper Peninsula of Michigan that was to eventually find its way into Green Bay. Whoever they were, they were the first Europeans to set foot on the soils of present day Wisconsin.

The French entourage may have journeyed to the Ontonagon River where after three days they could access the present day Brulé River that runs into the Menominie River, which flows into Green Bay or the newly discovered "third Lake." After crossing the "Peninsula," they would return to the Sault where they began. This would be the only way anyone could have known that this "Peninsula" separated Lake Superior from Lake Michigan. When these explorers returned they would have direct access to Ragueneau, who was the superior at Ste. Marie. This new discovery would appear in his journals of 1648.

Showing pestle with its two flat surfaces and a tool mark left to chip out an indentation for the thumb. Our user was right handed. (photo, In the Mind's Eye, L'Anse)

Both sides of the stone have grooves cut to accommodate the fingers, allowing it to fit the hand very comfortably. This memento was engraved and intentionally left behind, since it could no longer serve any utilitarian purpose, just waiting to be discovered 255 years later!

It was possible that Grosiller was not among those in the return venture, or if he was, it was as a soldier with the garrison that was a necessary escort for the safe return of anyone en route to Ste. Marie. Although he was epileptic, it may or may not have had an impact at this point in his career as an explorer. However, if he had been among the Bacon entourage prior to 1646 (that coursed Lake Superior without finding the river that was to have issued to the sea) it may have discouraged him from any further efforts to search Lake Superior. This all changed in 1648 when another lake ("third Lake") had been discovered!

The Iroquois War soon broke out in 1649, which completely eliminated all exploration for the French. Ste. Marie no longer existed, and the Hurons, as well as the French, were driven from Georgian Bay. A temporary truce occurred in 1653, and it was at that time Grosiller found new energies to request the assistance of his brother-in-law, Radisson, to join him in the "discovery he was to make."

This whole scenario makes sense when we understand the sequence of Radisson and Grosiller's journey in 1654. It was Grosiller who invited him to join in his quest to make a "discovery" in the "great lakes," only after he had made several journeys when he was in the service of the missionaries—a journey that had apparently taken him into Lake Superior. There is no doubt that these two were in search of the passage, as Radisson understood the Lake of the Hurons to be "upon the border of the sea." (1.)

Instead of accessing Lake Superior, they journeyed directly through the "straits" that separates Lake Huron from Lake Michigan and to the Fox River in Green Bay. They made their way down the Wisconsin River and into the Mississippi. The reason for their course is that Grosiller had probably already been in Lake Superior, and by this time they had exhausted Nicolet's report of a "great river" that was to have issued from it. News of the "third Lake" opened new opportunities for their "discovery."

It would only seem reasonable that if Nicolet had been in Green Bay in 1634, the French would have followed up his report of the "3 days journey to the sea" from this location. Instead, all the evidence indicates that their efforts were directed into Lake Superior (from Brulé's to those of the Bacon's). Consequently, we do not learn of the "third Lake" until 1648. It would seem obvious that the reason Radisson and Grosiller's journey was made directly through the "straits" to Green Bay in 1654 was that it was not known prior to 1648! Therefore, Nicolet could never have been in the "third Lake."

In 1647, while the French entourage was among the resident tribes at Green Bay (now called the Lake of the Puants), they would have learned of the route up the Fox, to the Wisconsin and Mississippi Rivers, which would have led to the sea. The likely choice for Radisson and Grosiller, who were also looking for the passage, was to go directly to the "third Lake" and begin their exploration there, a journey that was to eventually lead them "to a spot sixty leagues beyond *the lake of the people of the sea*." (2.)

(1.) *The Explorations of Pierre Esprit Radisson*, Adams, 1961:79.
  At the beginning of Radisson's third journey, which would take him to Green Bay, he states:
  "Being come to Three Rivers, I found my brother [Grosiller], who the year before came back from the Lake of the Hurons, with other French; both were upon the point of resolution to make a journey a purpose for to discover the great lakes that they heard the wild men speak of; yea, have seen before; for my brother made several journeys when the Fathers lived about the Lake of the Hurons, which was upon the border of the sea. So my brother, seeing me back from those two dangerous voyages for this reason he thought I was fitter and more faithful for the discovery he was to make."
(2.) J.R. Vol. 46:69
  "He [native Captain] is making preparations here to conduct some Frenchmen, as soon as spring opens, to a spot sixty leagues beyond the lake of the people of the sea, [the Puans at Green Bay] . . . ."
  *The Explorations of Pierre Esprit Radisson*, Adams, 1961.
  This author advanced the theory that Radisson and Grosiller made two journeys to Green Bay beginning in 1654. This would reflect the intensity of their exploits to discover the passage as they delved deeper into the interior of Wisconsin and south on the "missi-sepe" (Great River).
  If we examine the courses pursued by Radisson it becomes evident that they are searching the western regions of the Great Lakes for a possible western route to the sea. This is demonstrated by their continued efforts to penetrate the Sioux country, both west of Lake Michigan and Lake Superior.
  As a result fo the 1647 journey to Green Bay, the French learned from the surviving Puans that, "they come from the shore of a far distant sea toward the North, the water of which is salt" (see pg. 117). This explains why Radisson returns to Lake Superior and redirects his search to locate the sea in the "Bay of the North," lest they be told a "fib." They eventually end up in Hudson Bay after exhausting all their efforts from the "second" and "third Lake."

*(continued on next page)*

They ventured far enough down the Mississippi to locate native people who had in their possession Spanish tokens that had found their way up river. They were convinced that the "River" only led to the Gulf of Mexico! It was upon the return of Radisson and Grosiller that the missionary Dreuillette was able to make the entry in his letters regarding the location of the Gulf of Mexico, which was believed to be 300 leagues from western Lake Superior. It was at this juncture in the French exploration of these western waters that Dreuillette explained the concerted efforts that had previously been made to locate the sea from the western end of Lake Superior. (1.)

Just as Brulé opened the way into Lake Superior for Nicolet, so had Grosiller, Bacon and Radisson opened the way for exploration into the Green Bay region of Wisconsin for Marquette and Joliet. They used the same route to access the Mississippi as they also attempted to put to rest the long enduring myth of the "exceeding great River" that was to have issued from these "fresh-water seas" into the South Sea of China and Japan.

*(continued from previous page)*

After the French discovery of Green Bay in 1647, a return journey would have been discouraged due to the Iroquois advancement on the Huron country in 1648. In 1649 the French would burn the fort of Ste. Marie to the ground and flee to Christian Island (Island of St. Joseph). By 1650 the French and all the native populations would be driven from Georgian Bay.

Radisson and Grosiller would brave the advances of the Iroquois in ascending and descending the Ottawa River from 1654-1660. The Iroquois War would not officially be terminated until 1667 with the importation of elite French battle-seasoned troops. After this period, exploration would again advance with the traders and missionaries activities expanding into the regions of the Great Lakes where many of the refugee native groups had concentrated. Marquette and Joliet would make their journey into the Mississippi and would produce the most comprehensive map of the Great Lakes.

(1.) J.R. Vol. 44:247, Dreuillette, 1658. (see Chapter 8:102)

# 10

# THE CONNECTION

The historic and archaeological knowledge of the Ouinipegou now provides us with many clues to the area's mysterious features that have been the subject of much debate and speculation over the years. They are:

(1.) The Pequaming cairns.
(2.) A well used trail to Huron Mountain.
(3.) A cactus that grows only on Huron Mountain.
(4.) A mysterious stone altar located on Huron Mountain.
(5.) Thousands of ancient copper mine pits located on Isle Royale and the Keweenaw Peninsula.

These features have provided much intrigue for the prehistory researcher of Lake Superior and its inhabitants.

The geographical location of Sand Point to many of these features strategically identifies the Ouinipegou with all of them, but what evidence exists that would make them contemporaneous?

The archaeological evidence established the Ouinipegou as copper industrialists. What other evidence would connect them to the remaining features? Many questions can be answered by combining the archaeological with the historic evidence.

The most logical place to begin our analysis is with the importance of copper to the Ouinipegou at Sand Point; not only was it utilized within their own culture, but it was a vital component for trade with other native groups. The Hurons would travel from the southern shores of Georgian Bay to trade tobacco and corn for copper. They not only would trade from their shores but would travel great distances to barter this commodity. In fact, they may have traveled as far away as the ancient city of Cahokia, located near the Mississippi and Missouri Rivers. Trail systems connected river routes that provided access to areas very distant from Keweenaw Bay.

The most distinguished aspect of the Ouinipegou, however, was that they were mound builders, identified with the Late Mississippian Culture. Can the knowledge of other mound cultures serve us to understand those that resided at Sand Point?

Our efforts will entail making evidentiary *connections* that will attempt to answer these questions. What is most significant about the Ouinipegou is that they resided within the region of the Great Lakes that because of its copper was totally unique to any place else in North America. It may be the very reason they still occupied Sand Point. At one time this culture may have extended east to include the great fishery at the Sault. Possibly, the Ouinipegou were driven west but held fast to this region as they refused to relinquish the culture that made them the guardians of copper.

*Copper Culture—archaeological evidence*

The archaeological report established the Sand Point site as the site of a copper industry. This should not surprise us since this site was ideally located to the proximity of the greatest native copper bearing source in the world, an industry that would have supplied copper to the well established trade centers of Aztalan and Cahokia. But were they actually miners who extracted or worked copper from the mine-pits that predate the existing native American tribes to the region?

The report is ambiguous as to whether their efforts consisted primarily in retrieving surface or "float" copper as compared to the actual working of copper from a mine or pit. The several thousand shallow pits in the Keweenaw Peninsula and Isle Royale have been the subject of much debate.

Probably the most significant evidence to warrant our ascertaining the Ouinipegou at Sand Point as actual miners is provided by the physical anthropological examination of the 117 skeletal remains collected. The report identified a disease that can be considered an occupational hazard due to the methodology employed in the mining process. The report revealed that infection from bone inflammation was quite common. Of particular interest was that 25% of the adult population suffered from varying degrees of *periostitis*. Since most of the remains were recovered from burials where the bones of different individuals were commingled en masse, made it difficult to determine what gender group was most affected by it. However, one mound that was totally excavated contained five adult male individuals who were all affected by this disease.

Periostitis is a bone disease that may or may not be fatal. The most common cause of this disease is by physical trauma. The bones most affected by periostitis were highest among the tibia bones, followed by the fibula and femur. When we examine the process involved in prehistoric mining of these pits, we can understand how these industrious people were heavily engaged in the physical extraction of copper from the veins of rock. (The physical comparisons with the Robinson site fail to show any presence of this disease despite the similarity in culture, physical characteristics, and use of copper. See *North Lakes Project*).

Archaeologists pick through a pile of used hammerstones on Isle Royale. These simple devices were the principal tools for mining copper by ancient people. (photo, courtesy of Bill Deephouse)

Also among the prehistoric mine pits are thousands of "hammerstones." They existed at both Isle Royale and on the Keweenaw Peninsula and were the tools of the mining process. There has been much speculation as to how the copper was actually worked from these pits.

Two principal efforts have been made to study the mine pits of Isle Royale. The first in 1961 by Prof. Drier of Michigan Technology University, the second in 1963 by Tyler Bastian. These two studies are quite interesting since Bastian's research is critical of the 1961 effort. (1.)

While Bastian was conducting his archaeological survey on Isle Royale, he employed one of his field crew members to engage in prehistoric mining with an actual hammerstone recovered from the site. Acting the part, he assumed a

(1.) *Prehistoric Copper Mining in Isle Royale National Park*, Michigan; Bastian, 1963.
*Prehistoric Copper Mining in the Lake Superior Region*, Drier & DuTemple, 1961.
   Bastian excavated the very same pit that Drier did. Drier never excavated to the bottom, where Bastian continued beyond the level of Drier's.
   Bastian is critical of the estimates that Drier claims were extracted from the pits. He stated that they erroneously assumed the average pit was 20 X 30 feet deep, with estimates of 1000 -1200 tons of ore removed per pit with averages ranging from 5 -15 percent copper taken from an estimated 5,000 pits. "An early engineer estimated that the early workings represented the efforts of 10,000 men working for 1,000 years." Drier & DuTemple 1961:17, 30.
   Bastian claims that Drier's estimates are exaggerated due to the utilization of copper bearing percentages used by modern mining technologies and were not a valid standard for the percentages that actually existed in these shallow surface pits. Bastian estimates that from 560,000-750,000 pounds of copper were removed from Isle Royale.

squatting position only to learn that the shorts he wore were totally inadequate protection from the chunks of flying stone that were projected by the impact of the hammerstone. Not only were a pair of trousers necessary to offer protection to his shins, but he also included a pair of gloves for his hands. A handle affixed to the sledge would have been even more beneficial. (1.)

Interestingly, the hammerstones on Isle Royale differ dramatically from those found on the Keweenaw Peninsula. Those of Isle Royale lacked grooves that were apparently employed to fasten handles (hafting) and used as sledge hammers. Most agree that these more developed hammers were typical of a period of more recent use than those of the Isle Royale sites. Devices that would be more contemporaneous with the late Mississippian period and that of the Ouinipegou occupation of Sand Point.

Tyler Bastian's conclusions to his survey indicated he found no conclusive evidence that the use of fire and water (spalling) was employed to fracture the rock loose from its foundation. In fact, his findings revealed that the process was not necessary. Most of these pits are no more than six or seven feet deep. The crew member who experimented with the hammerstone was very effective in crushing the rock without the use of anything but the use of his sledge. Bastian theorized that because of glacial compaction on the surface of the bedrock caused the rock to become granular, allowing for the ease at which the rock could be crushed. At a depth of approximately nine-ten feet the rock changes consistency and becomes much harder making it difficult to continue by merely hammering. This also lends credence to the fact that the depth of most of these pits are less than nine feet deep.

No data has been made available for the multitude of mine pits of the Keweenaw Peninsula where the most concentrated number occur along the Ontonagon River. They extend fifteen or twenty miles along the range, each way, from where it crosses the river. It was this location that the famous Ontonagon boulder was removed and now rests in the Smithsonian Institute. This is also the area of the initial discovery of the first prehistoric mine pit. (2.)

*Copper Culture—historic evidence*

The Keweenaw Peninsula sites are of particular concern. They are the most convenient and accessible to the Sand Point site, mine locations that could definitely be attributed to their use. Most of the pits are located near the Ontonagon River, which is corroborated by the historic evidence.

---

(1.) Crew member Dave Olen was successful in removing 25 cubic feet of amygdaloid rock in 30 hours using two one-handed hammerstones. He found the one handed stone to be more practical than the larger stones requiring both hands to use. His fingers were more prone to being smashed being restricted to the confines of the bottom of the pit. All of the tailings accumulated were without the aid of fire. This is consistent with Bastian's theory that the lack of tailings at the sites was due to the bedrock being crushed rather than by fracturing, as would be the case with the use of fire.

(2.) *The Annuals of Science*, Whittlesey, 1854.

Field crew member Dave Olen engaged in the ancient method of mining copper with the use of a hammerstone on Isle Royale. He wears only a pair of shorts, probably all that the early miners would have worn. (photo, courtesy of Bill Deephouse)

Olen continues to work mine pit the second day. Note the addition of trousers and a pair of gloves. The hammerstones on Isle Royal lacked grooves for hafting. (photo, courtesy of Bill Deephouse)

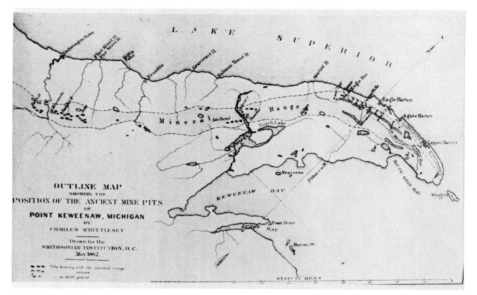

Charles Whittlesey Report (1862) showing the greatest concentration of copper mines adjacent to the Ontonagon River on the Keweenaw mainland. (M.T.U. Archives and Copper Country Historical Collections, Michigan Technological University)

Evidence of copper from the Lake Superior region was finding its way down to Quebec with the initial arrival of the French. Many reference are made in the French journals of the "mines" and copper mining, although the exact origin of its source eludes us.

Champlain's map of 1616 clearly identifies Isle Royale in the legend (no. 25) as the "Island where there is a mine of copper."

Champlain, however, makes mention of a "river" and "lake" on his 1632 map describing a location pertaining to the "mystery lake" of Lake Superior. In the legend, Footnote 33 states:

> River of the Puans, that is coming from a lake where close to it there is a mine of copper.

The first mention of copper finding its way down the Ottawa River was from Champlain who was presented a piece of copper by two native people. From his journal in 1613 he states:

> . . . the Algonkin Savage, one of chief, drew from a sack a piece of copper a foot long, which he gave me. This was very handsome and quite pure. He gave me to understand that there were large quanities where he had taken this, <u>which was on the bank of a river</u>, near a lake. He said they gathered it in lumps, and having melted it spread it in sheets, smoothing it with stones.

It was after Brulé and Crenole had returned from their journey above the falls into Lake Superior that the missionary Sagard was informed by Crenole, that he had visited the place where the Indians were "taking copper from a mine." Sagard (1621) further reported that:

> There are also mines of copper which should not be slighted . . . about eighty or one hundred leagues from the Huron country there is a mine of red Copper, of which the Interpreter showed me an ingot on his return from a voyage he made to that country.

After the death of Champlain, Monsieur the Chevalier de Montmagny, directed sorties into the copper region to "reconnoiter" the mines. The French donné Bacon, along with his Huron guide Armand, ventured into western Lake Superior to retrieve samples of copper and suspected gold ores. But where was this "river" and "lake" that was located eighty or one hundred leagues from the Huron country?

Champlain's 1632 map of the Grand Lac provides very convincing evidence that the river he displays as the, "Grand River that flows from the south," is none other than the Ontonagon River of western Lake Superior. The Intendant of Justice of Canada, Talon, wrote to Colbert in 1671, who was the Minister of the Colonial Department in France:

> The copper which I sent from Lake Superior and the river Nantaouagan [Ontonagon] proves that there is a mine on the border of some stream. More than twenty Frenchmen have seen one lump at the lake which they estimate weighs more than eight hundred pounds.

The Huron or "good Irocois," had been trading copper with the Algonkins, who had promised Champlain if he would accompany them they would show him where this appointed place of business was. Keeping their promise, they escorted Brulé and Crenole into the "River of the Puans," only a couple of years later, under the direction of Champlain to explore for "mines." In 1634 the Hurons would again escort Nicolet into the very same waters "above" and "beyond" the Sault to make a peace with the Nation of the Puans, who were identified on Champlain's 1616 and 1632 maps as occupying the western region of Lake Superior. They would prove to be the Ouinipegou of Sand Point, who were identified as copper industrialists.

## Pequaming Cairns

The Ouinipegou were mound building people classified with the Late Mississippian Culture. These industrial people not only were earth-working people, but also miners who worked copper from the veins or fissures of amygdaloid rock. Their familiarity with working and handling rock may lend credence to the mysterious man-made rock monuments that exist directly across Keweenaw Bay from Sand Point, at a location called Pequaming Point.

Aerial view of Pequaming Point. Cairns are located on the eastern tip called, Rock Beach Point or Picnic Point. Pequaming is located directly across the bay from Sand Point. At one time it was apparently an island.

These rock structures have been identified as *cairns* or calendrical structures that were used by prehistoric people to mark regular events by alignment with celestial bodies in the sky. These early people regarded the sun, moon and certain stars, as religious deities or gods.

There were approximately a dozen of these structures that stood until destroyed by a logging operation. Presently, they exist as piles of stone rubble that still mark their locations. There is evidence to substantiate that the cairns aligned with the Equinox and Summer Solstice. The present land owner has left them undisturbed and is currently engaged in reconstructing them.

Not only did this peninsula, called Picnic Point or Rock Beach Point (located on the northeast shore), provide the necessary resources to construct the cairns, but the peninsula itself is a rare location whose geography enables an observer to view especially the horizons. There are few locations in this region that are so accessible to Sand Point that offered this convenience, especially with the terrain consisting predominantly of hills and trees.

Located on the opposite southwestern point of this mushroom shaped peninsula (most probably an island then) was another cairn. This "stone ridge" existed with the initial settlement of the community of Pequaming in 1879. It ran from Mr. Hebard's house to the sawmill that was the nucleus of this community. It has long since been destroyed by development, as has most of the

The stone cairns as they originally stood in 1906. These calendrical features were used to observe the locations of celestial bodies, such as the rising sun, to depict the equinox and summer solstice. The structures were positioned on the edge of Lake Superior to the rear of the picnicker's, facing the eastern sky. (photo, courtesy of Pat & Dr. Peter Carmody)

The cairns were destroyed due to a logging operation. Efforts are being made by the current land owner to reconstruct them. (photo, courtesy of Pat & Dr. Peter Carmody)

native prehistoric evidence. Historical accounts claim that it was used by native people as a defensive bulwark resulting from the constant wars they were engaged in.

Its construction, location and orientation may indicate that it had a more important role in the lives of these early dwellers. This man made feature may have been constructed similar to those on Rock Beach Point, piled rocks, approximately four feet in height. The fact that these two features were located on the two existing points would indicate that they held a similar purpose. The most important aspect, however, is that it ran approximately 40 or 50 yards from the water's edge in a near west to east direction, giving it a solar orientation—also similar to those on Rock Beach Point. Because it bisected this narrow point and ran perpendicular to the shore line suggests that it would have been impractical for defensive purposes.

During the early historic development of Pequaming an "underground house" was discovered that may have been contemporaneous with the early dwellers. Although many legends and myths were connected to it, it may have served as a food storage for a sedentary occupation. This facility may have been used in conjunction with the evidence of reported "garden beds" that were also identified and still visible during the early 1920's. Evidence of these features has also been destroyed (1.)

If we compare the Sand Point Ouinipegou with other known locations of the Mound Culture that were contemporaneous, we may be able to answer some of the mystery of the Pequaming cairns.

Archaeologists were able to definitely link Sand Point to the southern Mississippian Culture that had greatly influenced most of the eastern half of the United States. Mr. Moore was able to state:

> . . . finding pottery and other artifacts [at Sand Point] which are Mississippian definitely links this northern range to the great Mississippian civilization. We believe that we have found enough Mississippian material so that we would say that Mississippian peoples were once at Sand Point. Had only a few Mississippian things been found we might have concluded that the objects were traded and that the Mississippian people themselves were not there. But the material unearthed was such that the actual presence of Mississippian peoples seems likely. (2.)

Mr. Moore reported several outstanding examples of Mississippian artifacts recovered from Sand Point. A pot sherd showed exactly the same design element as a pot recovered at the ancient city of Cahokia. Numerous small arrow points are typical Cahokian points in contrast with triangular Woodland points. A carefully carved slate ear spool was recovered and was much like ear spools found in the central and southern Mississippian Valley, never before

(1.) *The History of Pequaming*, Doyle & MacFarlane, 1999:4, 37, 38.
(2.) *Baraga County Historical Pageant*, Moore, 1972:18.

found this far north. The burial mound construction of Sand Point is similar to those of the south and in all probability, are related to Mississippian ideas of the appropriate treatment of the dead. The ramp, the burned structure, the use of the yellow colored sand—all find expression in burial practices at Cahokia. (1.)

Cahokia is significant because discovered among this well organized culture were numerous similar structures to the cairns at Pequaming. Although not constructed of stone they served similar purposes. Understanding the presence of these mysterious structures at Cahokia may give us some understanding of their correlation and use at Sand Point.

At Cahokia, five of these circular structures were of different diameters. Four were thought to have consisted of 24, 36, 48 and 60 posts that made up their construction. The fifth contained 72. All five circles were formed of multiples of twelve posts thought by some scholars to calculate the observance of the lunar cycles. Because of their resemblance to the famous English megalithic monument of Stonehenge, these wooden post structures at Cahokia have come to be known as "woodhenges." The circle represented with 48 posts was 410 feet in diameter and dated just after 1100 A.D. Archaeologists suspect that these structures were utilized by a priest to observe sunrises along the eastern horizon aligning with particular perimeter posts at the equinoxes and solstices. On the equinoxes the sun would have risen over the front of the principal mound (Monks Mound) possibly symbolic of the bond between the earthly ruler and the solar deity. Other posts may have marked other important dates, such as harvest festivals or moon and star alignments. (2.)

Is it possible that the cairns at Pequaming were utilized in conjunction with planting crops, harvest festivals or other ceremonial events?

Archaeologists are comparing historical evidence of the Natchez Mound Culture to answer some of the mysterious questions surrounding the finds at such sites as Cahokia. What makes Natchez so unique is that it still existed into the historic period, and the site was observed by early French missionaries in 1699. What comparisons may be made with these late Mississippian Mound dwellers that may provide insight for many of these mysterious remains? Although Sand Point is considered an outlining mound building culture, it appears that it was influenced by the greater centers it had contact with in the south.

The Natchez site was the last of the known mound cultures to have formally still been in existence as late as 1730. It was located on the bank of the

(1.) *Baraga County Historical Pageant*, Moore, 1972:18.
     Mr. Dorothy reported that the Mississippian ceramics found at Sand Point were a minority class and may represent trade vessels. He also stated that in shape and decoration they appear to more closely resemble the Middle Mississippian pottery of Aztalan and Cahokia than Upper Mississippian (Oneota) pottery (*The Michigan Archaeologist*, Vol. 26. Nos 3-4, 1980:69). Moore positively identifies at least one Mississippian sherd "showing the exact same design element as a pot recovered at the ancient city of Cahokia." Since Dorothy identified the Mississippian ceramics as trade vessels it implies that the Cahokian pot was actually *from* Cahokia and not a local expression of the Sand Point people.

(2.) *Archaeology*, Iseminger, 1996:35. *Condé Nast Traveler*, Fay, 1995:154.

Mississippi River, 330 miles from where it flowed into the Gulf of Mexico. French missionaries provided an excellent account of their observations of this rather organized and fascinating culture, which they claimed "is the only one on this continent which appears to have any regular worship," and was in certain points similar to that of the ancient Romans. A temple was filled with idols and an order of guardians who maintained a "perpetual fire," a system with strict observances to ritual and ceremony. A "great Chief" supplied important officers or ministers to his state to execute his will, such as war chiefs, masters of ceremony for the worship of the temple, officers charged with treats of peace, public works inspector, and those responsible for the arrangement of public festivals for entertaining guests.

The Natchez people looked upon the "great Chief" as "absolute master, not only of their property but also of their lives, and not one of them would dare to refuse him his head"; they "blindly obey the least wish of their great Chief." The most profound aspect of their religion provided that his servants honor his funeral rites by dying with him, in order that they may also serve him in the other world.

The *Sun* was the "principal object of veneration," whereas, "they cannot conceive of anything which can be above this heavenly body, nothing else appears to them more worthy of their homage." For the same reason the great Chief takes the title of "brother of the Sun," and maintains himself in despotic authority. In order that the great Chief and the Sun can converse together they raise a mound of artificial soil, on which they build his cabin, that is the same construction as the temple. The door faces the east, and every morning the great Chief honors by his presence the rising of the sun (his elder brother), and salutes him. He orders that the sacred pipe be lit, offers three puffs, raises his hand above his head as he turns, first to the east, then to the west, and shows the sun the course it is to take. The great Chief was the brother of the Sun and master of the Temple.

The great Chief and his sisters were the only ones allowed the liberty of entering the temple. Contained in the temple were the bones of many of the common people. During a certain time of the year, a ceremony was allowed in order that a food offering could be made to the temple in memory of their deceased. The fact that "this ceremony lasts only *during one moon*," suggests that some method of celestial time keeping was utilized to identify which "one moon" would serve for this event, a system that would require tabulation of the lunar phases in conjunction with the horizontal progressions of the sun. The temple also played a ceremonial role in the presentation of the harvest, as well as the seed for planting.

Archaeologists cite parallels that deal with human sacrificial rituals that are suggested among the remains of burials located at Cahokia. Most of these remains involved women.

Can we make any comparisons with the Ouinipegou to these other cultures that may explain some of the archaeological evidence found at Sand Point; for instance, the elaborate ritual ceremonial funerary pyre that involved four youths; was this suggestive of human sacrifice? (1.)

The missionaries of Natchez described an incident involving the temple being struck by lighting, reducing it to ashes. While it was ablaze, seven or eight women "cast their infants into the midst of the flames to appease the wrath of Heaven." This recorded event may give us cause to wonder why the archaeologists were unable to locate burial remains of infants, which were disturbingly under-represented among the burial remains at Sand Point. (2.)

What event among the Ouinipegou would have instigated the elaborate celebration of cremating the remains of four youth? This had to have been a significant event. Was it only isolated to this one incident, or do remaining linear mounds at Sand Point hold additional secrets?

Were the cairns instrumental in determining the proper time for the final mass burials? Was the sun instrumental in the construction of the elaborate funerary cribbing that was facing the southern sky so it would coincide with honoring the Sun deity at the proper moment it was set ablaze?

*Stone Altar—Huron Mountain's "mystery stone" and trail system*

In addition to the stone monuments at Pequaming is a stone monument located to the east of Keweenaw Bay on Huron Mountain. Much debate has centered around whether this controversial feature is natural or man made. This stone feature consists of a large rock, one meter long, measuring approximately 5.7 cubic feet in volume, weighing about 900 pounds, and is perched precariously atop three individually spaced smaller stones.

Those who dismiss this feature as man-made classify it as a natural phenomenal creation of the last receding glacier. The problem with this theory is that there are an awful lot of these "glacial erratics" existing in North America. There are approximately 40 or more of these "erratics" on the east coast, one in Colorado and one in Minnesota. But there are other extenuating circumstances that cause us to recognize this structure for what it is. The most convincing evidence is that of the prevalence of human activity in this area. The heavy presence of human activity, in conjunction with the location of this feature, is reasonably convincing evidence that identifies this stone monument as a man-made feature. However, to accept that fact places an extreme burden on those advocates to explain it, whereas, those who dismiss it are afforded the leisure of any further consideration.

---

(1.) *The Winnebago Tribe*, Radin, pg. 269.
"The ceremonial unit in all Winnebago societies consists of four bands, four representing the sacred number [the four cardinal points] . . . ."
(2.) J.R. Vol 68:121-153, (Natchez).

Huron Mountain located on the north shore of Mountain Lake with Lake Superior in the background. It is the highest of the Huron Mountain group. The stone altar sits on its south end overlooking Mountain Lake.

The "mystery stone" or dolmen as it still stands today. Its purpose is still a mystery although it was probably instrumental as an offertory for herbs that were considered sacred to its users.

For those advocates that identify it as a man-made feature classify it as a dolmen or "stone table" or altar, suspected of having correlation to similar structures found principally in Europe among the Celtic cultures.

Local people familiar with the stone have called it the "mystery stone." Author and Marquette historian, Fred Rydholm, has written extensively of the stone and the area surrounding Huron Mountain, with which Fred is very familiar. He provides us with a great many details in his book, *Superior Heartland*, including a history of the region surrounding the Huron Mountains. Of particular interest was a "well used trail" that began at the Lake Superior shore and led to Huron Mountain, that shows up on early survey maps of the area. Fred also describes in detail the construction of a foot trail by Cyrus Bentley, blazed from Deer Lake, near the north branch of the Peshekee River, to the south end of Mountain Lake, where Huron Mountain is located.

It is the significance of this trail that Fred calls the "Bentley Trail" that draws our attention to Huron Mountain on Mountain Lake. It would historically appear that Mr. Bentley was the originator of this trail, however, there is earlier historic evidence that indicates it existed much earlier since it shows up on a French map of 1688 (see Franqualin map of 1688, p. 174)—a trail system that connected the shores of Lake Superior with that of Green Bay in Lake Michigan.

Trail systems are very important references for understanding the activities of prehistoric people as well as the first historic exploration of this region; they were the highways of early travelers. They consisted of foot trails, or foot trails used in conjunction with lakes and rivers. Travel was accomplished by portaging the small vessels from one body of water to another, eventually reaching their destination. Many of these ancient trails were still very obvious during the original government surveys and show up on many of their maps.

This trail system led from the shore of Lake Superior to Anne Lake, from where it then proceeded to Mountain Lake. At the south end of Mountain Lake it continued south to the North Branch of the Peshekee River where the main branch runs into Lake Michigamme. It continued down the Michigamme River to the Menominee River where it entered Green Bay of Lake Michigan. This is the "chemin" that shows up on the 1688 map. But who were the travelers that kept this route so "well used?" If the French were aware of the existence of this route; it was obviously used long before they learned of it or were making use of it.

The use of altars, even stone altars, was not unique to prehistoric people. The Ouinipegou, as miners, were workers of stone as well as earth-workers. One answer may lie in the technology to construct a so-called dolmen, which the Sand Point people would have possessed. How does any human or group of humans manage to raise rocks that weigh from 900 pounds—30 or 40 tons, which precariously end up perched atop three other smaller stones!

Sometimes the simplest techniques can be just that, almost too simple to recognize. The method is similar to the simplicity of boiling water in wood bark containers, without burning the container.

A dolmen was constructed the very same way that engineers theorize the great stones of Stonehenge were set in place, by the use of earth working. A large rock acting as the table was located near the location where it was to be constructed. The three smaller stones were set in place, measured out to accommodate the capstone, then covered with soil. This would provide a ramp, not to lift the huge stone, but to *roll* it onto the carefully placed smaller stones. The use of only three stones acting as pedestals is convenient since it *always* provides a solid base upon which the larger stone rests. Try doing this with four stones.

Not only would logs be used as rollers, but the use of levers and wedges were employed by these people. Located near the Ontonagon River was a mine shaft that was approximately 20 feet in depth where early miners left a large copper boulder suspended about five feet off the bottom. It had been raised with the use of oak log cribbing and wedges. The Ouinipegou even employed the use of helical-twist copper drill bits.

The location of the stone altar is probably the most important evidence in determining its significance to humans. It is positioned on the southern end of Huron Mountain, directly above Mountain Lake, which is located to the south of it. Huron Mountain is the highest point in the Huron Mountain group and is also visible from Lake Superior. This was undoubtedly a very sacred site for the Ouinipegou who could frequent it on every occasion that they passed through the area. But there is one more convincing piece of evidence that leads us to understand the significance of this location and the people that used it, it is the presence of a unique cactus that grows nowhere else in Michigan!

*Huron Mountain Cactus*

Located on the south side of Huron Mountain, between the stone altar and the shore of Mountain Lake, is the cactus *Opuntia fragilis*, also called Brittle Prickly Pear Cactus.

A patch approximately one acre in size grows nowhere else in the vicinity, even though there are other sites in the region that would be conducive for its habitation. In fact, the most northern range of this plant is the Dells of Wisconsin, along the Wisconsin River.

It is protected by the Endangered Species Act in Michigan and is listed as threatened in the state of Wisconsin. Although it occurs more abundantly in Wisconsin its distribution is restricted only to certain areas. It grows on thin rocky soils of granite or quartzite outcrops and occasionally in sandy soil or on sandstone ridges. Its normal range extends from British Columbia, eastward to Manitoba, and south to Texas and Arizona. (1.)

Brittle Prickly Pear Cactus is not toxic and was used by many of the western groups as a winter or starvation food source. It is very unlikely that it ever served the same purpose for the Michigan and Wisconsin users since it grows so small. Western cattle ranchers burned off the spines and fed it to their cattle in times of drought.

The Brittle Prickly Pear Cactus is listed as rare though locally abundant in select locations of Wisconsin. This may have some significance since it appears that Wisconsin is out of its normal range, suggesting that it may have been introduced to Wisconsin from the western regions. This is probably the reason that it appears so stunted, where it has become naturalized compared to its size in its normal range. If this is the case in Wisconsin, then our Huron Mountain cactus is definitely out of its element. (2.)

Since the cactus on Huron Mountain is so small and restricted, it is unlikely that it would have served any substantial use as a food source. One study found that its stems were roasted over a fire, peeled and eaten as dessert by children. It is more likely the cactus served to honor this natural temple that faced the southern sky. (3.)

It appears that the frequency of human travel has been instrumental in translocating this species into the northern reaches of Lake Superior. This may have even occurred inadvertently; however, since the cactus is so strategically located, it would suggest otherwise. This "well used" area of sacred significance was a special place that held a great deal of meaning and reverence for its users.

*Ouinipegou Trail Systems*

For us to understand the connection of Sand Point to the regions to the south, where the central controlling trading centers were located, we must know how the copper reached its destination. It was through a network of foot trails, lakes and rivers. These important highway systems can be helpful in explaining the demographics of its people.

There were several routes that would lead the Ouinipegou from Sand Point and the copper range along the Ontonagon River to their southern relatives and beyond, to Aztalan and Cahokia.

The most direct route for transporting ore directly from the copper mines was to continue directly south on the Ontonagon River, where it heads out near Lac Vieux Desert. Lac Vieux Desert is the headwaters of Wisconsin River that flows the entire length of Wisconsin and into the Mississippi, where the major

(1.) *Preliminary Reports on the Flora of Wisconsin*, Ugent, 1962, Vol. 51:83-134.
(2.) *Grays Manual of Botany*, Fernald, 1950.
(3.) *Ethnobotany of Native America*, Moerman, (Data base). Turner, Nancy J., Laurence C. Thompson and M. Terry Thompson et al. 1990:194.

Enlargement of Franquelin's map of 1688 showing the Huron Mountain Trail (Chemin) leading from Lake Superior to Green Bay, Lake Michigan. This "well used" trail was a principal access route between these two bodies of water that was still in use well into the 1600's. (State Historical Society of Wisconsin)

Huron Mountain group showing south end of Mountain Lake where trail exited and followed Cedar Creek. Huron Mountain is in upper left of photo.

View of Sturgeon River from the Lac Vieux Desert Trail (Tibits Falls). This walking trail connected Sand Point to the headwaters of the Wisconsin River, Lac Vieux Desert.

Jim LaPointe fords the Sturgeon River at the Lac Vieux Desert Trail just below the Tibits falls. Once used by native people, today, it is only a deer crossing.

trade centers would be accessed. This trail system was still in use when Henry Schoolcraft entered the Ontonagon River in 1820.

Another trail that led directly to Lac Vieux Desert ran north to Sand Point. Referred to as the Lac Vieux Desert Trail, it was the most direct route from the settlement at Sand Point to the Wisconsin River system. It was strictly a foot trail with no river routes in between. (1.)

A more western trail system originated at Lake Superior near the Apostle Islands and proceeded south. It also shows up on the 1688 map of Franqualin and was called the "Trail of the Illinois." It ran all the way to the Illinois country south of Wisconsin. This was the route that Marquette implied when he described the thousands of Illinois who traveled this route to trade with the French at Chequamegon. It was strictly a foot trail that took them 30 days to *walk*! This was also the route that Radisson took on his southern winter snowshoe trek from the Sauteurs (Ojibway), who had migrated to western Lake Superior.

Even as late as 1831 Douglas Houghton reported accessing the Mississippi River "no less than three times along the south coast of Lake Superior . . . that were widely separated from each other . . . journeys made through a complete wilderness, uninhabited except by savages . . . ." (2.)

We have already discussed the trail system through the Huron Mountains connecting Lake Superior with Green Bay of Lake Michigan. This trail consisted of several canoe portages, hopping from lake to lake with an eleven mile portage from Mountain Lake to the north branch of the Peshekee River, and floating it down to the Menominee River where it would enter Green Bay.

All of these routes accessed the region of Wisconsin, particularly Green Bay, where historically the Winnebago have been demographically restricted. This occurred due to the misinterpretation of the historical journey of Nicolet. This single incident alone has contributed to a chain of historic interpretations, over a period of almost 150 years, that have made the understanding and the knowledge of the Ouinipegou (Sea People) impossible.

*North Lakes Project*

In addition to the historic evidence being misconstrued, the archaeological evidence was also subject to the same errors. One of the most difficult errors to explain is how archaeologists derived that the Sand Point people were "probably Algonquian" and not Sioux, when it is in contradiction to the evidence presented in this research effort.

To do this we have to examine the comparisons that were made to other investigations of other sites that preceded the Sand Point discovery. We must also bear in mind that the means of ethnological determination was based solely on physical anthropological comparisons. In examining the other sites that

---

(1.) *Documented Records of the Historic use of the Lac Vieux Trail*, Dompier, 1984.
(2.) *Memoir of Douglas Houghton*, Bradish, 1889.

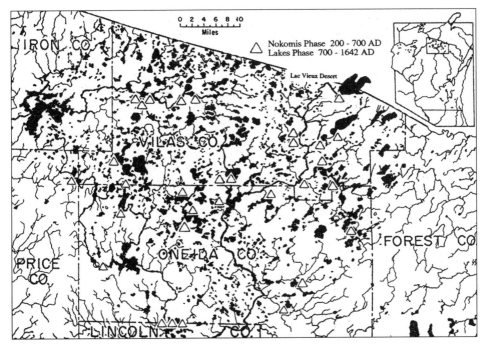

**Northern Wisconsin locations of the Sea People.** The archaeological study area (North Lakes Project) revealed many other related sites to those of Sand Point connected by the Ontonagon River and a trail that led directly from Sand Point to Lac Vieux Desert. The Lac du Flambeau and Wisconsin River systems, both leading to the Mississippi, are represented, as well as the Menominie River which flows into Green Bay. These related sites represent the beginning of ceramic pottery and extensive copper usage. During the Lakes Phase period burial mounds became evident.

were compared, we also discover information that was not obvious to the investigators, principally by what we are able to confirm from Sand Point.

The course of events that led anthropologists to ascertain that Sand Point and other related sites in the region were Algonkin was due to the extensive effort to reestablish previous physical comparative analyses that were considered inadequate. The study that was pivotal to this effort was The North Lakes Project that was conducted in Wisconsin in 1964. The region under study consisted principally of the northern Vilas and Oneida Counties, located in the multi-lakes area of the Flambeau Flowage and Wisconsin River headwater systems that also border on the watershed of the Ontonagon River. (1.)

The project revealed 82 archaeological sites. The specific site that was excavated and utilized in the physical analysis study was the Robinson site, located on Lake Nokomis, contiguous to the Wisconsin River. It was from this site that numerous skeletal remains were examined and used in the comparative study. This is an extremely crucial site in relationship to Sand Point since there

(1.) *Aspects of Upper Great Lakes Anthropology*, Johnson, (Salzer), 1974:40.

are many cultural and physical similarities. The crucial task was to determine the ethnology of its inhabitants.

As the T-score system evolved, physical comparison of the Robinson site remains were made. When they were compared with the western plains Sioux they differed dramatically; consequently, comparisons to any of the Sioux people were excluded. It therefore left them to search for an Algonkin group that would meet the expectations of the analysis, and a group of skeletal remains were located that compared very similar to those of the Robinson people. They were from a cemetery located on Old Birch Island in the far reaches of Georgian Bay, Ontario, that were deemed to be "most likely" an Algonquian speaking people. It is here that the real problem lies.

The ethnological conclusion of the Old Birch Island Cemetery is mostly conjecture and lacks evidence to support that its users were Algonkin or Ojibway. This assumption was based solely on the historic occupation of Georgian Bay by predominately Algonkin inhabitants. Archaeological evidence of the cemetery, however, showed no similarity to the suggested Ojibwa culture, which was to have inhabited it in modern times; despite the fact the cemetery was used during the historic period (1750 -1800; during a period when European influence had integrated its way into native genetics also producing metis). In fact, the burial customs and artifacts more closely linked them to people of southern Ontario and New York taken to represent an evolved Point Peninsula (Focus) culture, which is regarded as contemporary with the late Hopewellian, and closely related so-called Intrusive Culture of the Heinisch Mound. However, even these "similarities are far from conclusive." Additionally, "the trait list of Old Birch Island offers but a tenuous identification at best." Since there was no habitation associated with the Old Birch Island Cemetery, it is pure speculation that its users had an occupation anywhere on Georgian Bay during the period of 1750 -1800. The only definite conclusion was that the site fits that of a "Woodland Pattern" and "can not with finality be placed in any cultural division below the pattern level." (1.)

The historic artifacts prove that Old Birch Island cemetery was not used prior to 1750 and was considered strictly a historic site. The question is, where were these people prior to that time, and where was their habitation, since none were located on the island? After 1650 all of the residing groups on Georgian Bay were scattered to various places in the Great Lakes region—some never to return—or were assimilated into other cultures. The area surrounding Old Birch Island had long been used as a thoroughfare for trading groups, and since it was located directly on the trade route between Montreal and Sault Ste.

---

(1.) *Old Birch Cemetery and the Early Historic Trade Route*, Greenman, 1951:62.

*North to Lake Superior*, Penny, (Carter & Rankin), 1987:62.

At LaPointe, in 1840, there were 86 dwellings, 300 native people, and 300 American and French—a population so mixed that "all the different races are so mingled that a classification would be impossible."

Marie, it is more likely that the cemetery was used to accommodate a transient people who were active beyond 1750.

To attempt to establish an ethnology for Old Birch is impossible. It is just as possible that they may have been from Siouan stock, or akin to the Iroquois of southern Ontario and New York, where the Petun, Huron, Neutral, and Iroquois tribes resided long before the arrival of any Europeans.

Despite the ambiguities of the Old Birch Island cemetery, it was the determining factor in deciding that the Robinson site consisted of Algonkin people rather than Sioux. It poisoned all the ethnic wells of Wisconsin and the Upper Peninsula of Michigan. Archaeologists failed to include in their comparisons the close physical similarities of the Winnebago Focus with those that existed among the Robinson and Sand Point people—a culture that was Sioux but very physically dissimilar to the plains Sioux. (1.)

It would seem more appropriate for the archaeologists to have used the known Sioux speaking Winnebago as a basis for comparison, especially since they were more geographically and contemporaneously proximal, as well as sharing equally similar physical characteristics, with the Old Birch site represented by so few samples. Also, the Siouan genetic similarities may have endured a greater test of time since they were not exogamous as compared to the integrated Algonkin clans with their totemic systems.

Although no habitation was evidenced on Old Birch Island the closest habitation was at Great Cloche Island, located four miles away. This camp site contained small fragments of pottery and flakes of quartzite and flint, which were located a quarter mile west of a cemetery also located there; that indicated occupation in "precontact times." Located 400 feet from the camp site, in an open plain along the shore, was a large rock that stood approximately five feet high. On its top were "five circular cuplike depressions" approximately 3.5-4.75 inches in diameter and from 2.5-3.5 inches deep. They were positioned in a straight line running nearly east and west and 2.5-4.75 inches from the edge of one to the edge of the next. A dozen or more similar holes of somewhat smaller dimensions were elsewhere on the top and side of the rock. Archaeologists have no explanation for this structure. (2.)

At the Robinson site, located on a ridge above the lake shore, on the southeast side of the peninsula, archaeologists removed the skeletal remains of 81 individuals. Of these, 30 were found to be buried simultaneously en masse. Among them (nine) were the only instances of trauma discovered among the skeletal remains. Six of them displayed bone deformations similar to those of Sand Point, distinct impact fractures from a sharp piercing

---

(1.) *The Michigan Archaeologist*, Vol. 27., Nos 1-2, 1981:18 & 19.
(2.) *Old Birch Island Cemetery and the Early Historic Trade Route*, Greenman, 1951:13.

**The North Lakes Project revealed a "Woodhenge" that was mistakenly identified as a house. These celestial observatories were mere modifications of the Cahokian models, made of stone (cairns) or wood posts.**

implement in the same skeletal regions of the cranium, evidence that this instrument was the cause of death. (1.)

In the course of removing the remains of the mass burial of the 30 individuals, a structure was discovered that was mistakenly identified as that "certainly used as a house." It was described as "an oval subterranean structure" that was approximately nine by eleven feet in size with a flat floor containing "a series of large, centrally located posts." The subterranean layout was approximately three feet below the normal ground level. This so-called house was without a hearth and there was no indication of the use of fire within the structure. It is difficult to ascertain that this could ever have been a "house" used as a place of habitation, especially with the absence of the most necessary element of native cultures, the fire. (2.)

The structure is more characteristic of a modification of a Cahokian "woodhenge," a celestial observatory. The recessed level would allow the observer to sit comfortably upon its ledge in order to wait for the observations to align

(1.) *An Analysis of a late Woodland Population in the Upper Great Lakes*, Melbye, 1969:91.
(2.) J.R. Vol. 28:295.
    "The Savages hold scarecely any assembly without the calumet filled with tobacco in their mouths; and, as fire is necessary to the use of tobacco, they nearly always kindle fires at all their assembles—insomuch that it is the same thing with them to light a council fire, or to keep a place suitable for assembling, or a house for visiting one another, as do relatives and friends."
    Much historical mention is made of the fire being the center of social life since it almost constantly contained a kettle of food for any occasion.

themselves with the centrally located posts. Interestingly, of the 82 sites located, 80% of these were located on lakes near outlets, on peninsulas, and they preferred islands, and particularly "*eastern*" lake shores (facing the rising sun). For the first time in this region, the Late Mississippian period saw the introduction of burial mounds. (1.)

Among some of the other sites identified in the North Lakes Project, archaeologists discovered structures they identified as "cairn-type hearths." These were presumed to be associated with the processing of copper implements that are so prevalent among all of these sites. However, it would appear that these rock structures were similar to the cairns that were identified at Pequaming Point, adjacent to Sand Point, that were utilized as celestial observatories, structures that were mere modifications and local expressions of the Cahokian model.

What may prove to be most interesting is that the Robinson site woodhenge structure was found below that of the burial mound complex. Since archaeologists established that the use of the burial mounds in the North Lakes Project area did not appear until after 700 A.D. (Lakes Phase), it would suggest that the Nokomis Phase (200-700 A.D.) structures (cairns and woodhenge), would predate those found at Cahokia!

W e must not undermine the importance of the scientific utilization of anthropological physical comparisons; however, their applications are limited, especially in establishing ethnical identities. As much as we would like to think that the Old Birch users were Algonquian speakers, they possessed physical characteristics that were comparable to the Winnebago Sioux. Many of the historic traders spoke more than one language in order to consummate their trading enterprises. Just the same, it is also just as possible for the prehistoric Winnebago to have originated from Algonkin stock and evolved into a Sioux speaking people with the advent of the historic period. Even during the historic period they underwent a transitional process that involved an acculturation from Siouan to an Algonkin transformation. Whereas, it is dubious as to what ethnic physical comparisons would be demonstrated if we were to analyze the existing Winnebago people as we know them in modern times.

The region of Wisconsin in the western Great Lakes is typical of an ethnic and linguistics potpourri that complicates the anthropological sorting and classifying of prehistoric groups. But how do we understand the origin of the use of celestial observatories that are part of this copper related culture. Does it begin with the ceramic period in this region? How does it relate to the major cultural centers of Cahokia and Aztalan of the Mississippian periods? Did their use begin in the Great Lakes region and find their way to the Mississippi, or vice versa? One of the great archaeological mysteries of Cahokia is where its

(1.) *Aspects of Upper Great Lakes Anthropology*, Johnson, (Salzer), 1974:49.

inhabitants went after its decline. Is it possible that some of them may have found their way into Wisconsin and Upper Michigan, explaining the expansion of occupation in these northern locations that were identified with the "Lakes Phase" of the North Lakes Project?

The identity of the Ouinipegou of Sand Point may shed some light on these celestial structures and their origins. Were they introduced from intrusionary peoples that may have traversed the sea? Why were they called Sea People, and did this reference for a people extend to those that may have had a profound impact on the great culture of Cahokia?

*Sea People*

Many of the historic names for the native groups leave us mystified as to who many of them were and where they were located, especially with the rapid displacement taking place during the historic period.

The names supplied by the French were often conjured to accommodate their ability to identify one group from another. What is particularly fortunate for us is that the name used by the French to identify the Sea People (Ouinipegou) was a *prehistoric* reference supplied by the Algonkin and Huron groups they had formed close alliances with.

The Algonkin word "Ouinipeg" and the Iroquois (Huron) word "Aweatsewaenrrhonon" meant Sea People, which the French explained were "so called because they came from the coast of a sea of which we have no knowledge."

This was no mythological reference which other groups implied in the course of preserving their origins (totem or clan lineage) through the Medicine Society. This is a *literal* reference, meaning their ancestral origin actually took place in some place distantly removed—"from the coast of a salt sea."

When Dr. Paul Radin engaged in the three year study of the Winnebago, he learned of their prehistoric origin, although he did not understand the full implications of their profound statement of having "come from over the sea." He was nonetheless uncertain as to whether it was a mythological account, preserved in their legends, or an event that historically would reveal a possible "over the sea" journey to North America. Had Radin the knowledge of the prehistory evidence supplied by the French missionaries, he could have given more credence to an otherwise skeptical account of their legendary ancestral origin that was but "a vague memory of some historical happening," supplied to him some 270 years after their near demise by the Illinois. (1.)

It was the Ouinipegou themselves who would lay claim to their origins as they would inform the French that they had "come from the shore of a *far distant sea* to the North"—information that would confuse these early explorers

---

(1.) *The Winnebago Tribe*, Radin, 1990:2. (Originally published as part of the Thirty -Seventh Annual Report of the Bureau of American Ethnology, Smithsonian Institution, Washington, 1923.)

looking for the passage. It would eventually prompt Radisson to venture to Hudson Bay to confirm whether or not they were being told a "fib."

The French believed because they were the Sea People, they would lead them to the sea. Champlain had no problem understanding that they had come from "over a sea," only he envisioned a sea to the west, thinking they were Asian or "Tartary." After all, he had just come from over a sea himself!

Who were the ancestors of the Sea People that had come from "over the sea?" When did they arrive and how did the intrusion of these foreigners integrate themselves into the interrelationships of Paleo-people?

Much speculation surrounds the marvels of the Mississippian culture, especially that of Cahokia. A great deal of uncertainty surrounds the origin of this marvelous ancient culture that was so well established with its large earthworks and highly organized social system. Who were they and where did they come from? Were the "Mississippians," Sea People, so called because "they came from the coast of a salt sea of which we have no knowledge?"

How did these sun-worshipping cultures, who utilized celestial observatories, originate? Was it a natural developmental process of the collective unconscious that evolved from paleo-peoples? Or was it introduced by the intrusion of a "Stonehenge" people versed in solar worship, who were already conscious of the numerological aspect of dividing the solar progressions into equal lunar phases? Possibly the presence of cairns and dolmens may offer some clues as to who they may have been. (1.)

There is a growing number of pre-Columbian enthusiasts who advance the idea that North and South America were subject to intrusions by Euro-Mediterranean seafaring people. The stone altar or dolmen of Huron Mountain would surely suggest the introduction of an overseas visitation by a people who were influenced by some Iberian culture. With all the archaeological and historic evidence available, are we missing or ignoring something here? The Euro-Mediterranean search is not the scope of this investigation; however, no serious objective researcher should ignore or dismiss the evidence despite their former schools of thought. (2.)

(1.) *Off the English Coast, a Seaside Stonehenge*, Miles, 1999.
   A recent discovery of a "Seaside Stonehenge" off the English coast was identified as a British Bronze Age religious structure. Constructed of 55 oak tree trunks that formed a 22-foot circle, it is the first such structure ever discovered on the Isle made of timber. Some call it "Seahenge."
(2.) *The Celts, Europe's Founders*, Severy, 1977.
   No other culture had a greater influence on the development of Europe, even the Greeks. They were earth workers, built effigy mounds, cremated their dead in "bone fires," sacrificed infants, constructed dolmens. An excavated Celt cargo vessel was found to be 60 feet long. Even Viking vessels were twice the size of the French ships that plied the Atlantic on a regular basis. Archaeologists were surprised to find that LaSalle's ship was merely 51 feet long and 14 feet wide! (National Geographic, Vol. 191, No. 5, 1997:78.).

Efforts continue as we attempt to understand the dynamics of native American populations, their religions, socio-economic relationships, wars, etc. Anthropologists and ethnohistorians categorically define ancient human populations through classifications of designated archaeological sites, geographical linguistics, chronological periods, traditions, foci, phases, expressions, manifestations, intrusions, etc., all with a scientific intent or basis. Unfortunately for science, what we fail to understand is that the complexities of human behavior are anything but static.

Archaeologists have continually struggled in their attempts to explain the Effigy Mound Tradition of Wisconsin and its developing role to other so-called Oneota classifications—foci identified as the Koshkonong, Grand River, Lake Winnebago and the Orr. It is uncertain what foci the Sand Point site may belong to, if not deserving of a separate focus yet to be decided. Only a reevaluation of the site will determine if it, along with other northern sites, requires reclassification. What is certain is that the Sand Point site was associated with the historic location of the "Ouinipeg." But just who was included among this so-called group of Sea People may prove to be an even greater mystery.

We might compare this example to another large lower Michigan group, the eastern Algonkin and Huron, referred to as the Fire Nation. It consisted of a large constituency of combined Algonkin tribes. They were the historic Potowatomi, Mascouten, Miami, Kickapoo, Fox and Sauk, possibly even the Illinois, all Algonkin speaking people. Likewise, these same eastern Algonkin and Huron possibly referred to the combined Sioux speaking people on the western border of the Great Lakes as the Ouinipeg, or Sea People. It probably did not just include those that archaeologists identified as the Lake Winnebago focus, but possibly all of the Sioux speaking people contained in the region. In fact, it may have even included the so-called Mississippian cultures bordering the "exceeding great river" that led to the sea.

Meanwhile, archaeologists continue to debate the mysterious Effigy Mound Tradition, or fail to offer explanations for the linguistic complexities of the Algonkin and Sioux in this region. Is it possible that the Effigy tradition itself was a result of an intrusion from "over the sea," as was articulated by some of Radin's Winnebago?

We will probably never be able to explain fully the ethnological transformation of development of this region, try as we may, because of the "confusion arising from our inability to decipher the information contained in our data." The results stemming from the inconsistent dynamics of aboriginal behavior make it virtually impossible to resolve and explain because of the complexities of constant cultural flux.

# 11

# DREAMS
## (AND THE USE OF SIMPLES)

*"Tradition fades, but the written record remains ever fresh."*
—Clements Library of American History, U.M.

I might truly say that Dreams are indeed the God of these poor Infidels, because it is they who command the Country—they alone are obeyed and honored by all. If they have any fears, hopes, desires, passions, and affections—everything they do is a result of their Dreams. J.R. Vol. 23:171.

It would be improper to research the progenitors of the Winnebago tribe without mention of the extensive research that was conducted by the noted Dr. Paul Radin and the publication, *The Winnebago Tribe*. The purpose for mention is to emphasize Dr. Radin's difficulties in attempting to solicit traditional information that was a result of a three year autobiographical study of the so-called Winnebago descendants. He identifies the problems and inconsistencies that he encountered during the course of interviewing the elders of this tribe, who by this time, had been scattered as far away as Nebraska. (1.)

Radin makes a very through effort to identify categorically the ethnological aspects of the Winnebago with his biography. He uses the archaeological remains of Wisconsin (the mound structures—effigies) in conjunction with what he is able to learn from his interviews, with what he purports to be surviving descendants of the Winnebago. Dr. Radin is very candid with many of his findings due to the problems dealing with consistent and reliable information based on myth and oral traditions. He acquired at great deal of information that he attempted to correlate as Winnebago, however, he was deficient regarding the early French historical documentation of these people. By the time of Dr. Radin's work, the original Ouinipegou culture was nonexistent, and had been so since their near demise in 1642. What he produced were the results of a great conglomerate of many different native groups that had incorporated themselves under the Winnebago ethnic umbrella. Influences were mostly

(1.) *The Winnebago Tribe*, Radin, 1990.
    Originally published as part of the Thirty-Seventh Annual Report of the bureau of American Ethnology, Smithsonian Institution, Washington, 1923.

Algonkin, Sauk, Fox, Potowatomi, not to mention the European cultural influences that adulterated the ideologies of the original Ouinipegou, that really began with the introduction of European trade goods in the early 1620's. European technologies were quickly followed by the introduction of their religion. If anything, we should distinguish the Winnebago from the Ouinipegou, since there is virtually no way of really asserting what the similarities are. Certainly, the Ouinipegou that Nicolet knew in 1634 are not the same Winnebago that Dr. Radin was attempting to identify.

Because of the very rapid changes that were taking place among native groups, which were grasping for acceptance of these new and profound European influences, they were simultaneously losing a grip on their own. It is for this reason that any attempts to learn the most unadulterated aspects of these early cultures, even through historical accounts, can be difficult. What these early observers saw and recorded were certainly not products of objective anthropological study. They are, however, the best evidence we have despite the prevailing European attitudes that were colored with shades of exploitation (economic) and proselytization (religious). More importantly, historic documents have not changed since their compilation, which cannot be said of oral tradition and myth that get passed down from generation to generation. The process of preserving history through word of mouth can easily deviate with each narrator, be modified for individual groups, or totally changed by new positions in power.

Despite this fact, many anthropological studies of native American cultures are based on the results of traditional mythological information that was passed down through oral communications believed to have survived the perils of human error and time. Additionally, because this line of history is rooted in oral concepts, not only is it subject to error or deviation, but societal secrets are subject to loss as well. If not lost, they can never be confirmed, since the secrets are not a matter of written record. Such is the case with a secret society that was referred to as the Great Medicine Society.

## Dreams, Simples, and the Medicine Society

It has been the general consensus of anthropologists that native groups of the Great Lakes Region did not employ the use of hallucinogenic plant substances as part of their culture observance. Much historic evidence, however, alludes to the practice as we present documentation of the ritual use of medicinal plants that the French called "simples." In conjunction with the use of these so called "simples" was revealed another most intriguing aspect of native American culture, the emphasis placed upon their dreams. (1.)

The historic records repeatedly mention the great dependency they gave to their dreams. This illusionary apparition, because of its mysticism, was considered paramount to their lives as they sought good health, spiritual power,

(1.) *Aboriginal Relationships Between Culture & Plant Life in the Upper Great Lakes Region*, Yarnell, 1964:47.

and prophetic guidance. To oblige the illusion of a dream would seem absurd for us today, if not a little bit scary, but it portrayed the spiritual essence of everything, since all life and all things were spiritual. The dream, or unconscious state of mind, was the spiritual connection, or medium, between the physical world and the spirit world.

It is through documenting the observations of early historic writings that we can combine the understanding of the importance of the dream to the relationship of plants, as portrayed through the knowledge of the Medicine Society. It was through the organization of this society that the knowledge of the use of the plants was preserved. The knowledge of the most sacred and powerful of these plants, as medicine, was to be a highly regarded secret. In effect, the same spiritual state that was produced by a dream during sleep could be entered through the use of a hallucinogenic substance produced by a medicinal plant. The relationship of medicinal plants and prophetic apparitions of dreams had a profound effect not only on their physical health, but on their spiritual well being. It was this spiritual well being, which was most revered above all else, that provided the native American with a unique temperament.

## Guardian Spirit, Manito

If we are to understand the prehistoric Indians, it is necessary for us to document the earliest historical evidence possible. By focusing our efforts on records available from the initial French occupation made with the native people during their exploration of the Great Lakes Region, we may access the most unadulterated information we can prior to the cultural revolution that was occurring.

What is important, if we are to know anything of the individual lives of prehistory peoples, is to understand that the dream or dream state was central to their lives. The emphasis of the dream appears to have been universal among all aboriginal peoples. Once this central fact is understood, then the remaining aspects of the lives of native people and their culture can be more comprehensively appreciated.

The letters of Radot in 1709 explain this paramount point, as he states that they:

> . . . are much given to dreams and are so well persuaded that it is their spirit who gives them to them, that they absolutely must carry them out. It is dreams which oblige them to undertake wars, to make great voyages, to abandon war parties which they have undertaken against their enemies and to return from them to their cabins. It is also these dreams that give them their spirit, which they imagine takes care of them in all acts of their lives. (1.)

(1.) *Memoir*, Pease, IHC, Letter 30 (1709), Radot.

It was important that every individual have a guardian spirit "which takes care of them." This aspect of spirituality is taught at an early age. Radot continues to describe this concept:

> ... as soon as there is one of them who has reached the age of ten or twelve years and who can use the bow and arrow, his father says to him that he is of an age to get a spirit and to choose a manito for himself, and he gives him at the same time the instructions necessary to succeed in this.

> For the purpose he has him 'mattach' or paint his face black with crushed charcoal and requires him in this state to fast for several days in order that, having the brain empty he can more easily dream during his sleep, which is the time that this god ought to disclose himself to him and strike his imagination with some extraordinary thing or some animal which holds the place of a divinity for him. The father, anxious to know the dream of this child, watches the time of his awakening in order that he speaks to no one before him and questions him privately on what happened in his imagination during the night: if nothing has appeared, he counsels him to continue his fast, saying to him that on this occasion he must give marks of his firmness and his strength. Finally, his weakened brain represents to him some object such as the sun, the thunder, or other extraordinary things of which he has often heard his father or other elders speak.

> When this child has dreamed he runs to carry the news to his father, who strongly recommends to him not to divulge it and encourages him with many reasons to accept this dream and honor this idea which he takes thenceforth from his childhood for his divinity, for his manito, for his protector, and continues during his life to worship it by sacrifices, and by feast which he gives in its honor. (1.)

Raudot continues to explain that this ritual is performed by the young girls as well.

For us to fully appreciate the spirit world of early native peoples, we must first understand the nature of his everyday environment. It was literally a natural environment that consumed his existence, being in a world where his dependence was on the very elements necessary for his survival—namely, the creatures that he shared the earth and sky with. There was perceived a spiritual connectedness with everything that existed within the natural scheme of things. He, along with the other creatures of the earth, shared a spiritual place in its grand order. His vision through the "quest" of a certain animal or thing, became his guardian spirit.

All things, however, possessed a spirit—rocks, trees, birds, water, etc. Everything in creation was connected spiritually by a "spirit that dwells in all things." The association of animal and human forms is referred to as anthropomorphism.

---

(1.) *Memoir*, Pease, IHC, Letter 30 (1709), Radot.

The dream world held all the mysteries of knowledge and power. It contained the answers to future events (prophesies) and was responsible for one's good or ill health.

Vision in dreams extended power. In fact, if any central theme existed in native American spirituality, it was the giving of life through the transmission of spiritual power. All of which was presided over by a Great Spirit who was the "superior being." (1.)

As we continue to emphasize the dream as the medium for understanding the spiritual connection, in 1719, Pachot describes this relationship with the superior being:

> These savages adore only the sun, the earth, and the thunder because they say that these are the things attached to the superior being whom they call the master of life . . . . The Illinois call him Ketchesmanetoa, which means the spirit master of life; the Outavois call him the same as the Illinois with a little different pronunciation. They gave confidence only in their manitous because they believe that they give them ideas coming from the superior being and that it is he who shows them in their dreams the animals which they take for their manitous because he wishes to use them to lead them, which is the reason also that <u>for their medicine they only use their simples to invoke their manitou</u> by their song, because they believe that their manitou communicated to the plants the virtue they have to cure and that these plants would not have it otherwise. (2.)

This reference is very explicit towards the important relationship of plants to the native people. We see that not only did the spirit world communicate through animated symbols, but also through the use of plants. Here, plants were used to "invoke their manitou," which was to restore them to health, an implication that medicinal plants could supplement where dreams may not suffice to convey a manitou to lead them. In fact, the native person was more committed to the plant community for spiritual well being than anything else in his environment. Plants were powerful medicine that could spiritually invoke physical well-being. Spirits were the cause of either good or ill health, and the knowledge of plant use to influence the spirits was considered sacred. (3.)

So important was the plant community to the aboriginal that in order to perpetuate the mystical knowledge and skill relating to their herbal uses, they organized a secret society that would not only insure their good health, but would also provide continuity among the tribal community as well.

The most significant aspect of this society, referred to as the Great Medicine Society, was that the knowledge was indeed secret. For that reason, the use of the most powerful substances used to "invoke their manitou," have been suc-

(1.) *Ojibwa Myths and Legends*, Coleman, 1961:59.
(2.) *Memoir*, Pease, IHC, 23:363, Pachot, (1719).
(3.) *The Winnebago Tribe*, Radin, 1990:123.
"My son, if you are not able to fast, try at least to obtain some plants that are powerful. There are people who know the different plants, who have been blessed by the spirits with this knowledge."

cessfully concealed from the knowledge of not only early European observers, but from the modern day anthropologist and historian as well.

For us to appreciate fully the maintaining of secrecy of these sacred herbs, preserved in the knowledge of this society, we only have to cite the reference by William Warren. Warren, who was an Ojibwa and could speak the language fluently, had intimate knowledge of this rite. He states:

> The grand rite of Me-da-we-win (or, as we have learned to term it, "Grand Medicine") and the beliefs incorporated therein, are not yet fully understood by the whites. This important custom is still shrouded in mystery, even to my own eyes, though I have taken much pains to inquire, and made use of every advantage, possessed by speaking their language perfectly, being related to them, possessing their friendship and intimate confidence, has given me, and yet I frankly acknowledge that I stand as yet, as it were, on the threshold of the Med-da-we-win lodge. . . . Amongst the Ojibways, the secrets of this grand rite are as sacredly kept as the secrets of the Masonic Lodge among the whites. Fear of threatened and certain death, either by poison or violence, seals the lips of the Med-da-we-win initiate, and this is the potent reason why it is still a secret to the white man, and why it is not more generally understood. (1.)

The emphasis on the role of plants to the native community is reiterated in this account of Deliette who describes to us the ritual initiation rite of the assemblage of the secret Medicine Society:

> . . . All of them, the medicine men and the medicine women, remain for the time being in the cabin of one of their confreeres, waiting for all this to be arranged, and planning together, what to do in order to easily hoodwink the young people and keep alive the faith in their magical powers, both for the rewards which they get for attending to the sick and also with a view to keeping the younger generation under their influence when they wish them to do something for the security of their village or the repose of their wives and children. After these preliminaries, they enter gravely into this enclosure, their dresses trailing, having their chichicoya in their hands and carrying bear skins on their arms. They all sit on mats which are spread for them. One of them rises, the chichicoya in his hand, and speaks in a chant before the whole assembly: 'My friends, today you must manifest to men the power of our medicine so as to make them understand that they live only as long as we wish.' Then they all rise and, waving the chichicoya chant, 'This buffalo has told me this, the bear, the wolf, the buck, the big tail:'—each one naming the beast which he particularly venerates. Then they sit down again, still shaking the gourd. Immediately three or four men get up as if possessed, among them some who resemble men who are on the point of dying. Their eyes are convulsed, and they let themselves fall prostrate and grow ridged as if they were expiring. Another falls also, and rises with an eagle's feather in his hand, the barbs of which are reddened and form a figure suggesting that he has been wounded therewith, but has been saved from the conse-

(1.) *The History of the Ojibwa People*, Warren; 1885:65.

quences by his medicines, and wishes to inject it into the body of one of the band, who then falls to the ground and expels a quantity of blood from his mouth. The medicine men rush to give him help, tear away the feather which issues and inch out of his mouth, spout medicine all over his body, and then have him carried off with great solemnity to his cabin, where he is treated like men who have been poisoned. They make him swallow a quantity of drugs, and five or six of them lay hold of him and pull him by the arms and legs, uttering loud yells. They shake him for a long time in this manner without his coming to; finally he vomits a quantity of water, and they at the same moment throw down a little rattlesnake. A medicine man picks it up and shows it to the spectators and chants: 'Here is the manitou that killed him, but my medicine has restored him to life.' The whole assembly come like people filled with amazement to see this serpent and chant: 'Medicine is the science of sciences. (1.)

This is a most fascinating account of the medicine ritual. The observance of the use of "drugs" is well documented with the final emphasis on "Medicine" (plants or herbs), as "the science of sciences." There is a great deal of symbolism beside the use of "medicine," incorporated into this rite. It is the symbolism of the "little rattlesnake" that might escape our attention if we were not privy to its significance, as it will be demonstrated later. The "medicine," that is portrayed as the "science of sciences," will prove to be a powerful plant that was used as a cure for the bite of the deadly rattlesnake. This plant also had the notorious distinction of being used as a hallucinogenic, and was the most universally used plant known to man.

The peculiar conduct of the participants in this rite deserves attention. They are apparently under the influence of the "drugs" that were such an instrumental part of this ritual. The medicine men (or women) in charge of conducting these rituals were very influential in the guidance of the community. In 1634, the French missionary, Father Paul LeJune, informs us of this importance and provides a very vivid description of his witness to the peculiar conduct of the Medicine man or Sorcerer:

> . . . He immediately began to soar, and talk about the power, the authority, and the influence he had over the minds of his fellow savages. He said that since his youth they had given him the name, *Khimouchouminau*, meaning 'our sire and our master; that everything was done according to his opinion, and that they all followed his advice. (2.)

During LeJune's winter nomadic residence with the Montagnais, he described the hardships endured due to famine. The wife of the Medicine man became sick and was on the point of dying. It was at that point the Shaman-priest was consulted and LeJune provided us with a very articulate account of the event, as he described the behavior of the Sorcerer:

(1.) *Memoir*, Pease, IHC, 23:369-71, Deliette.
(2.) J.R. Vol. 7:129.

It was here that the Savages consulted their genii of light, in the manner I have described in Chapter four. Now as I had always shown my amusement with this superstition, and on all possible occasions had made them see that the mysteries of the Sorcerer were nothing but child's play . . . this unscrupulous man, the day afterward, went through with the performance I am going to describe.

My host having invited all the neighboring Savages to the feast, when they had come and seated themselves around the fire and the kettle, waiting for the banquet to be opened, lo, the Sorcerer, who had been lying down opposite me, suddenly arouse, not yet having uttered a word since the arrival of the guest. He seemed to be in an awful fury, and threw himself upon one of the poles of the cabin to tear it out; he broke it in two, rolled his eyes around in his head, looked here and there like a man out of his senses, then facing those present, he said to them . . . . 'Oh, men, I have lost my mind, I do not know where I am; take the hatchet and javelins away from me, for I am out of my senses.' At these words all the savages lowered their eyes to the ground, . . . This Thrasco [braggart] redoubling his furies, did a thousand foolish acts of a lunatic or of one bewitched; sometimes he would cry at the top of his voice, and then would suddenly stop short, as if frightened; he pretended to cry, and then burst into laughter like a wanton devil, he sang without rules and without measure, he hissed like a serpent, he howled like a wolf, or like a dog, he screeched like an owl or a nighthawk—rolling his eyes about in his head and striking a thousand attitudes, always seeming to be looking for something to throw . . . .

The next evening at the same hour he seemed disposed to enter into the same infuriated state, and to again alarm the camp, saying that he was losing his mind. Seeing him already half-mad, it occurred to me that he might be suffering from some violent fever; I went up to him and took hold of his arm to feel the artery; he gave me a frightful look, seeming to be astonished, and acting as if I had brought him news from the other world, rolling his eyes here and there like one possessed. Having touched his pulse and forehead, I found him cool as a fish, and as far from fever as I was from France. This confirmed me in my suspicion that he was acting the madman to frighten me, and to draw down upon himself the compassion of all our people, who in our dearth, were giving him the best they had. (1.)

It is obvious that these symptomatic reactions, based on the very vivid description of the Medicine man observed by LeJune, are typical of the effects of the influence of a substance capable of producing mind-altering states of abnormal behavior. The results of a strong narcotic capable of producing hallucinogenic states of mind. LeJune, who was totally ignorant of the secrets of the culture, dismissed all of this to superstition, child's play, and a plot to frighten him. He failed to recognize what was really transpiring between the visionary Sorcerer and the spirit world in which he had placed himself in order to communicate the prophecies necessary for their survival. This incident was not isolated to a single event, but was repeated the following evening. The

(1.) J.R. Vol. 7:117-123.

native people not only refused to teach LeJune their language, but were also unwilling to divulge the secrets of their most sacred and powerful medicines.

Peculiar behavior associated with the rituals of the medicine men was also observed by Champlain among the Algonkin and Montagnais. Although Champlain lacked the eloquent literary flair of LeJune, he describes their actions as:

> ... monkey tricks, and incantations, and writhing, in such a way that often they are beside themselves, as if they were mad and out of their senses. They throw the fire from one side of the cabin to the other, now eating burning coals—having held them some time in their hands, then throwing red-hot ashes into the eyes of the spectators. When the noise and din are over, each one goes away to this cabin. But the wives of those who are possessed, and the inmates of their cabin, are in great fear lest they burn all that is in it, so they take out everything that is there. For when they come in they are perfectly wild, their eyes flashing and terrible. Sometimes they stand and sometimes they sit, just as the impulse moves them. They grab everything that they find, or run up against and fling these things about from one side of the cabin to the other. Then they lie down and sleep for a while; then, waking up with a start, they grab some fire and stones, which they hurl about on all sides without any regard. This fury passes off in the sleep that comes upon them. While they are in the sweat, they sing all the time. And since they get very thirsty, they drink great quantity of water, and gradually change from madmen to sober ones. (1.)

The use of plants among the natives was apparently intriguing to early Europeans. They doubted the spiritual implications that were connected with them, but many records attest to the medicinal effects of their use. As we refer back to Deliette, here is a continuation of his account in his *Memoir*:

> ... Most often they do not cure the sick, although assuredly they have admirable drugs, because they are ignorant of internal maladies. It is only a mere chance when they succeed. Their medicines they use for purging have all the effectiveness possible. There are some who use coloquinte [Hawthorn—bitter apple], with which the wilderness abounds in autumn when they gather their seeds. In the healing of wounds some of them are very skillful. I have seen them cure some surprising ones and in a very short time. However full of pus a wound may be, they clean it out entirely without inflicting much pain. They take the precaution of putting a little powder in their mouths; but when they draw out the worst of it, they no longer do so, but continue to suck at the wound until it appears ruddy, after which they chew up some medicine which they spit upon the wound merely wrapping up the whole by day, while leaving the wound to suppurate. At night they wrap it also. When a man has been wounded by a gunshot or by an arrow through the body, at the bottom of the neck or opposite a rib, they open his side, after taking care to raise the skin a little so that on being lowered again the opening will be between two ribs. They pour into him a quan-

(1.) *The Voyages and Exploration of Samuel De Champlain*, Bourne, 1911, Vol. II:136-138.

tity of water, in which they have diluted some of their drugs, after which they have the patient make motions and inhale, and sometimes they even take hold of him by the arms and legs, pushing him to and fro between them, and they make him eject all this water through his wound, expelling along with it fragments of clotted blood, which otherwise, doubtless, would suffocate him. Then they sprinkle him with some of their powdered herbs, which they put into their mouth as I have said already, and they never close up the wound by day. I have seen two men who were healed in this way. (1.)

This account documents the application of powdered herbs, being chewed and placed in the mouth, to treat certain maladies. It would appear that the powdered substances placed in the mouth would serve a dual purpose; by sucking out any infection, relieving pain, and the prevention of infection to the attending physician.

As the early Europeans observed the use of their "simples" we get very few actual descriptions of what these most powerful plants were or how they were prepared. In fact, there was an obvious indication from the records that the native people withheld this knowledge, in secret, and were not willing to divulge it to outsiders.

An example was recorded by Cadillac:

Nevertheless, one thing is quite certain, namely that the Indians are most skillful and very experienced in healing all kinds of sores and wounds, of whatever kind they may be, by means of simples, [herbs] of which they have an excellent knowledge. They also have remedies for burns, frostbite, and the stings and bites of snakes and other venomous animals; but the best of it is that they stop and drive off the mischief as quickly as it came. They are very good anatomists; and so, when they have an arm or any bone broken, they treat it very cleverly and with great skill and dexterity, and experience shows that they can cure a wounded man in a week better than our surgeons can in a month, perhaps because the former have better remedies and are more straightforward, while the others are actuated by the desire to turn their talent to their own profit. As to venereal diseases, they laugh at them, for those who are attacked recover in ten or twelve days at the furthest, by taking certain tasteless powders, which they swallow in hot water, and for this reason one never sees a woman among them who has syphilis; but they are malicious enough to refuse to teach the French their secrets, though they do not refuse them their remedies in case of need. (2.)

Because the knowledge of the use of plant substances was denied the French, they were not able to identify them or know their properties. The early observers understood the reverence the native people held for them, but did not fully understand why. What they observed during the ritual consumption

(1.) *Memoir*, Pease, IHC, 23:369-71, Deliette.
(2.) *Relation of the Indians*, Cadillac, MS, Edward Ayers Collections.

of these plants was not fully understood, mainly because of the secrecy surrounding the source and the effects of these medicinal substances.

Radot made this evident while among the Illinois:

> . . . Many rattlesnakes are to be found on the prairies . . . . Its bite is very dangerous, and if one is not promptly cared for by the savages, who know the simples [herbs] which cure it, one soon dies. (1.)

Undoubtedly, the sacred plants and their powerful applications were not something that the native people wanted the Europeans to be privy to. The secrecy made it just as difficult then, as it is today, to ascertain whether native peoples of the Great Lakes Region utilized plants containing certain drugs to enhance or induce the dream state. It would entail the use of plants, whose properties contained certain narcotics that caused altering states of mind, which produced hallucinations. Once taken, the dreamer then entered the visionary spirit world.

Recent studies reveal that Shaman or Medicine men would enter the spirit or dream world to diagnose a person inflicted with a disease. It was thought that diseases were caused by ominous spirits and that the only way to dispose of them was to treat them spiritually.

Tobacco was something that native peoples used extensively. The merits of tobacco among them is undisputed, as it was very highly esteemed. It was considered sacred and was used in performing many rituals. They raised a great deal of it, and it was used as a form of money in trade. They were incessant smokers who introduced its effects to the New World inhabitants, where today, modern smokers continue to bear the consequences. (2.)

The type of tobacco (*Nicotia Rustica*) used by native people was unlike the modern type commercially grown today. It was more potent and was inclined to produce a more euphoric state, although it did not induce a dream state or cause hallucinations. Still, tobacco had its share of mystical properties, for much of it was used for sacrifices, either being cast upon the waters or ending up in fires symbolizing its spiritual effect.

---

(1.) *Memoir*, Pease, IHC, Letter 30 (1709), Radot.
(2.) J.R. Vol. 7:137.
    "The fondness they have for this herb is beyond all belief. They go to sleep with their reed pipes in their mouths, they sometimes get up in the night to smoke; they often stop in their journeys for the same purpose, and it is the first thing they do when they reenter their cabins. I have lighted tinder, so as to allow them to smoke while paddling a canoe; I have often seen them gnaw the stems of their pipes when they had no more tobacco. I have seen them scrape and pulverize a wooden pipe to smoke it. Let us say with compassion that they pass their lives in smoke . . . you tell me that tobacco satisfies hunger . . . and I had to draw out the last bit, not without astonishment at seeing people so passionately fond of smoke."

everal studies in recent years have been conducted that demonstrate the use of narcotic plants for various purposes, especially with those tribes of the west. (1.)

Unfortunately, the archaeological recovery of organic substances from the soil, at best, is not entirely comprehensive or a completely reliable one. In addition to the difficulty of attempting to recover organic substances, archaeologists many times fail to look for them.

According to a study conducted in 1964, most of the ethnobotanical data available for Upper Great Lakes Indians was to have been obtained from the Ojibwa, Menomini, Sauk-Fox, and Potawatomi, which omits any of these groups from partaking in hallucinogenic plant use. Very little information of this type is available for the Winnebago, Kickapoo, Mascouten, Ottawa, Huron, Petun, Neutral, or Miami, nor are the Illinois mentioned. (2.)

There is, however, evidence that would indicate that tribes of the Upper Great Lakes region did in fact utilize medicinal plant substances of a hallucinogenic nature. It is understandable how this evidence could evade even the most astute historical researcher, because it is so fragmented in minute references. To complicate our efforts, we can also add the erroneous editing of previous historical researchers.

The historic evidence that directs us to the particular plant that was used by those groups is found in the *Relations* and was observed by the missionaries Allouez and Marquette. It has eluded us for two principal reasons. One, because the editors dismissed the virtues of the plant as somewhat exaggerated, and secondly, they were unable to identify it accurately. It should not surprise us to know that this plant was used as a treatment for the poisonous rattlesnake bite, which was the "manitou" that was so symbolic in the Grand Medicine ritual. The fatal effects of its bite were symbolic of its life threatening power, which could only be counteracted by this most powerful drug, which, without its use, "one soon dies." A "Medicine" that was the "science of sciences."

This extraordinary plant was first introduced to Father Allouez in Green Bay, who then informed Marquette of its uniqueness. It was Marquette, however, who provided this very excellent description of the mysterious plant that was so revered:

> I also took time to look for a medicinal plant which a savage, <u>who knows its secret</u>, showed to Father Allouez <u>with many Ceremonies</u>. Its root is <u>employed to Counteract snakebites</u>, God having pleased to give this antidote Against a poison

(1.) *Ethnobotany of Native America*, Moerman, (Data base reference).

Apache, White Mountain ceremonial medicine root. Regan, 1929:156 Hopi, Hallucinogenic root—induce vision by medicine man while making a diagnosis. Colton, 1974:396. Navajo, Hallucinogen and ceremonial medicine. Vestal, 1952:42. Paiute, Hallucinogenic root, taken to have visions, especially visitation from the dead. Steward, 1933:318. Shosohni, Hallucinogenic root taken to become unconscious and have visions. Murphy, 1990:50.

(2.) *Aboriginal Relationships Between Culture & Plant Life in the Upper Great Lakes Region*, Yarnell, 1964:47.

which is very common in these countries. It is very pungent, and tastes like powder when crushed with the teeth; it must be masticated and place upon the bite inflicted by the snake. The reptile has so great a horror of it that it even flees from a Person who has rubbed himself with it. The plant bears several stalks, a foot high, with rather long leaves; and a white flower which greatly resembles the wall flower. I put some in my canoe, in order to examine it at leisure while we continued to advance toward Maskoutens, where we arrived on The 7th of June. (1.)

The editors of the *Relations* mistakenly identified the description of this plant with that of Virginia and Seneca snakeroot. The plant just described, however, is none other than Datura. Anyone with any knowledge of plants can easily interpret this description so adequately provided by Marquette. Datura can reach a height of five feet under desirable conditions, although Marquette stated that is was only a foot high. We must remember that his observation took place at Green Bay in June, when it would only have been a foot high and bore its first flowers (see photo). It would grow a great deal more before it produced seeds in the fall. (2.)

Marquette apparently located the plant somewhere above the rapids at present day Wrightstown, on the Fox River. If not on the Fox, its location was at least in the region north of Lake Winnebago. The region above the rapids opened up into prairie and it was in this country that Marquette made a special effort to go ashore to recover a sample. Allouez must have known exactly where this plant was growing for Marquette to be easily directed to its source. These two missionaries must have considered it a significant plant, worthy of their consideration, since it was shown to them by the natives "with many

(1.) J.R. Vol. 59:99.
(2.) This plant even escapes the identity of the Lewis & Clark Expedition. Stephen Ambrose (*Undaunted Courage . . .* ), emphasizes the importance of a plant that bore a root called, "white wood of the prairie." So important that Lewis made it the subject of a separate letter. It reportedly was used to counteract bites of snakes and mad dogs. Lewis sent several pounds of it to Jefferson to be analyzed by the Society.

The plant has been misidentified as that of Purple Coneflower by later researchers. This medicinal plant and its prescribed application was not revealed by the native Mandans, but by a British fur trader, Hugh Henney, who was living among the tribes of the Assiboine River. He prescribed a similar application to that of Marquette:

"the way of useing it is to scarify the part when bitten to chu or pound an inch or more if the root is small, and applying it to the bitten part renewing it twice a Day. the bitten person is not to chaw nor Swallow any of the Root for it might have contrary effect."

Of particular significance is that the root was *not to be swallowed*! Lewis explicitly instructs that it was to be applied externally. A definite precaution with Datura, however, not with Purple Coneflower. Also the name, "white wood of the prairie" is explicit in describing the dried stalks of Datura, whereas, the same can not be said of the latter. The specimens that were collected were apparently dried (Feb. 28) and consisted of several pounds. The green chlorophyll layer of Datura fades upon drying, whereas, the roots are very white and large! Also, the large stalks of the dried plant become very hard and woody, hence "white wood." Most likely, Lewis's only specimens were those provided during the winter months, which were cured or dried and difficult to recognize or associate with a plant that also grew in the eastern United States. This may also explain why there is no evidence that Jefferson had it analyzed.
References:
*Undaunted Courage*, Stephen E. Ambrose, Touchstone, N.Y. 1996:207.
*History of the Expedition under the Command of Lewis and Clark.*, Elliott Coues, 2 vols. Francis P. Harper, N.Y. 1893:347-48.
*Lewis and Clark: Pioneering Naturalists*, Paul Cutright, Univ. of Ill. Press, Urbana: 1969:122, 273, 408.

Datura at one month bearing its first flowers. This is the long leaf plant with several stalks that Marquette observed in the month of June at Green Bay.

Plant with long ominous leaves that Marquette described with "a white flower which greatly resembles the wall flower."

Ceremonies." The fact that the plant was revealed to Allouez with such ostentation, would suggest that its use was not only limited to the application of snake bite.

The French trader Perrot, in the same region, established an alliance with the Miamis by the observance of a feast. Perrot and the chief got into a religious debate over whose God (Manitou) would be adorned to secure the alliance. He described the importance of plants as they were used to invoke manitous as spiritual inspirations for their dreams:

> . . . the chief of the Miami, an altar had been erected, on which he had caused to be placed a Pindikosan [medicine bundle]. This is a warriors pouch filled with Medicinal herbs, wrapped in the skins of animals, the rarest that can be found; it usually contains all that inspires their dreams. (1.)

Perrot refused to eat things that were sacrificed to "evil spirits" or the skins of animals. He agreed to share in the meal only after the Miami chief silenced his Manitous.

Two species of Datura are most prominent in the United States. Both have the same medicinal properties. Common names for them are many; Jimson weed, Jamestown weed, devils trumpet, sacred thornapple, mad apple, apple of Peru, Indian apple and stink weed.

Herbal literary sources provide a variety of medicinal uses for the plant. It is narcotic and was used as a powerful antibiotic and local anesthetic. What must be remembered, however, is that plants with very toxic properties are also extremely poisonous! There is a curious interest, especially among adventurous young people, to experiment with controlled substances, who have suffered grave consequences due to their involvement with this plant. The results are catastrophic!

The entire plant is toxic, especially the seeds, which are contained in its hard, prickly fruit. It has a long history of poisoning in man. The symptoms are spectacular and include: unquenchable thirst, enlargement of the pupils, delirium and apparent insanity. Cases of overdose produce convulsions and coma, which precede death! There are many poisonous plants in our part of the world, but this one tops the list. A curator of the herbarium at Eastern Michigan University reported nose bleeds just from handling specimens. (2.)

The people who live in the farm country of the midwest and the east coast know the plant with a common disdain for its ability to propagate so profusely. It is a weed that plagues agriculture production. Many farmers, at least the ones who know what it is, attempt to eradicate it from their farms because it is also fatal to cattle. It grows predominately in areas that are conducive to agriculture and will not tolerate shaded woods. It can be found growing in barnyards,

---

(1.) *The Indian Tribes of the Upper Mississippi Valley & Region of the Great Lakes,* Blair 1911, I:332.
(2.) *The Sinister Garden,* Wyeth Laboratories, 1966.

along ditch banks, and in open sun. The farmers call it stinkweed or stinky weed, because it is unmistakably pungent, just as Marquette describes it.

The mature Datura plant can grow to five feet, has several stalks with large ominous looking leaves, and beautiful trumpet shaped flowers. Due to its size, a great deal of medicine could be secured from a single plant. Dried and ground into a powder, it would provide an ample supply for native people to use abundantly. Various parts of the plants were used in different ways and for different purposes. The medicine men of the Hopi tribe would chew the root to induce visions while making a diagnosis of a sick member. The Luiseno tribe used the root juice in a boy's puberty ceremony to induce stupefication. (1.)

Interestingly, Marquette must have tasted the plant to be able to state that it tasted like powder. The only powder that he could be relating to was that of gun powder, which would correlate very well with the pungent smell of this plant and as it would compare to the sulfurous (rotten egg) taste of black gun powder!

An account that is similar to that of Marquette's was reported by Father Mathurin de Petit while among the Mississippi Mound Culture of the Natchez. Again, the importance of a medicinal plant that overpowers poisonous snakes. He reported the medicine men had in their bundles remedies that contained:

> . . . a certain root, which by its *smell* can put serpents to sleep and render them senseless. After having rubbed their hands and body with this root, they take hold of these reptiles without fearing their bite, which is mortal. (2.)

Radin's study of the Winnebago (Sioux) revealed a medicinal plant only identified as "stench-earth medicine." He was never able to determine what it was. The "stench-earth" medicine men could cure the sick, but they also used it to poison people. In more modern times they considered it "bad medicine," workings of the devil. (Radin was excluded from the most sacred aspect of the Medicine ceremonial.) (3.)

Radisson's journal reveals the use of a narcotic drink reported to him that may identify a Sioux tribe along the Missouri:

> They live only upon corn and Citrulles [pumpkins] . . . . They have fish through-out the year . . . . Their arrows are not of stone as ours are, but of fish bones, and other bones that they work greatly, as other things. Their dishes are made of wood . . . . They have great Calumets of great stones, red and green. They make

(1.) *Ethnobotany of Native America*, Moerman, (Data base).
    Colton, 1974:306; Sparkman, 1908:229.
(2.) J.R. Vol. 68:153.
(3.) *The Winnebago Tribe*, Radin, 1990:216.

Mature Datura at a height of five feet. Grown in the Upper Peninsula of Michigan only a short distance from Sand Point. This large plant would produce an ample supply of medicine for a great many people.

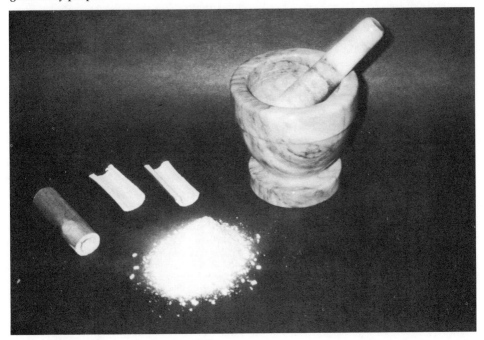

Datura mortised into a powdered medicine.

**Roots are white with green stalks bleaching white upon drying. Thorny seed pod that contains a multitude of highly toxic seeds.**

a store of tobacco. They have a kind of drink that makes them mad for a whole day . . . . (1.)

There are many recent studies of various tribal uses of Datura in a decoction or brew for drinking the substance. The Apache made a juice, or powdered the roots, to make a fermented, intoxicating drink. The Navajo used it to make a drink that would "make you drunk like whiskey." The Papago ground the roots, infused it, and used it to make a beverage. The Havasupai used the leaves or seeds to make a person "intoxicated for a day or more." (2.)

What recent studies have shown, more than anything about Datura, is that it was the *most universally used hallucinogenic and medicinal plant know to man!* (3.)

From the historic evidence, we may conclude that Datura was used by many of the tribes occupying the Great Lakes and surrounding region. We may infer that the Ouinipegou and Siouan related groups were pre-

(1.) *The Exploration of Pierre Esprit Radisson*, Adams, 1961:98.

 They are explained as a nation that "live in the other river." This information seems to have been gleaned from the Illinois (Aliniouek, J.R. 44:247), who had "retired" to present day Illinois from the continual threats of the Neutral, Ottawa, as well as the Iroquois. Possibly the Illinois may have previously resided in lower Michigan, northern Ohio or Indiana. At one time they had to have been part of the Fire Nation contingency.

(2.) *Ethnobotany of Native America*, Moerman, (Data base).

 Regan, 1929:151; Vestal, 1952:42; Underhill, 1935:26; Seaman, 1985:239.

(3.) Ibid. Bean & Saubel, 1972:60.

scribers to its use since the plant was indigenous, as well as accessible, to the area they had always inhabited around Green Bay. Today, Datura is found only in the lower two tiers of counties in southern Wisconsin, adjacent to the Wisconsin and Mississippi River systems.

The plant that native people revered with such great esteem would be later regarded by Euro-American agriculturists as a nuisance weed. Ironically, this plant still thrives in many agricultural areas today, just as it did during the agricultural practices of early aboriginal peoples. It would have had a respected place in the cultivated plot, where its importance may have exceeded many of the necessary food staples.

The geographical distribution of Datura suggests that it is likely that the Formative Cultures of the mound builders, who were extensive farmers, may have contributed to the present day distribution and densities. For this plant to grow in the midwest and eastern U.S. requires that it be cultivated, or it will not survive. Its proliferation has been perpetuated by agricultural ground disturbance necessary for this plant to grow in full sun and reproduce as an annual (*Datura Stramonium L.*).

One of the most intriguing questions about Datura is its origin. Classified as an Asian plant, it appears to have been introduced to the Americas, where it has become naturalized. From Asia, we know it found its way to the Western world of Greece in very early times. Ironically, Grecians entombed their dead in burial mounds also. We may only speculate as to how this mysterious plant found its way to the North American continent. (1.)

We conclude our research on "dreams" by establishing some conclusions. The core of the Native American belief system was based on the absolute importance of medicinal plants and the dominant influence of dreams or spirits. It was the effects of medicinal plants, as well as their fascination with the unconscious state of mind, which mystified the native person's thinking. This is to interpret the "dream" not only as a condition of sleep, but as an altered state of mind that could be produced either by the influences of a narcotic substance, or fasting, which caused illusions or imaginary visions. It produced a condition of the mind that stimulated and enlighten the prophetic knowledge of the soul. A belief that was manifested through visionary symbols that would act as guiding forces for people who attempted to explain the mysteries of the natural world, which, totally consumed their existence and they depended on for survival.

Plants and animals were equal parts of the natural equation and the guiding forces, or messengers, for the "spirit master of life." The secrets of life were

(1.) *Grays Manual of Botany*, Fernald, 1950.
    The Tholos (temple), c. 490 B.C. of Greece contained the most ancient and influential oracle, consulted on all important issues. The presiding deity was Apollo, god of prophesy. The use of Datura as the prophesy plant, to produce visions-hallucinogen-via inhaling of burning leaf smoke.

attainable through a medium with the spirits or "manitous," who could render guidance from the master. His most powerful medicine was produced from plants, which were considered "the science of sciences." The secrets could be revealed through visions produced by the most sacred of medicines; the most powerful was the "master of life's" own creation—Datura. The knowledge of plant use was as revered as their effects and they were preserved in secrecy through the Medicine Society.

The principal reason for our lack of knowledge of these narcotic plants was due to the secrecy surrounding their use. Secrecy enhanced the mysteries associated with these powerful plants; sharing the secret would share the power. It was power and courage that primal peoples depended on to strengthen and preserve their cultures, elements, which were most essential for survival in a very hostile world.

*Life is but a Dream*

In recent years there has been increased interest in researching botanics with the hope of finding chemical properties that may offer new opportunities for the medical field, the discovery of new drugs extracted from plants that provide alternatives to the present use of synthetics.

Additionally, attention has focused on the native American community to study the various uses of plants that were employed as food and medicine. This particular area of exploration of the botanical field is still relatively new, as researchers attempt to probe for the secrets of these substances and study their reported effects.

Also becoming popular is the resurgence of native American idealism and cultural tradition, not only among native people, but non-native as well. Attempts are being made to reclaim the traditional concepts that are currently being blended into what can be expressed as New Age. The surviving native American community has been struggling with the reintroduction of the use of narcotic plants, particularly peyote, that began at the turn of the century.

We should learn something from the past history of the native people. It is easy for historians to get lost in interpreting the impact that Europeans had on the native communities with their arrival. Too often this escalates into a romantic facade for the native culture and lifestyles. Since no historical information exists, it is convenient that only uncertainty and speculation avail themselves for explaining the mysterious circumstances that surrounded the cultural rise and fall of prehistoric Americans.

The history of the Ouinipegou was a classic example of native American dynamics. A fierce people, who believed themselves invincible, subjected themselves to what appeared to be totally irrational behavior that practically destroyed their entire nation.

What is especially important for us to be aware of is the social impact that certain plant substances had on native communities. Substances that would hallucinogenically produce altered states of mind could certainly have a profound effect on an entire culture. (Especially in cases where the entire community confided in a single person—Shaman-priest, Medicine man, a great Chief or a Master of a Temple—who relied on the arcane effects of narcotics to provide the destinies of entire social groups or tribes). Visionary apparitions were consulted to provide solutions to problems that were without intelligent reason or logic—a schizophrenic prophecy that would be infinitely capricious, leaving their destinies to fate. The long term use of these substances would also take its toll on the acuity that was so critical for survival-based decisions. If wars were not successful in the eventual decline of cultures, the disturbing intertribal conflicts erupting within would provide a catalyst for its failure and dispersal.

It is very possible that the reliance on dreams, or spirit-oriented substances, may have been a greater contributing factor to the decline of large social structures, such as the great Mound Culture, than the impact of disease and declining resources. When formative populations depended on their mysticism to resolve the calamitous effects of agricultural deficiency, eventually, natural casualty would expend itself to the detriment of the whole community. When the group finally lost confidence in its mysticism, conflict arose, systems broke down, they diffused and separated. New cultures evolved and modified what previously was not successful. What was unpopular was abandoned, and new *spiritual avenues* were incorporated; as one culture died, another was born, thus, the cycle of life. Life *is* but a dream.

THE END

*"In darkness dwells the people
which knows its annals not."*

*—William L. Clements Library, U.M.*

# BIBLIOGRAPHY

Adams, Arthur T., ed., *The Explorations of Pierre Esprit Radisson*, Ross & Haines, Inc., Minneapolis, Minnesota, 1961

Ambrose, Stephen E., *Undaunted Courage, Meriwether Lewis, Thomas Jefferson, and the Opening of the American West*, Touchstone, N.Y. 1996

American History Class of L'Anse High School, *The History of L'Anse Township*, L'Anse Sentinel, 1922

Anonymous, *The Pioneer Letters*, Keweenaw Press, 136 S. Iroquois St., Calumet, MI. 1994

Bastian, Tyler, *Prehistoric Copper Mining in Isle Royale National Park*, Michigan, Dept. of Anthropology, University of Utah, 1963

Beers, Henry Putney, *The French in North America*, Louisiana State University Press, Baton Rouge, 1957

Blair, Emma Helen, *The Indian Tribes of the Upper Mississippi Valley & Region of the Great Lakes*, 1911. University of Nebraska Press, Lincoln and London 1996

Bourne, Edward Gaylard and W.L. Grant, *The Voyages and Exploration of Samuel De Champlain*, (1604-1616), Toronto, The Courier Press Limited, 1911

Bradish, Alvah, *Memoir of Douglas Houghton*, A.M. 1889

Bremness, Lesley, *Herbs*, Dorling Kindersley, London-New York-Stuttgart, 1994

Burden, Philip D., *Mapping of North America*, Raleigh Publications, 1996

Butterfield, C.W., *History of the Discovery of the Northwest by John Nicolet*, Cincinnati, OH: R. Clarke & Co., 1891

Butterfield, C.W., *History of Brulé's Discoveries and Explorations*, 1610-1626, The Helman-Taylor Company, Cleveland, Ohio, 1898 (Grand Rapids, Mich. Reprinted by B.L.B. Black Letter Press, 1974)

Cadillac, Antoine De La Mothe, *Relation on the Indians*, Edward Ayer Collection, Newberry Library, Chicago

Callender, Charles, *Social Organization of the Central Algonkian Indians*, Milwaukee Public Museum, Publications in Anthropology 7:1962

Carter, James L., *Baraga County Historical Pageant*, "L'ANSE SHOWN ON 1668 MAP." Baraga County Historical Society, 1969. (Michigan)

Carter, James L., & Ernest Rankin, *North to Lake Superior,* The Journal of Charles W. Penny, 1840. The John M. Longyear Research Library, Marquette, Michigan, 1987.

Chaput, Donald, *Baraga County Historical Pageant,* "Europeans Enter The Lake Superior Country," Barage Co. Historical Society,1969 (Michigan)

Chuinard, Eldon G., *Only One man Died, The Medical Aspects of the Lewis and Clark Expedition*, The Arthur H. Clark Company, Glendale, Cal. 1979

Coe, Michael, Sean Snow & Elizabeth Benson, *Atlas of Ancient America*, Facts On File Inc., New York, 1986

Coleman, Bernard, Sister, *Ojibwa Myths and Legends*, Minneapolis, MN; Ross and Haines, 1962

Coues, Elliott, *History of the Expedition under the Command of Lewis and Clark*, Francis P. Harper, N.Y. 1893

Cutright, Paul, *Lewis and Clark: Pioneering Naturalists*, University of Ill. Press, Urbana 1969

Dever, Harry, *The Nicolet Myth*, Michigan History Magazine, Vol. L, no. 4., 1966

Dompier, James, *Documented Records of the Historic use of the Lac Vieux Trail*, Baraga County Historical Society Press, MI, 1984

Doyle, Earl L. & Ruth B. MacFarlane, *History of Pequaming*, Ontonagon Historical Society, Book Concern Printers, 1999.

Drier, Roy Ward, and Octave DuTemple, *Prehistoric Copper Mining in the Lake Superior Region*, Calumet, MI. 1961

Dunbar, Willis Fredrick, *Michigan: A history of the Wolverine State*, W.B. Ferdmans Pub. Co., Grand Rapids, 1965

Eccles, W. J., *France in America*, Harper & Row, New York, Evanston, San Francisco, London, 1957

Fay, Stephen, *Condé Nast Traveler*, Feb.1995, "Close Encounters of a New Kind: Stonehenge," Richard D. Beckman, Publisher 1995

Fernald, M.L., *Grays Manual of Botany*, New York American Book Company, 1950

Halsey, John R., *Miskwabik—Red Metal*, The Roles Played by Michigan's copper In Prehistoric North America, State Archaeologist, Bureau of History, Michigan Department of State. Reprinted from *Michigan History Magazine*, Sept./Oct. 1983. Published in 1992 by the Keweenaw County Historical Society.

Ho-Chunk Nation, *A Brief History*, Revised: 1997
    website: http://www.ho-chunk.com/HCHistory.htm

Hunt, George T., *The Wars of the Iroquois*, The University Press, 1940

Hurley, William M., *Anthropological Papers, Museum of Anthropology*, University of
    Michigan, No. 59. Ann Arbor. (Effigy Mound complexes in Wisconsin)

Hutchens, Alma R., *Indian Herbalogy of North America*, Shambhala, Boston & London,
    1991

Iseminger, William R., *Archaeology*, May/June 1996, "Mighty Cahokia," Archaeological
    Institute of America Publication

Johnson, Elden, *Aspects of Upper Great Lakes Anthropology*, Series No. 11., Minnesota
    Historical Society, St. Paul, 1974 "The Wisconsin North Lakes Project: A
    Preliminary Report" Robert J. Salzer "Origins and Relationships of Woodland
    Peoples: The evidence of Cranial Morphology" N.S. Ossenberg

Johnson, Ida Amanda, *The Michigan Fur Trade*, Michigan Historical Commission, 1919

Jury, Wilfrid and Elsie McLeod, *Sainte Marie Among the Hurons*, Oxford University
    Press Canada, 1954

Karpinski, Louis, *Manuscript Maps of European Archives*, Michigan History Magazine,
    vol. 14:1930

Karpinski, Louis, *The Bibliography of the Printed Maps of Michigan*, Michigan History
    Commission, 1931

Kellogg, Louis, P., *The French Regime in Wisconsin and the Northwest*, Madison:
    Wisconsin State Historical Society, 1925

Kershaw, Kenneth A., *Early Printed Maps of Canada*, (1540-1703), Kershaw Publishing,
    Ancaster, Ontario, 1993

Kinietz, Vernon W., *The Indians of the Western Great Lakes*, 1965, (Raudot, Letter 53,
    1710) Ann Arbor, MI. University of Michigan Press, 1940

Krochmal, Arnold and Connie, *Field Guide to Medicinal Plants*, Random House Inc.,
    New York, 1984

LaRoe, Lisa Moore, *National Geographic*, "LaSalle's Last Voyage," Vol. 191, no. 5,
    National Geographic Society, 1997

Lust, John, *The Herb Book*, Bantam Doubleday—Dell Inc., New York, 1974

Melbye, Floyd Jerome, *An Analysis of a Late Woodland Population in the Upper Great Lakes*, University of Toronto, 1969

Mentrak, Thom and Rev. Raymond A. Bucko, S. J., Dept. of Sociology and Anthropology *The Jesuit Relations and Allied Documents* (1610-1791) Le Moyne College, Jesuit College of Central New York and Ste. Marie Among The Iroquois, a facility of Onondaga Co. Parks. website: http://vc.lemoyne.edu/relations/

Michigan Archaeological Society, *The Michigan Archaeologist*, East Lansing, MI., Vol. 26, Nos. 3-4, 1980. Vol. 27, Nos. 1 -2. 1981

Miles, David, *National Geographic*, "Off the English Coast, a Seaside Stonehenge," Vol. 196, no. 5, (Geographica) National Geographic Society 1999

Moerman, Daniel E., University of Michigan—Dearborn, "Ethnobotany of Native America" (Data base reference—Datura) Bean, John L. & Katherine S. Saubel, Chumash;1972 Colton, Harold S., Hopi;1974 Murphy, Edith V.A., Shosohni;1990 Regan, Albert B., Apache;1929 Seaman, Steven A. & P. David, Havasupai;1985 Steward, Julian H., Paiute;1933 Turner, Nancy J., Laurence C. Thompson and M. Terry Thompson et al. 1990 Underhill, Edward F. & Ruth M., Papago;1935 Vestal, Paul A., Navajo;1952

Moore, Charles, *History of Michigan*, The Lewis Pub. Co., Chicago, 1915

Moore, Winston D., *Baraga County Historical Pageant*, Baraga County Historical Society, Mich. "In Search of Baraga County's Ancient Past" 1972

Ontario Ministries, *Archaeological Report*, "Algonquin Subtribes and Clans of Ontario," 1922

Pease, Theodore C. and Raymond C. Werner, *Memoir Concerning the Illinois Country*, Coll. Ill. State Hist. Lib., (IHC), 23, French Ser., I (1934); 302 -95. Memoir Concerning the Different Indian Nations of North America, Letter 30, *Relation par lettres de l' Amerique Septentrionale* (Paris: Letouzey it Ane, 1904)

Perry, G.W., *Transactions*, Wisconsin State Horticultural Society, Madison, Wisconsin 1877

Radin, Paul, *The Story of the American Indian*, Garden City Publishing, New York 1927

Radin, Paul, *The Winnebago Tribe*, University of Nebraska Press, Lincoln and London 1990

Rodesch, Jerrold C., *Voyager*, "Jean Nicolet" Brown County Historical Review, 1984 Green Bay, Wisconsin

Rydholm, Fred C., *Superior Heartland*, 1989, 221 Lakewood, Marquette, Michigan

Severy, Merle, *National Geographic*, "The Celts, Europes Founders," Vol. 151, no. 5, National Geographic Society 1977

Schoolcraft, Henry R., *Narritive Journals of Travels from Detroit Northwest through the Great Lakes Chain of American Lakes to the source of the Mississippi River in the 1820*, Albany; E & E Hosford 1821

Scull, Gideon, *Voyages of Peter Esprit Radisson*, The Prince Society, Boston, 1858

Shea, John Dawson Gilmary, *Discovery and Exploration of the Mississippi Valley*, Albany, Joseph McDonough, 1903. (2nd edition, 1861)

Stonehouse, Frederick and Daniel R. Fountain, *Dangerous Coast: Pictured Rocks Shipwrecks*, Marquette Avery Color Studios, 1997

Sulte, Benjamin, *Wisconsin Historical Collections*, "Notes on Jean Nicolet," Vol. 8. 1877, Madison, Wisconsin

Thwaites, Ruben Gold, ed. *Jesuit Relations and Allied Documents*, 73 Vols., Cleveland: Burrows, 1899

Ugent, Donald, *Preliminary Reports on the Flora of Wisconsin*, Wisconsin Academy of Science, Art and Letters, Vol. 51, no. 47:1962

Warren, William, *The History of the Ojibway People*, Minneapolis, MN: Ross & Hains, 1957

White, Richard, *The Middle Ground*, Cambridge, MA: Cambridge University Press, 1991

Whittlesey, Charles, Report; 1852, *The Annuals of Science*, Cleveland, Harris & Fairbanks, 1854

Williams, Mentor L., *Narrative Journals of Travels from Detroit Northwest through the Great Lakes Chain of American Lakes to the Source of the Mississippi River in the year 1820*, Michigan State College Press 1953

Wilson, Clifford P., *Minnesota History Magazine*, "Where Did Nicolet Go?," Minnesota Historical Society, Minneapolis, Vol. 27, no. 3, 1946

Wisconsin State Historical Society, *Wisconsin in Three Centuries*, Madison, Wisconsin, 1906

Wrong, George M., *The Long Journey to the Country of the Hurons*, by Gabriel Sagard, Champlain Society, 1939, edited by George M. Wrong, Greenwood Press Publications, Toronto, 1968

Wroth, Lawrence C., *An unknown Champlain map of 1616*, IMAGO MVNDI, A review of early cartography, ed. by Lew Bagrow, Anno dni MCMLIV, vol. XL

Wyeth Laboratories, *The Sinister Garden*, Division of American Home Products Corps. New York, 1966

Yarnell, Richard Asa, *Aboriginal Relationships Between Culture & Plant Life in the Upper Great Lakes Region*, Anthropological Papers, Museum of Anthropology, University of Michigan, no. 23, 1964